PRELIMINARY NOTE

This book integrates scientific and philosophical terminology that, at first, may seem challenging to read. However, it is designed for the readers to take possession of these concepts as they advance in the first chapters and quickly discover an agile, precise, and profound lecture. In other words, it is suitable for beginners and experts alike.

To my dear wife, María Eugenia, with all my love.

Grateful to my children for the inspiration they give me, Andrea for her courage and determination, Mariana for her prudence and artistic creativity, and Juan Carlos for his discipline and strength.

To my grandchildren Ilión and Teseo, my new life force and hope for a better humanity.

Carlos Chávez

To my father, the soul of this book.
With special gratitude to my grand team: my mother, sisters Andrea and Mariana, and my partner and love of life Agneta

Juan Carlos Chávez

STRATEGIC BIOINTELLIGENCE

Economic Ethology, Business Model Generator, and Behavioral Biology in decision making.

Carlos Chávez and Juan Carlos Chávez

"For all of us who love Creativity and are interested in understanding how and why behaviors can be modified, Strategic Bio-intelligence is an intelligent and fresh lecture in which Carlos and Juan Carlos Chávez help us better understand how emotions, feelings, and decision processes are triggered in the fascinating and changing world of Marketing."
- CARLOS VACA, *Former CEO and President of BBDO— recognized as one of the most creative agencies in the world.*

"A piece that certainly challenges the common assumptions of those dedicated to the strategic development in Commercialization and Marketing. With a multidisciplinary focus, Juan Carlos Chávez and Carlos Chávez expand the traditional understanding with which Finance, Statistics, and Economics approach the theory and practice of decision making."
- DR. ARTURO PICOS, *Dean Professor of Human Factor at IPADE Business School.*

"Throughout this extraordinary treatise on human behavior and desires, I have found a sustained understanding of how to influence interactions related to brand promise, value definition, and consumer relevance."
- GABRIEL HIDALGO, *Associate Professor of Marketing at IPADE Business School.*

CARLOS CHÁVEZ

Dean Professor of Marketing and Finance at *IPADE Business School*, with over 2,000 sessions imparted to business leaders and young graduates.

Endearing athlete, exemplary husband, father, and grandfather convinced of the power of ideas to change lives and improve the World.

Researcher and writer with over 50 academic cases and hundreds of published articles.

He has been an advisor to more than 150 companies in his career as a consultant, where some of the most important on the continent stand out.

Creator of the *Business Model Generator*, a strategic map that offers a well-structured and privileged perspective on the fundamental variables impacting profitability.

Professional with extensive managerial experience in notable academic and banking institutions.

Chemical Engineer from the Faculty of Chemical Sciences of the *Autonomous University of Mexico (UNAM)* with a Master's in Business Administration from *IPADE Business School* and certified in Participant-Centered Learning by Harvard Business School.

JUAN CARLOS CHÁVEZ

Writer and Professor of Creativity and Economic Ethology.

Current PhD in Psychology, Master in Business, and Communication Graduate. He is also a father of two children, an animal rights defender, and a musician. He has published 5 books in 2 languages and dozens of articles. He is an advisor to national and international companies, teaches academic programs at a post-graduate level, and lectures for different industries.

Co-author of the book © *Strategic Bio-Intelligence* (2023), a text structured to understand the biology of human behavior as a fundamental factor for business management, economic research, and human development.

Author of the book © *Creative Intelligence* (2022), a detailed model that systematizes a comprehensive perspective on the creative faculty and the concept of freedom with an epistemological basis focused on mechanical causality. His research objective is to elucidate the creative faculty's ontology, teleology, and etiology. Or, in other words, creativity's origin, purpose, and essence. To do this, he considers information from disciplines such as ethics, genetics, psychology, neurobiology, philosophy, and physics.

Author of the book *Multi-Self: Searching for Meaning* (2021), a mechanical theory where he proposes living beings are made up of different overlapping layers—differentiated by their etiology (origin) and teleology (purpose)—that influence behaviors synchronously. In this book, he deeply addresses why we desire? focused on human well-being with solid scientific and philosophical foundations.

Creator of the © *Psyche-Marketing* model and author of the book of the same name (2020). Designed to identify, based on the biology of human behavior, conscious and unconscious forces affecting actions and decision-making in an economic context.

Author of the book *Creativity: The Most Powerful Weapon in the World* (2019). A free and short text that explores what creativity is, how we have used it throughout humanity, and how we can develop it on an individual level.

PROLOGUE

By Roger Schweizer

Professor in International Business
School of Business, Economics, and Law at the University of Gothenburg

Effective decision-making is crucial in business for several reasons. It determines the allocation of resources, shapes strategic directions, and impacts financial outcomes. Well-informed decisions enhance productivity, minimize risks, and foster innovation. Moreover, timely and thoughtful choices allow businesses to adapt to dynamic markets, gain a competitive edge, and achieve long-term success. Ironically, we still know little about what influences decisions made in a business context, among others, since researchers' focus has been relatively narrow. Hitherto, research on decision-making within the business literature has drawn on disciplines such as psychology, economics, management science, behavioral economics, organizational behavior, cognitive science, and operations research. Despite the prevailing efforts to include several disciplines, decision-making has remained a 'black box.'

In this pioneering book, Chávez and Chávez contribute to opening this box—or rather redefining and questioning 'the black box'—by adding insights from different research areas—such as ethology, phylogenetics, ontogenetics, cultural history, anthropology, sociology, neurobiology, physics, philosophy, linguistics, and Marketing—that previously have been ignored when explaining decision-making within an economic context.

At the heart of the authors' exploration lies the theoretical foundation of Strategic Bio-Intelligence—a critical-realism-based model that acknowledges the existence of a reality beyond the observer. It is a recognition that consistent patterns and observations are windows into an external world waiting to be understood. In an inspiring and pedagogical manner, with many illustrative examples from the business world, the authors convincingly elucidate the causal interrelation of biological conditionings in human behavior and decision-making within an economic context—thereby not only providing a conceptual map, categorizing the biological elements that influence decision-making but also offering various ready-to-be used strategic models that support business intelligence.

By highlighting our biological and behavioral conditionings, the book offers insights that help decision-makers to steer clear of harmful biases, fosters critical thinking, facilitates the flow of crucial information, nurtures creativity, and—maybe most importantly today—also invites us to reflect on the importance of conscious and empathetic leaders to be able to tackle our many current societal challenges.

During the last ten years, Roger Schweizer has studied decision-making in the context of firms' internationalization and within multinational companies. He currently works as the Chief People and Culture Officer in a scale-up FBA operator in the Amazon space—Go North—where he applies many of the insights in this book.

INDEX

ACADEMIC ABSTRACT

THESIS

Understanding the biology of human behavior is a fundamental factor for business management, economic research, and human development.

CONTEXT

Carlos Llano Cifuentes (1998) states that the director's competence is a function of interrelation synthesis in decision-making processes. For this reason, it is so significant to delve into the elements influencing these processes within the framework of a commercial effort.

Mainly, disciplines such as Statistics and Finance have been prioritized within the managerial exercise and economic research. The latter has created a gap in causal understanding between business intelligence and other fields of study—apparently distant but directly correlated—such as Genetics, Neurobiology, Psychology, and Ethology, among others; the advances that (as humanity) we have achieved in these areas are extraordinary and admit a privileged vision to understand and optimize decision-making.

In relation to Neurobiology, the afferent and efferent processes (of communication and stimulation) between the brain and the rest of the body directly influence choices. It is a reactive system cured for over four billion years, determining the physiological response to proprioceptive, interoceptive, and exteroceptive stimuli. Learning the somatic frameworks (bodily states) that our biological-emotional programming detonates, which the mind interprets as feelings, is crucial to understanding and driving behavior. Hence, considering neurophysiology, neuroanatomy, and neuropsychology is essential to trigger a purchase, motivate teamwork, or achieve any goal involving human interaction.

Regarding Genetics, the coding, integrating around three billion "letters" (nucleotide bases) forming over twenty thousand "chapters" (genes), instructs the phenotype of the organism (how we look) as well as fixed action patterns and innate behavioral tendencies (how we act) that have represented survival advantages in the past. Visualizing phylogenetic and ontogenetic phenomenology allows us to anticipate its titanic impact on our thoughts and human actions.

Regarding Psychology, it is essential to know the behavioral conditionings and biases determined by how our mind processes and retains the information received by our perceptive channels. It is equally important to estimate the interactional impact of the unconscious, preconscious, and conscious to provide consistency to man's determination.

Ethology, the study of behavior, is vital for outlining intelligent economic and business tactics.

On the other hand, in the second part of this book, we will expose a particularly pragmatic cartography detailing the primal factors for a business model, and we will link it with bio-economic variables.

METHODOLOGY

The central objective of the research is to elucidate the causal interrelation of biological conditioning in human behavior and decision-making in an economic context to present strategic models supporting business intelligence. On a broader level, to unify contemporary information based on the contributions of some of the most relevant exponents of the following disciplinary bases:

Ethology, Phylogenetics, Ontogenetics, Cultural History, Psychology, Anthropology, Sociology, Neurobiology, Physics, Philosophy, Linguistics, Cognitive Sciences, Economics, and Marketing.

The theoretical basis of *Strategic Biointelligence* is critical realism. Accordingly, it assumes that the observations, which attend to the identification of consistent patterns, correspond to a reality outside the subject.

ECONOMIC ETHOLOGY

PART 1

ECONOMIC ETHOLOGY

PART 1

INTRODUCTION

Despite the perceived control over ourselves, human beings are actually loaded with biological conditionings and biases guiding our thoughts and behaviors—ironically, that same delusional perception is one of them. Being the dominant species on the planet and—apparently—the most intellectually advanced does not mean absolute autonomy in commanding our choices.

The latter happens by an almost axiomatic principle: we are free to choose based on our desires, but we are not free to choose what we desire.

Understanding what biologically influences our desires is an immensely effective exercise to make much more intelligent decisions in any area.

We must seek a broad vision and an adequate critical focus to discern this phenomenology. First, scrutinize the parts comprising us as living beings and species. Second, consider how we think and why we act. Third, elucidate what desires are and how they influence the processes. And Fourth, identify our systematized behavioral tendencies, integrating contextual, biophysical, physiological, psychological, neurobiological, social, and cultural variables.

As we establish the above, attending to the theme of this book, we will be able to consolidate the biology of human behavior in an economic context with reflexive objectives to make intelligent decisions. Likewise, we will review intersubjective modeling tactics that allow forging shared individual appreciations to determine positionings (or "realities") allied to the highest probability of goal fulfillment.

In addition, in the second part, we will complement what has been exposed with a *strategic business model generator* that signifies an essential development and guiding map for financial profitability in any project. Understanding the biological influence behind human decisions has a strong economic impact that can be measured with the variables of said generator.

The following ideas represent powerful management tools that must be used responsibly and ethically; their primary intention is to signify important associates to forge a more conscious, intelligent, creative, and empathetic humanity.

1.0 HERMENEUTICS OF CONSCIOUSNESS

How do we interpret what we desire, think, and do?

Desiring, thinking, and acting are not isolated processes; together, they represent the basis of our conscious existence as *Homo sapiens*. Nevertheless, few identify their proportional correlation, and even fewer question their nature.

When we delve deeper into human psychodynamics, the immensity of the unconscious and its dominant influence is revealed. What reaches our consciousness represents only a tiny part of the mental, biological and physical structure.

If we observe from a very open and abstract perspective, the map displaying our decisions is relatively simple:

1) The Will, composed of unconscious biological conditionings, shows itself in the form of desires in the conscious.

2) The possibility of fulfilling (or not fulfilling) these desires is sublimated into ideas about experiential situations.

3) Potential experiences—which symbolize the conquest of desires from the unconscious—are combined to form "ideal" scenarios (templates) of our perceived reality.

4) We take actions and decisions based on the possibility of "materializing" these scenarios.

Desiring-thinking-acting consolidates a perpetual dynamic dance.

Following, let us review how the human mind operates in its psychological layer.

1.1 Unconscious, Preconscious, and Conscious

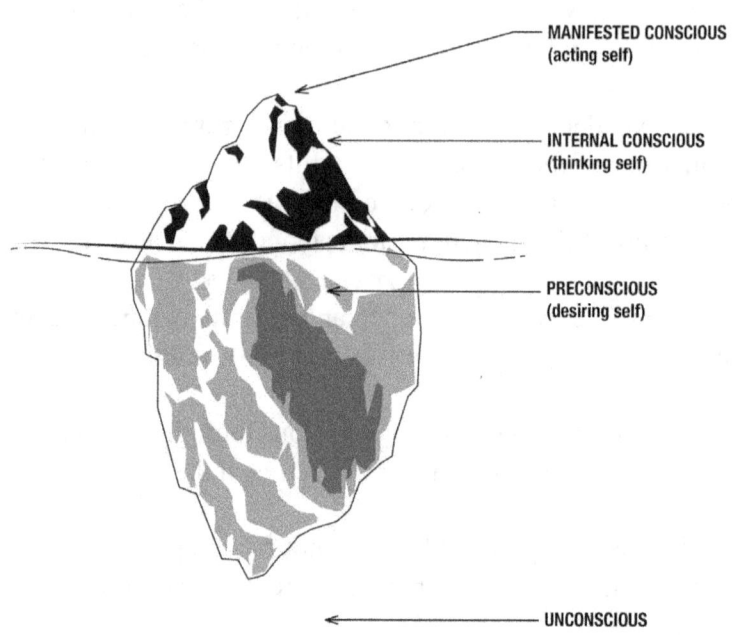

Figure 1: Analogy of the Manifested Conscious, Internal Conscious, Preconscious, and Unconscious.

With a slight adjustment, the classic metaphor of the iceberg is very didactic to visualize the role played by the unconscious, preconscious and conscious in the mind.

Let us start at the tip of the tip. There we will find the self that acts, or in other words, the ***manifested conscious*** that connects with the *intersubjective topology* conformed by shared experiences. It is about the part of us that speaks, expresses, and mobilizes.

From the first position, we can already detect the ego is fragmented: in each location of the psycho-phenomenological map, there is a different self. This effect is interestingly reflected in language; for example, when we use the future perfect to refer to ourselves as distinct persons: "in a week, I will already have been a father."

The *desiring self*, the *thinking self*, the *acting self*, or the *self* of the past, present, and future are not the same. Psychologically, the being is multifactorial.

In the second location, we find the base of the tip, the network of conscious thoughts to which only the subject has access: the **inner conscious** or *thinking self*. The difference between thinking and doing is noticeable.

On the third axis, at the broad base of the frozen body, we find the **preconscious**, comprised of neural activity that does not perceive itself (although it potentially could). As we can see, this section is much broader than the superficial ones. It is the main field of action of the *desiring self*; Jacques Lacan (1958) builds a very similar concept he refers to as the Other (with a capital "O"). Particularly against the Other is that the most colossal psychological battles are fought: the conscious self using all its willpower to mitigate its biological conditioning exposed in the form of desires. To be or not to be! Hamlet would convey. But, also, it is the source of an endless number of sentient gratifications given when such passions are fulfilled. Similarly, in language, we see the projection of this duality when we talk to ourselves.

Finally, marked with the immensity of the ocean, we locate the **unconscious**, or rather, the interconnection—inaccessible to consciousness—of the mind with everything forming us as an organism, inside and outside of it.

In summary, the hermeneutics of consciousness we propose in this book, considering Freudian and Lacanian foundations, categorizes the psychological layers of the mind into:

1) *Manifested Conscious*: what our mind perceives about itself and is expressed.

2) *Internal Conscious*: what our mind perceives about itself but does not necessarily is expressed.

3) *Preconscious*: what our mind does not perceive about itself but potentially can.

4) *Unconscious*: that which influences our mind but cannot perceive directly.

First Bio-Strategic Tool: understand that the dominant influence on conscious decisions comes from the preconscious and unconscious, its broader structural bases.

1.2 Will, Sublimation, Modeling, and Behavior

Based on Lacanian foundations, I present the *human psychological systematization* map, a superlatively practical tool for understanding Sapiens's mental processes and behaviors.

Everything starts from the Will, the origin of desires. Primarily unconscious, it is about the structural biological mechanics of the Being. The Will integrates everything that influences the mind inside and outside the organism; it unites the forces that motivate thoughts, actions, and decisions. Considering its essence, Sigmund Freud refers to this phenomenon as *unconscious*, Baruch Spinoza as *conatus*, Arthur Schopenhauer as *will*, and Richard Bandler and John Grinder as *deep structure*; we are talking about the engine moving the vital gear. Later, we will decode some of its central pieces.

Continuing, from birth—and even before—a process of **sublimation** begins: the Will manifests itself in the form of desires, and our—conscious and preconscious—mind assigns the possibility of obtaining them to what we experience as objects, subjects, and situations. In other words, ideas of people, things, and experiences symbolize the possibility of fulfilled or unfulfilled desires.

Based on the latter, our consciousness undertakes a process of **modeling** exemplary *templates*, integrating (or eliminating) those elements that signify consolidated (or lost) desires. We imagine our "ideal reality."

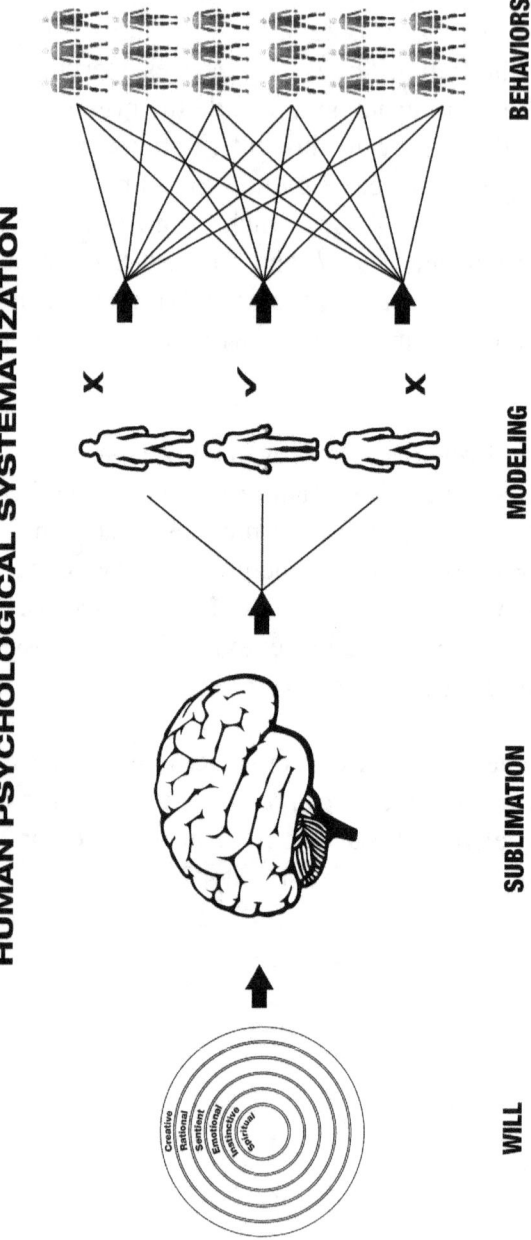

Figure 2: Human Psychological Systematization Map.

Lastly, our behaviors are regulated by the possibility of "materializing" these templates with various tendencies in the face of variable contexts: how we present ourselves is diversified depending on the circumstances (alter egos) but always aligned to base objective models. For example, how we behave in an academic classroom or in a family environment is different.

The process could be staged as follows: 1) the Will, at the unconscious level, instructs an innate desire to belong, 2) in the preconscious, the idea of a sports team is correlated (sublimates) with the fulfilled desire, 3) the conscious "decides" to support said team and 4) we attended a game.

In other words, sublimated desires form ideals that regulate decisions in an incessant omnipresent loop.

Second Bio-strategic Tool: understand that unconscious desires sublimated in things, persons, or situations, moderate all thoughts, actions, and decisions.

1.3 Meta-Value

From a neurobiological point of view, thoughts are synaptic maps programmed with information we receive through proprioceptive, interoceptive, and exteroceptive channels. In other words, they are data on stimuli from inside, outside, and the body itself that form interconnected electrical imprints in the brain.

Thoughts, based on the *Creative Intelligence* model, can be categorized into two main modes:

1) *Logical thoughts*: are quantifiable, and their primary function is to allow us to detect rational causes.

2) *Homeostatic thoughts* (feelings): are unquantifiable, and their primary function is to regulate behavior procuring homeostasis (the maximum point of physiological and psychological well-being).

With this information, something very relevant is revealed: each logical thought is accompanied by homeostatic thoughts, and vice versa: every idea, however rational it may be, causes an emotion (corporal reaction) that causes a feeling (mental reaction) with more or less intensity depending on its importance.

As we previously reviewed, conscious notions symbolize fulfilled, preserved, unfulfilled, or lost desires, which will mark the positive or negative character of the homeostatic trace following it.

In synthesis, within the idea of any *object, subject,* or *experience*, is sublimated the possibility of satisfying (or not) and preserving (or not) a biologically programmed desire that triggers an affect at a conscious, preconscious, or unconscious level. And also, other ideas are juxtaposed.

For example, the neural image of a luxury watch can be merged with other brain maps representing the fulfilled instinctive desire for dominance (to perceive ourselves better than others), the feeling of empowerment, the idea of being recognized, and many more symbolic values. The latter is what we call **meta-values**; it is about those notions that go far beyond the rational or functional significance of an object, subject, or experience.

Brief examples and counter examples:

Object: Convertible car.
Meta-values: fulfilled instinctive desire for discovery, a feeling of independence, and the idea of arguing that nothing limits me.

Object: Ultimate smartphone.
Meta-values: fulfilled instinctive desire to belong, a feeling of wonder, and perceiving myself as successful.

Object: Medical expenses insurance.
Meta-values: fulfilled instinctive desire for control, a feeling of tranquility, and the idea of being protected.

Object: Household cleaning product.
Meta-values: fulfilled instinctive desire for family and protection, a feeling of confidence, and the idea of taking care of my loved ones.

Object: Electric car.
Meta-values: fulfilled instinctive desire for cooperative altruism, a feeling of satisfaction, and the idea of being part of a movement that protects the Planet.

Subject: President of a country.
Meta-values: lost instinctive desire for freedom, a feeling of helplessness, and the idea of future financial problems.

Experience: Graduation.
Meta-values: fulfilled instinctive desire for learning and power, a feeling of hope, and the idea of a better future.

Third Bio-Strategic Tool: understanding the meta-value is a fundamental element strongly influencing decision-making.

1.4 Conclusion

In short, our bio-systematization integrates instructions appearing as desires in consciousness that influence every thought, action, and decision.

The latter happens to become a blunt survival tool. Desires, which trigger feelings, operate as a sophisticated rewards program to ensure the organism follows the protocol representing the most significant possibilities of resistance and prevalence of Life.

Unraveling the biological essence of the mind, desires, instincts, emotions, feelings, reason, and creativity allows us to decode the primary variables that influence decision-making, which come mainly from the unconscious.

Regarding the managerial exercise, the interpretation of psychological phenomenology allows us the possibility of working with meta-values, connecting with deep desires, motivating the conscious through the preconscious and unconscious, detecting psychosomatic biases present when making own decisions, creating *constructs* that unify ideas, complement meaning, and facilitate understanding, and more.

By recognizing that the self is not a linear and independent element but complex and dynamic, a universe of constructive possibilities opens up. It is not the same I, in "I love you" or in "I am here," Lacan would say. Individuals are an extraordinary *multi-self* in which each part presents different needs and tendencies. Conquering the diverse selves, whether to sell, motivate or make intelligent decisions, begins by seeking a broad and profound vision of the biological nature of the Being.

Fourth Bio-Strategic Tool: delving into psychological processes, detecting the **multimodal quality of the Being**, and recognizing the dominance of the unconscious, is essential to understand why and how we make decisions.

2.0 COMMERCIAL BIOEQUALIZATION
How to align a commercial offer to human biological conditioning?

By definition, an equalization process (from the Latin *aequalis*: equal) implies adjusting variables for the reproduction of a signal; it is about seeking an ideal uniform balance.

On the other hand, decision-making is deeply conditioned by distinct biological aspects such as biophysical, genetic, neurophysiological, and psychological factors.

Consequently, *commercial bio-equalization* signifies configuring strategies adequately aligned to the biological programming of the *Homo sapiens*.

Such variables include innate instructions determined a *priori* phylogenetically, but also cultural and experiential causes established a *posteriori*. Together, the latter explains and motivates every human thought and action.

Considering these fundamentals, we will review the main forces comprising the Will to determine potent management tactics.

Based on the *Multi-Self* model, we will differentiate the diverse influences by their etiology (evolutionary origin) and teleology (purpose). For further reference, I have documented the specificity of this model with ample detail in the books *Creative Intelligence*—on the biology of the creative faculty—and *Multi-Self*—on the biology of desires.

Taking all of the above into account, we will be able to determine strong Purposes connecting with the depths of the vital essence, establish intersections between the commercial offer and the instinctive triggers, anchor emotions and feelings to the strategic positioning, use rational values correctly, synchronize with the cultural codes, and enhance the creative impetus to shape the future.

Following, allow me to present the primary motivators of human behavior.

Fifth Bio-Strategic Tool: Allying with behavioral biology to make strategic decisions exponentially increases the probability of completion.

2.1 Spiritual Drivers

Determining a strong Purpose, as the flag of a commercial effort, is essential to compete in the current market.

In other words, a project that does not show how it protects the integral, collective, and future well-being of life as a whole loses its most potent catalyst.

Spiritual drivers correspond to the influence—on behavior—imposed by the connection with everything surrounding us. It is a biophysical phenomenon of interrelation that affects acting and thinking from the depths.

Establishing a mission-vision in the company has been an almost bureaucratic requirement for a long time. Nevertheless, mostly, these statements end up forgotten and archived. The vast difference is that a Purpose honestly reflects a penetrating intention of its founder, as well as an objective of mass interest. If either of the two previous characteristics is not met, this field is disabled.

How, then, to build a solid Purpose that conquers the utmost unfathomable fibers of the human spirit? The answer is paradoxically simple: ensuring it protects all of Life.

Let me explain it further, all living beings share a common biological origin and function; we are systematized to support Life to resist and prevail. Modern physics has detected a constant property of existence denominated *entropy*—it even refers to it as *the second law of thermodynamics*—that disorders, disperses, and cools everything. Life defies said "law" and fights to maintain order to avoid a frozen and divided destiny: it perseveres to resist and prevail.

Therefore, a motto accompanying a commercial team that defends what we all strive for as living organisms will become an idea with scope for mass construction (or destruction).

Examples:

To accelerate the world's transition to sustainable energy...
-**Tesla**

To revolutionize space technology, with the ultimate goal of enabling people to live on other planets. -**SpaceX**

To make a contribution to the world by creating tools for the mind that advance humankind. -**Apple** (Steve Jobs)

To give people the power to build community and bring the world closer together. -**Facebook**

The previous Purposes clearly protect the evolution and transcendence of Life, which is why they are so robust and have represented a colossally influential tool to connect en masse.

So, what is the Purpose of your company or project?

Sixth Bio-Strategic Tool: Understanding that a strong Purpose protecting the resistance and prevalence of Life—in all its manifestations—is one of the most potent business tools.

Practical Note: determine the Purpose that mostly moves you (individual and business) and always keep it in mind as a source of inspiration and potency (for you, your team, and your clients).

2.2 Genetic Drivers

The human genome is made up of more than three billion "letters" (nucleotides) (A, C, T, G) organized into more than twenty thousand "stories" (genes) instructing the formation of proteins. As a species, we share 99.9% of the genetic code identically, a formidable correlation that proves the irrefutable similarity between us. What makes each one different is the—approximately.1%— genetic differential, which also reveals something remarkable: the vast scope of the effects of every "letter" of the instructions.

This epic manual has been written for three to four billion years based on the learnings that have meant the best chances for survival and reproduction of the gene. As a side note, it is not about the species for the species but of the gene for the gene; Richard Dawkins masterfully documents this phenomenon in his book *The Selfish Gene* (1976).

Fundamentally, DNA details the guidelines for the physiological formation of organisms (phenotype), as well as innate reactive factors determining behavioral tendencies (instincts).

With this background, we can distinguish that every human thought and act—largely, although not uniquely—is genetically influenced.

Therefore, matching the orders from the genes implies exponentially increasing the possibilities of predicting and promoting behaviors. Also, recognizing their interference signifies clarifying the panorama to make more intelligent decisions of our own.

We can detect these conditionings with what I call *sentient validation*: we will know a disposition—very probably—has a phylogenetic origin when practically all of humanity receives the same emotional guide when it is executed or not.

For example, all of us *Homo sapiens* experience a positive feeling when we perceive ourselves as safe: we instinctively desire control.

In a commercial context, the key is found when we understand that the correct intention is not to sell products or services but, in this case, the opportunity of satisfying genetic instructions.

Harley Davidson doesn't sell motorcycles; it sells an *instinctive desire* to *belong* fulfilled.

Rolex does not sell watches; it sells an *instinctive desire for domination* (to feel better than others) fulfilled.

Volvo does not sell cars; it sells an *instinctive desire for control* (safety) fulfilled.

Disney does not sell movies or theme parks; it sells an *instinctive desire for discovery* fulfilled.

Cybex does not sell baby products; it sells an *instinctive desire for protection and family* fulfilled.

History Channel doesn't sell documentaries; it sells an *instinctive desire for learning* fulfilled.

An investment fund does not sell returns; it sells an *instinctive desire for power* fulfilled.

The Red Cross does not sell medical services; it sells an *instinctive desire for cooperative altruism* fulfilled.

Twitter does not sell a digital platform; it sells an *instinctive desire to be heard* fulfilled.

A gym does not sell sports facilities; it sells an *instinctive desire for recognition* fulfilled.

The chart below shows what I call the *12 instinctive triggers*. It is a guide of some behavioral genetic conditionings—identified by *sentient validation* and inter-species coincidences—that we can use to connect with a commercial offer.

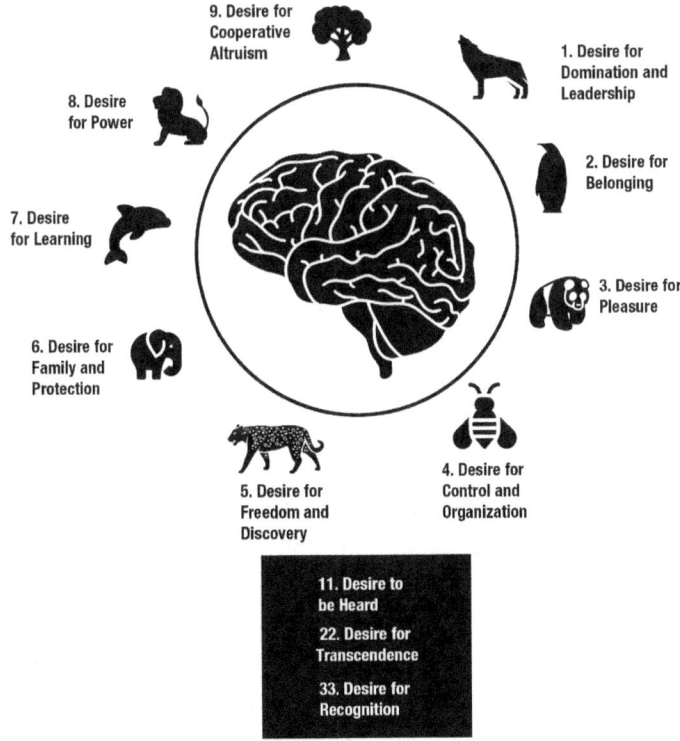

9. Desire for Cooperative Altruism

1. Desire for Domination and Leadership

8. Desire for Power

2. Desire for Belonging

7. Desire for Learning

3. Desire for Pleasure

6. Desire for Family and Protection

5. Desire for Freedom and Discovery

4. Desire for Control and Organization

11. Desire to be Heard

22. Desire for Transcendence

33. Desire for Recognition

Figure 3: The 12 Instinctive Triggers.

Seventh Bio-Strategic Tool: understanding that *genetic drivers* permanently influences decision-making.

Practical Note: identify (and communicate) the instinctive trigger that your commercial offer can better satisfy to strongly motivate.

2.3 Neurobiological Drivers

Pavlov's famous dog experiment very well illustrates the effect we want to achieve concerning *neurobiological drivers*. It is about behavioral conditioning using preprogrammed physiological responses to specific stimuli.

In short, the Russian repeatedly synchronized the provision of food with the sound of a bell to eventually seek to obtain the same bodily reaction that triggers food with the isolated ringing. Iván Pavlov successfully turned an arbitrary audio cue into an anchor of hunger in the mind of his dogs.

To better understand the phenomenon, let us remember that emotions are states of the body, and feelings are states of the mind. In the latter case, the bell became a detonating anchor of an emotional response presenting salivation, gastric hormones, and acid secretion. This somatic framework is interpreted by the brain as the feeling of hunger.

An unrelated sound signal became synonymous with food in the neural maps of the dogs. The transcendental fact is that we can do this between all visual, auditory, olfactory, taste, or tactile stimuli and any emotion or feeling.

The specific way our body automatically reacts to the different proprioceptive, interoceptive, and exteroceptive stimuli is systematized a *priori* by nature. I refer to this phenomenological structure—which operates mainly from the unconscious—as the *biological-emotional programming* in the *Creative Intelligence* model and is the subject of study of the neurobiological disciplinary base.

Given the above, we can better visualize the economic applications regarding the subject in question. Fundamentally, we can make brands—or any related construct—a precursor anchor of emotions and feelings that encourage action. Just as *Coca-Cola* has done for decades, proving the significant potential of these tactics.

How to do it? With strategic definition and repetition: choose a sentiment—positive to seek sustainability—and connote it in the vast majority of your communications.

Eventually, the brand, product, or service will anchor the selected mental experience. Finally, when the potential customers are at the point of making a purchase decision, they will opt for the option generating greater sentient gratification, and, most likely, they will justify it with whatever rational argument.

It must be noted that the grandest value in understanding these ideas is providing us with information allowing us to mitigate our own behavioral biases to make smarter decisions.

For a deep understanding of the neurobiology of emotions, the entire bibliographical work of Professor Antonio Damasio and the *Polyvagal Theory of Professor* Stephen Porges are highly recommended.

Eighth Bio-Strategic Tool: understanding that **neurobiological conditioning** influences every decision and can be used to trigger emotions in front of the idea of brands, subjects, products, or services to increase the probability of action.

Practical Note: choose a feeling and make it synonymous with the construct you want to position.

2.4 Psychological Drivers

The unconscious influence of biophysical, genetic, and neurobiological conditioning in decision-making is profoundly significant. But, how we retain and process information in the mind is also a fundamental factor.

Particularly, in the commercial exercise, recognition (that we are remembered) and positioning (how are we remembered) are the primary variables determining the perceived value of a brand. Hence, studying psychodynamic processes is a necessary effort.

The *psychological drivers* represent the coincidence with the technical tendencies allowing us to think and remember. We can divide them into two main categories:

1) **Information processing:** the dynamics of the mind to make sense of the available data. Recommended related reading: *The Structure of Magic Vol I and II* by Richard Bandler and John Grinder.

2) **Information retention:** the phenomenology of memory. Recommended related reading: *The Seven Sins of Memory* by Daniel Schacter.

Contrary to common sense, representation and data storage in the neural system are non-definitive and malleable processes. In addition, they cause biases and specific conditioning that directly impact decision-making.

In other words, we believe we are in total control of these processes, but they have their own momentum loaded with unconscious influences.

In short—without our authorization—, as a survival instrument, the mind pre-makes automated decisions:

On the one hand, it tends to generalize, distort, and eliminate to favor understanding.

On the other hand, to prioritize, it carefully filters what is remembered. Memory is a multiple-distillation process that admits only what is frequent and/or generates a high emotional impact.

Thus, the options that the mind shows us to consciously "choose" are deeply mended a *priori*.

The most relevant thing about this subject is to detect such procedures to procure smarter decisions—by avoiding adverse influences—and, also, using them to connect vigorously with other human beings.

In subsequent chapters, we will review the above in more prominent detail.

Ninth Bio-Strategic Tool: understanding that psychodynamic processes drastically transform the conscious information we use for decision-making.

Practical Note: procure remembrance and a correct representation of your brand, product, or service with the aid of repetition, abstraction, and the triggering of intense emotions.

2.5 Rational Drivers

How many times do we allow ourselves to be guided by a cognitive unconscious, exercised and formed under the supervision of conscious reflection to keep and fulfill ideals, desires, and plans that have been consciously conceived? And how many, instead, are we guided by unconscious desires, appetites, and predispositions, ancient in biological terms and deeply rooted? I imagine that most of us, weak but well-intentioned sinners, function with both registers, although, depending on the situation and the different hours of the day, we do more with one than the other.[1]

- Antonio Damasio

Reason, or corticalization, has a specific biological function: temporarily mitigating innate impulses—instinctive and emotional—to make decisions other than those preprogrammed when they become adverse in a changing context; it is a survival tool.

To that end, nature has enabled us to consciously identify causes and effects to interrelate the phenomenology we ex-

---

1 Damasio, 2010, p. 418.

perience. *Rational drivers*, those forces encouraging us to find meaning, also promote actions.

The latter—for better or for worse—has allowed us to be the ruling species on the planet. Nonetheless, it is worth noting a very relevant point: logic is a weak element in the ecosystem of the forces that motivate a decision; it is only contrastably superior in cases of life or death.

For example, when faced with an indulgent food—let us think of the much-mentioned chocolate cake—our instinct will fervently ask us to consume it because of the energy it represents, but our reason could well avoid it by arguing counterproductive effects. In this case, we observe a corticalization process temporarily mitigating genetic behavioral instructions (Eibl-Eibesfeldt, 2007). However, if our nutritional habits were governed primarily by intelligent information, humanity would have a very different diet.

Now, the rational negative against innate conditioning is a rare case on a day-to-day basis; the vast majority of the time, reason justifies the underlying desires. Among other auto-indulgent, evidently permissive lines, we frequently find: "you deserve it," "everyone does it," "it's a good moment," etc.

Considering the range of biological influences on decisions, logical argumentation represents an indispensable but not very dominant factor.

For these motives, when we seek to encourage behavior, it is crucial to establish logical arguments to justify it, nevertheless they will only be of use if we conquer the spiritual, instinctive, and emotional layers first. The same should be considered when it comes to self-management; to seek intelligent decisions, it is essential to understand our unconscious catalysts.

Tenth Bio-Strategic Tool: understand **reason** is an indispensable ally in decision-making, but it does not represent the most influential behavioral guideline.

Practical Note: Clearly define and communicate *rational drivers*—which logically justify your strengths—as the final incentive in the decision-making process; however, always consider reason does not act alone in the human mind.

2.6 Cultural Drivers

From an ethological point of view, the information used by the mind of a human being to make decisions comes from three fundamental sources:

1) *Innate conditionings*: pre-programmed action guides based on what has represented the best chances of survival during more than four billion years of evolution. We are born with them; they correspond to the Being's instinctive, emotional, and spiritual plane.

2) *Individual experiences*: particular personal situations that complement the available data to determine actions. They are juxtaposed with innate conditionings. For the present, they are processed synchronously and stored in the memory for the future. They correspond to the psychological plane of the Being.

3) *Cultural learnings*: collective information heritage transmitted from person to person, group to group, and generation to generation. They represent socially modeled supra-instinctive survival tools and correspond to the social plane of the Being.

With this broad panorama, we can detect critical fields of study we must consider to understand and promote behavior: biophysics (vital interrelationship), genetics (instincts), neurobiology (emotions), psychology (information processing and retention), and sociology (culture).

In particular, to instrumentalize social guidelines, I refer to them as *cultural drivers*.

Neurobiologically, these motivators are supported by *consensus maps* (Zaltman, 2003) representing collective synaptic systems. In other words, neural information we structure and share between persons.

Cultural codes change from group to group, although there are many coincidences internationally in a globalized world like the contemporary one.

Culturally speaking, what we have to do or say to convince members from different countries (e.g., Scandinavian, Japanese, or Mexican) is different. Contemplating these codes in the strategic mix is necessary to facilitate the connection with other minds.

To fit in socially, telling stories using metaphors or archetypes while considering their shared significance is very pragmatic. The film and advertising industry do it all the time. For example, the alpha cowboy of *Marlboro*, the Santa Claus of *Coca-Cola*, the arches of *McDonald's*, the tiger of *Frosty Flakes*, the wise old man, the young rebel, and the dark force. All these references are symbols with shared sublimated values between individuals.

Eleventh Bio-Strategic Tool: identify and use codes with **sublimated-collectively-shared values** to connect with distinct cultural groups.

Practical Note: Use symbols with cultural meta-value to reinforce communications, whether to sell, motivate, or analyze your own thoughts.

2.7 Creative Drivers

The final piece of our behavioral biologic armory for behavioral understanding is integrated with the *creative motivators*, the forces encouraging us to change destiny.

After more than twenty years of seeking to get closer to the rational essence of this magnanimous concept, the most consistent definition I have managed to systematize is the following:

Creativity is about thoughts of thoughts impacting inside and outside of the mind to shape the future.

In more abstract terms, the creative impetus represents **transformative metathoughts**.

This extraordinary faculty has a specific biological function: allow the organism to adapt and become the constant change in an infinitely dynamic existential context like ours.

To strengthen and use the creative ability, it is imperatively relevant to consider that the thoughts comprising it include quantifiable rational ideas but also unquantifiable irrational such as feelings.

In short, an outstanding creative work masterfully fuses sensory stimuli, logical thoughts, and sentient experiences.

Likewise, it is essential to understand that these creations are not only needed to inspire the soul; they also allow us to conquer obstacles and form new realities.

Consequently, as a survival tactic, we humans are biologically designed to seek creativity in ourselves and praise it in others. Our most unfathomable essence drives us to become architects of sublime worlds.

Hence, it is essential to include this inertia for understanding decision-making. We will be predisposed to opt for paths that build the future in the way our two main cognitive modes direct it: reason and intuition. As a side note, within intuition, we find instincts, emotions, and feelings at a conscious and unconscious level; regarding reason, we encounter conscious logical thoughts.

For much greater detail and depth on the biology of the creative faculty, I have documented the book *Creative Intelligence* (2022) with a geometric model exploring this and other categorical questions such as Being and Freedom.

In the managerial exercise, devising new metathoughts that transform reality is a necessary effort to:

1) **Meet and maintain objectives** in all areas: managing the adaptation and conversion to ally with the infinite change.

2) **Add value:** creativity differentiates everything it touches; therefore, due to the supply-demand law, it will make it more valued—*the worth of things rises with scarcity and uniqueness.*

3) **Procure Affiliation:** motivate teams by carrying a flag of leadership representing new and better times to come.

4) **Generate attraction force:** energizing products or services with the possibility of improving lives in the distant and immediate future.

This phenomenon is clearly manifested in the interest and attractiveness generated by companies that have joined the human space race with satellite facilities and interplanetary resources. Among them are *SpaceX, Starlink, Google, Amazon, Virgin Galactic, and Blue Origin.*

Twelfth Bio-Executive Tool: understanding that adding creativity to anything means adding value exponentially.

Practical Note: Clearly identify and communicate how your efforts or offer represent a unique tool for improving the future.

2.8 Conclusion

To conclude a strategic bio-equalization aligned to the biological conditioning of the species in a commercial context, I propose the following process:

1) **Biophysical equalization**

Identify and define a strong Purpose behind the project and commercial offer, which demonstrates protecting Life—in all its manifestations—to endow them with an enormous power of attraction. Respond to other minds: why do you, the project, and everything around it, represent a movement worth supporting for the good of all? Inspire the depths of the human essence!

2) **Genetic Equalization**

Choose a core instinctive trigger that you can connect to most efficiently. To establish it, consider the innate behavioral tendencies—phylogenetically ordered—and the desires they channel in the mind. Once determined, connote—directly and indirectly—its fulfillment through the result you want to achieve (e.g., purchase, affiliation, vote, agreement, or more). In other words, clearly communicate the effect: doing X means satisfying the desire for (for example) domination, belonging, sensory pleasure, control, discovery, protection and family, learning, power, cooperative altruism, being heard, transcendence, or recognition. Essentially, clarify which instinctual desire you can best meet with your strategic offer and consistently convey it. For efficiency purposes, select only one to create a solid long-term alliance and a maximum of three per communication element.

3) Neurobiological equalization

The human organism is systematized to react physiologically in specific ways to the different stimuli it experiences. These bodily responses—better known as emotions—are interpreted by the mind as feelings. Team up with a catalyst that provokes a particular positive feeling experience (e.g., an image of a happy family, extreme sports, natural panoramics, etc.) to favor the decision you want to promote. If your brand, offer, product, or service triggers a positive emotion, it will gain significant preference. How to do it? With the help of repetition and changelessness, suggesting a feeling—and the release of its respective neurotransmitter—in the vast majority of your communications. Just like Pavlov did with his dogs. How do you want to make people feel whenever they hear from you? Define it properly.

4) Psychological equalization

Consider that, by nature, we are designed to save energy, simplify, prioritize, and streamline processes. For these reasons, the memory firmly filters, and the mind generalizes, distorts, and eliminates the information received; consider these phenomena to make intelligent decisions and communicate convincingly. Also, estimate the most potent influence of psychodynamic processes comes from the unconscious; conquer it first to access conscious choices.

5) Rational equalization

Congruently order the rational value of the decisive option you seek to highlight. Logically, why would someone choose what you intend to promote? These reasons are essential, but remember they represent the weakest influence in the de-

cision-making process; it is the final step after having convinced the deepest levels of the psyche.

6) Cultural Equalization

Recognize the sublimated shared values in the symbols regarding the group you are intercommunicating with. Use
such codes to clearly link them with the ideas you want to
convey. Always be careful to ensure these covert meanings
are really what you are trying to project.

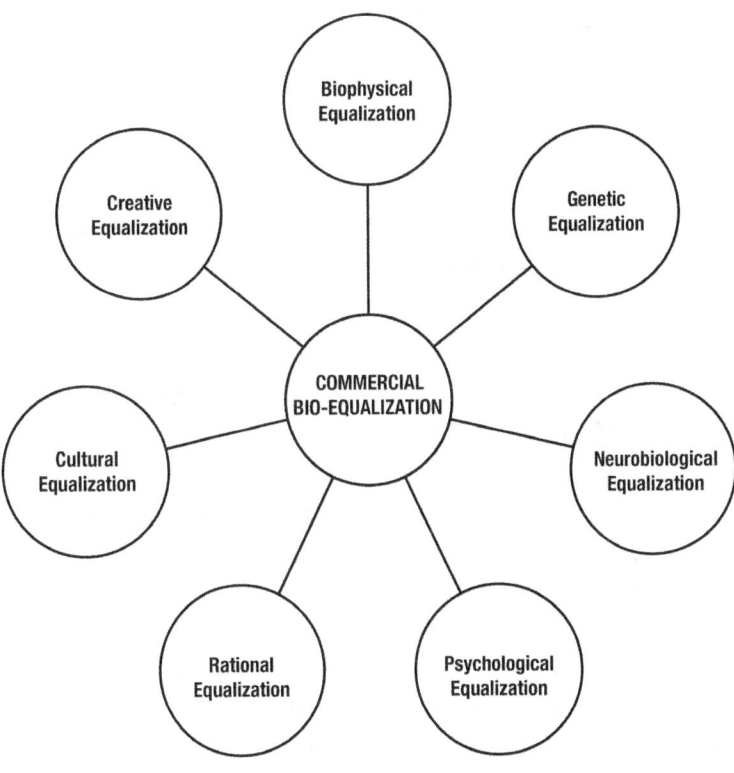

Figure 4: Elements of the Commercial Bio-equalization.

7) Creative equalization

Finally, pursue a significant differentiation through neural constructs comprised of thoughts—including feelings—that will impact inside and outside the mind shaping destiny. Clarify: what rational ideas and sentient experiences do you offer like anyone else? And how do they contribute to a better future for everyone?

This bio-equalization model is a compelling means of predicting and promoting behaviors, deeply enriching a commercial strategy or offer, positioning robust constructs in the mind, weaving shared perceived realities, and, above all, identifying selfish biases and personal conditionings to make wiser decisions. The world urgently needs a vastly more conscious and empathetic humanity to protect vital prevalence. The latter is the final purpose of the presented ideas; I sincerely hope they find the right hands and pave the way for a fruitful and compassionate future.

3.0 COGNITIVE AND BEHAVIORAL PHENOMENOLOGY

Following, we will review some traps that the mind plays on us based on the physical, genetic, neurobiological, and psychological conditionings of the Being.

To weld this exhibition, it is essential to start from the most fathomless point, seeking to answer epistemological questions such as: What is reality, matter, ideas, or desires? What motivates us? How does the mind present our perceived reality? How do we store and process the information we sense of existence? What are reason and intuition? And what reactions and behavioral tendencies do we have preprogrammed biologically?

As knowledgeable readers, you will agree there are no definitive answers to such perennial questions; however, with the help of modern philosophy and science, we have extraordinary information that allows us to get closer to their understanding. Therefore, the following ideas have a reflective and non-determining character; they are specifically designed to decode the mind and disarm the selfish biases commonly dominating our decisions

In addition, these notions represent key instruments to guide, determine, motivate, encourage purchase, build brands, structure strategies, configure concepts, create value, and many more applications in the managerial environment.

Contemporary leadership demands a creative, courageous, and profoundly reflective spirit; exploring the most remote territories of our comprehension is vital to conquering the present and future.

With you, the human cognitive and behavioral phenomenology.

3.1 Hermeneutics of Reality

3.1.1 Physical Paradigms

A dairy farmer is struggling with milk output on the farm and decides to ask a scientist at the local university for help.

For reasons that remain unexplained, they consult with a theoretical physicist. The physicist goes off to do some complicated calculations and returns with an impressive-looking stack of equations. "I have solved your problem, I think," says the physicist. "What is it? replies the farmer excitedly. "Well, first assume a spherical cow…"[2]

This anecdote told by Sean Caroll, one of the most recognized scientific communicators in the world, in his book on the biggest ideas in the universe, is very representative because it clearly illustrates one of the most fundamental cognitive biases of humanity. In short, it emphasizes that everything we think we know (including science) is based on baseless assumptions—properly referred to as axioms—shaping our conclusions.

In an effort to understand what we experience, we human beings have designed very pragmatic models acting as phenomenological maps; for example, classical mechanics is one of the most used in recent history.

Within this latter paradigm are the highly sought-after Newtonian mechanics and even the disruptive relativistic mechanics erected by Albert Einstein. Also, other not so well known models, such as Lagrangian and Hamiltonian mechanics.

Caroll explains it very well: *Classical mechanics says that the world is made by things with definite, measurable values, obeying deterministic equations of motion; it stands in contrast to quantum mechanics. Newtonian mechanics adds specific ideas about absolute space and time. It stands in contrast with "relativistic" mechanics, which is classical*

2 Caroll, 2022, p. 26.

but not Newtonian, and in which space and time become unified.[3]

The problem with classical mechanics is that it only asks what the system is doing at a particular moment but doesn't question more transcendental answers like what makes the system move?

On the other hand, quantum mechanics has started to tear down classical frameworks due to its focus on the smallest. The latter has allowed it to detect causes with a broader vision, but it has discovered phenomena that even defy logic. As which? Like subatomic "particles" acting like waves that exist and "do not exist" at the same time and that change their behavior once we observe them.

For reasons of efficiency, we will not delve into the world of contemporary physics; however, it is strongly recommended each reader seeks to soak up the theories that try to explain what we assume to be true. With this objective, I suggest the following readings: *Something Deeply Hidden* (Caroll, 2019), *The Biggest Ideas in the Universe* (Caroll, 2022), *A Brief History of Time* (Hawking, 1988), *Uncertainty* (Lindley, 2007) and *In Search of Schrödinger's Cat* (Gribbin, 1984).

In short, we cannot be absolutely certain of anything given our cognitive limitations as a species; what we know is part of interpretations based on axiomatic human models. Crucial observation: but the map is not the territory.

However, the grand "however" is that despite the latter, we do have access to an intersubjective (shared) reality with

---

3 Caroll, 2022, p. 18.

identifiable and constant patterns that we can corroborate between minds to get closer to the truth. Let's review this idea below.

Axiomatic Conditioning: the map is not the territory; comprehend the axioms that support your conclusions to make better decisions.

3.1.2 Objectivity, Subjectivity, and Intersubjectivity

As Antonio Damasio, an authority in the world of neurosciences, well notes: *Whether one likes it or not, all the contents in our minds are subjective, and the power of science comes from its ability to verify objectively the consistency of many individual subjectivities.*[4]

Consider: everything we experience happens within an interface we call the mind, where perceived reality is interpreted and restructured.

What is superlatively valuable is understanding that said interface—both personal and collective—is moldable with thoughts and actions.

Objectivity is derived from the word object and usually refers to ideas free from individual judgments and biases. But is this even possible? Strictly, it is an antinomy; an idea can never be objective because, by definition, objects do not have ideas. On the other hand, no matter how rational it may seem, a thought cannot be separated from the physiological

---

4 Damasio, 1999, p. 83.

(emotional) reaction it unleashes in the organism, much less from the mind itself. Thus, objectivity is a myth.

Now, if we admit every mental construction has emotional, sentient, and psychological frames, we can aspire to detect and contemplate their influences. If we only deny these effects, we will start from a fallacious and incongruous basis.

On the other hand, subjectivity suggests a high burden of individual convenience. It is impossible to think outside of ourselves; however, we can try to avoid selfish biases in our thoughts. Consequently, the central question is not about objectivity against subjectivity but egoism against open-mindedness to approach the truth.

In Kantian terms, for thought to be consistent with itself, it is pragmatic to differentiate our cognitive abilities as follows (Kant, 2017)[5]:

Understanding: corresponds to intuitive thoughts; they are unquantifiable.

Judgment: juxtaposes intuitive thoughts with rational thoughts.

Reason: rational thoughts; they are quantifiable.

---

5 Kant, 2017, p. 87.

Finally, if all human thinking is subjective, how can we access reality outside the self? Science has skillfully found this answer: validating with consistent intersubjective patterns.

Kant refers to it as subjective universality in his famous book *Critique of Judgment*:

The judgment of taste, in which we are aware of being completely disinterested, can, then, rightly claim a universal value, although this universality does not have a foundation in the objects themselves; or in other words, there is a right to a subjective universality.[6]

Then the last piece in this chapter is intersubjectivity: shared thoughts integrating intuitive and rational values, with which we can identify consistencies to assume models reflecting the possible reality outside of ourselves.

So, not everything is lost; we have the possibility of accessing the truth, maybe not in absolute terms, but in partial terms; that is what science and philosophy care of, the most remarkable patrimony of humanity.

Finally, the splendid peripety—already revealed at the beginning—is that we can model the intersubjective realm with our thoughts, actions, and decisions; we are the architects of shared worlds that we build with creativity impacting inside and outside the mind.

Additionally, taking advantage of the inertia of Kantian terminology, I conclude with a thought for those who like philosophy: we can rationally reflect on what is *good*, delight ourselves irrationally and individually with what is *pleasant*,

---

6 Kant, 2017, p. 30.

find shared glimpses of reality in what is beautiful, and approach together the infinity with the *sublime.*

Kant calls sublime that which is perceptible but incomprehensible because of being bigger than ourselves. Thus, it is in our hands, making the individual and the shared universe a sublime masterpiece that inspires the most profound depths of being.

Conditioning of subjectivity: All thought is a subjective judgment that integrates individual inclinations; detect and consider them to make intelligent decisions.

3.1.3 What is Value?

Previous note: Next, for efficiency purposes, I will summarize profound ideas; reviewing the chapter several times is recommended to favor its understanding.

The central premise is that value is not intrinsic but subjective and intersubjective. That is, the material or functional qualities of something are not what define its value but its accessibility and the human impulse to dispose of it.

Let us update the famous law of supply-demand, which proposes that the lower the supply and the higher the demand, the value rises, and vice versa. But what is behind each variable, and what modulates them? In synthesis: desires and availability.

I call it the *Law of Supply-Demand 2.0*, and it is very frank: the *Will* (conscious and unconscious forces that motivate) triggers *thoughts* originating *desires* in the mind generating collective *demand* that, contemplating the offer, moderates the *perceived value*.

In more technical terms, biological conditionings guide psychological dispositions by drawing up neural cartographies motivating their organisms to pursue—and endow with value according to their availability—objects and experiences that trigger sentient rewards.

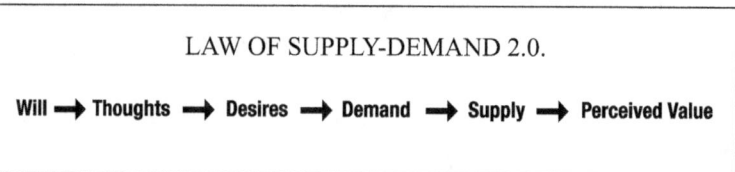

LAW OF SUPPLY-DEMAND 2.0.

Will ➡ Thoughts ➡ Desires ➡ Demand ➡ Supply ➡ Perceived Value

Figure 5: Law of Supply-Demand 2.0.

The latter is very relevant; we *Homo sapiens* value things mainly based on the feelings they generate.

It is essential to understand that the economic aspects, representing the valuation and access to goods and services, cannot be understood without the background of human nature and its social context; they are by no means purely rational phenomena, much less independent.

On this foundation, Karl Polanyi, author of *The Great Transformation*, one of the most influential books in the world of Economics, comments: *neither the birth nor the death of classes, neither their aims nor the degree to which they attain them; neither their cooperations nor their antagonisms can be understood apart from the interests of society, given by its situation as a whole.[7]*

Desires—biologically determined and psychologically and culturally specified—define value and the entire social structure. To increase the chances of survival, the vital impetus, instincts, emotions, feelings, psyche, reason, and culture—united—give shape to what we call the market and economy; all these elements are sub-instinctive, instinctive, and supra-instinctive tools of prevalence.

Now, based on the above and concerning value manifested in price: it represents the quantification of the availability of objects and experiences that reflect collective desires; it is a systematized measurement to favor exchange. This is what also Polanyi comments:

...money is just another name for a good used in exchange more frequently than another, and which is therefore acquired mainly in order to facilitate exchange.[8]

With another approach, something interesting happens if we analyze currency from a behavioral biologic point of view. Money means the *instinctive desire for power* symbolized, quantified, and materialized. Said fulfilled desire provokes the feeling I call *potency*; the same, that within the framework of the *Geometry of Feelings* (J.C. Chávez, 2022), is a joy in the face of the possibility of obtaining or preserving desires.

In short, currency provides a numerical value to the opportunity of obtaining positive feelings and avoiding negative

---

7 Polanyi, 2001, p. 159.
8 Polanyi, 2001, p. 137.

ones, which are at the service of the resistance of Life: it is a supra-instinctive survival tool (just like culture and social structures).

Computing these condensed ideas, we close the didactic cycle complementing the initial premise: value is not intrinsic but subjective and intersubjective and is modulated by the availability of collective desires that reward their creditors with sentient experiences.

Then, considering all of the above, how can we create value? Connecting with spiritual, instinctive, emotional, and rational desires with well-differentiated—and therefore scarce—creative products and services.

Conditioning of valuation: Value (or price) is a mental construct and does not have a direct material root. Human beings value based on biological desires; recognize the own and collective to make better decisions and/or generate demand.

3.2 Biological Dialectic

Next, a fascinating and penetratingly transcendent subject. It is the most fundamental observable essence of existence, a simple process that reflects the functioning of everything we experience, from the most micro—in subatomic levels—to the most macro—in cosmic planes.

Identifying this unique phenomenon becomes a heuristic tool that facilitates understanding biological, psychological, and economic processes.

Because of representativeness, I call it *biological dialectic*; the precursor genius of the concept, at the time, named it *dialectic materialism*. Although, in 1947, given the context and politicization of the term, he instructed that it be redefined as *energetic functionalism*. I am talking about Willhelm Reich, one of the most brilliant minds in the Western world, and he commented this way regarding the topic:

It will be necessary to add a preface to the publication of Die Bione which would point out the progress made in orgone research since its first publication, and, most important of all, to change the term "dialectic materialism" to "energetic functionalism" which it truly and really is. I could no longer afford, as I did ten years ago, to have my method of thinking and research termed dialectic materialism, since (1) the socialist and communist parties are still using the term without giving it any meaning; (2) I don't wish anymore to be confused with the Marxist political parties; and (3) energetic functionalism of today has as much to do with dialectic materialism as a modern electronic radar device with the electric gas tube of 1905.[9]

Reich's life was filled with controversy and opposition, as has happened with other privileged and revolutionary minds in history. Independently of that, one of the pillars of his extraordinary ideas will allow us exceptional insight.

The biological dialectic is a process present in the operation of everything observable about existence and, therefore, permeates physical, mental, and social aspects.

It consists of a simple and forceful dynamic:

---

9 Reich, 1979, Editor's Note.

TENSION - CHARGE - DISCHARGE - RELAXATION

I have identified some related examples in different areas:

In Physics, Chemistry, and Cosmology:

- The *tension* and *charge* in quarks (subatomic particles), caused by other forces, lead to the *discharge* of energy and *relaxation* in the form of protons and neutrons—the physical basis of existence.

- The *tension* and *charge* in atoms, caused by other forces, lead to the *discharge* of energy and *relaxation* in the form of the universe's elements, from light to heavy, such as iron.

- The tension and charge in galaxies, caused by other cosmic elements, lead to the discharge of energy and relaxation in the form of new galactic systems.

In Biology:

- The *tension* and *charge* on nutrients, caused by metabolic processes, lead to the *discharge* of energy and *relaxation* in the form of cell growth and reproduction—the functional basis of Life.

- The *tension* and *charge* in ecosystems, caused by the survival impetus of their living organisms, lead to the *discharge* of energy and *relaxation* in the form of evolved systems with greater probabilities of prevalence.

In Sociology:

- The *tension* and *charge* on social structures, caused by different interests, lead to a *discharge* of energy (frequently with violent manifestations) and *relaxation* in the form of new geopolitical and economic systems.

In Philosophy:

- The *tension* and *charge* in a thesis, caused by an antithesis, lead to a *discharge* of energy (thoughts are energy) and *relaxation* in the form of synthesis. The famous Hegelian dialectic.

In Psychology:

- The *tension* and *charge* in the neural processes, caused by mental experiences, lead to the *discharge* of energy and *relaxation* in the form of learnings.

In Climatology:

- The *tension* and *charge* in the climatic systems, caused by its dynamic elements, lead to the *discharge* of energy in the form of storms or natural phenomena and *relaxation* in the form of calmness.

In Behavioral Biology:

- The *tension* and *charge* in the Being, caused by spiritual, instinctive, emotional, sentient, rational, and creative desires, result in energy *discharge* in the form of actions (thoughts, behaviors, and decisions) and *relaxation* in the form of positive feelings.

Thus, the existential wheel turns incessantly, destroying and building to evolve, a sublime swing highlighted by its infinitely changing character. It is a masterpiece full of dissonances in search of harmony, just as the most august symphonies do; for this reason, music touches the deep fibers of our essence and represents another example of manifest biological dialectic.

And thus, the most majestic human faculty is also revealed, our ability to direct the dialectical cycle, consciously forming metathoughts triggering tensions discharging into new ideas that impact inside and outside the mind, sculpting destiny. Creativity is the most potent grant that *Homo sapiens* possess.

Regarding the managerial exercise in an economic context and other psychosocial issues, you will find below some cyclic analogous processes to biological dialectics. Identifying its parts signifies a necessary tool to channel its effects. A manager or leader must understand and seek a balance that generates energizing tension and renewing discharge to achieve exceptional results.

After all, there is no reward without effort.

Tension - Charge - Discharge - Relaxation	
Problem - Fear - Conquest - Learning	↻
Need - Innovation - Solution - Satisfaction	↻
Inflation - Austerity - Manufacturing - Abundance	↻
Desires - Demand - Supply - Wealth	↻
Objective - Effort - Achievement - Reward	↻
Low Energy - Hunger - Feeding - Satiety	↻
Scarce Resources - Work - Production - Stability	↻
Introduction - Conflict - Resolution - Outcome	↻

Figure 6: Cyclic analogous processes to biological dialectics.

Bio-dialectical conditioning: All physical, biological, and human processes are incessant dialectical cycles; the *Homo sapiens* is designed to seek harmonious resolution in every thought, action, and decision.

3.3 Phenomenology of Memory

As we reviewed in the section on psychological motivators, data storage in the neural system is a malleable process; it changes over time and is never definitive.

Memories are fragile but powerful products of what we can remember about the past, believe about the present, and imagine about the future[10], according to Daniel Schacter, professor of psychology at Harvard University and an au-

---

10 Schacter, 1996, p. 308.

thority on memory research. This quote implies something very relevant: memories are updated each time we think about them based on the current context.

Jeffrey Prager, Professor of Sociology at UCLA and member of the Southern California Psychoanalytic Institute, refers to them as *narrative fragments created to represent one's feelings and bodily*[11] *experiences*. In other words, not only are memories transformed every time we think about them but they are also born subjectively biased.

Memory represents a fragile storage system but still convincingly influences each of our thoughts

Added to all this, the brain integrates a network of *Zones and Regions of Convergence and Divergence* (Damasio, 1989) that act as a strict filtering system defining—among other things—what is remembered in the short or long term.

As we can see, entering in a defined fashion and prevailing in the mind is not a simple matter; it is a task full of imposing barriers.

In the economic field, *recognition* (to be remembered) and *positioning* (how are we remembered?) are variables directly impacting the perceived value of any construct (brands, subjects, products, services, etc.). So what can we do to be 1) remembered and 2) remembered the way we want?

The most crucial matter is understanding that the transition to long-term memory depends on two essential factors: repetition and sentient intensity. In other words, we will remember for a longer time what we have interacted with many times or what caused us an intense emotional experience—

---

11 Prager, 1998, p. 82.

positive or negative. With these reflections, a rule is deduced to impact the mind: repeat and thrill.

Regarding the immediate present, the qualities of memory determine biases and specific conditionings in behavior.

Therefore, creating value, motivating, existing in other minds, and making intelligent decisions depend on the phenomenology of memory.

Grounded on the book *The 7 Sins of Memory* by Daniel Schacter (2001), I list some memory phenomena with their respective antidote to ensure correct recall.[12]

1) *Transience*: Memories tend to fade over time. **Antidote**: repetition.

2) *Absent-mindedness*: what did not go through the mind is not registered. **Antidote**: Make sure you get attention.

3) *Blocking*: the mind is inclined to hide memories that cause negative effects. **Antidote**: connect mainly with positive feelings.

4) *Misattribution*: Memories combine with each other to form distorted representations. **Antidote**: clarity and frequency in communications.

5) *Suggestibility*: the mind tends to configure its perceived reality with what is constantly suggested. **Antidote**: Take the lead in shaping perception and memories.

---

12 J.C. Chávez, 2021, p. 164-173.

6) *Bias*: the mind tends to remember better what it perceives as convenient. **Antidote**: connect with conscious and unconscious desires to represent the most significant benefit.

7) *Persistence*: the mind remembers more what is constantly presented to it. **Antidote**: frequency.

Memory fragility conditioning: Memories strongly influence behavior and are formed based on what we frequently experience or generate a high sentient impact. Maxim to permeate long-term memory: repeat and excite.

3.4 Psychological Programming

3.4.1 Generalization

As human beings, we create models of perceived reality to find meaning and survival tools. Frequently, these models are very incorrect and create barriers that limit our actions and thoughts; detecting and overpowering them with broad perspectives is much needed. In the end, all ideas are inaccurate neural interpretations, but when they become too detached from shared and consistent reality, then they become adverse.

Richard Bandler and John Grinder (2005), precursors of neurolinguistic programming, well detect some psychological phenomena that lead to cognitive restrictions in their book *The Structure of Magic, Vol. 1 and 2*; one of them is generalization, and this is how they expose it:

One of the universal processes which occur when humans create models of their experiences is that of Generalization. Generalization may impoverish the client's model by causing loss of the detail and richness of their original experiences. Thus, generalization prevents them from making distinctions which would give them a fuller set of choices in coping with any particular situation. At the same time, the generalization expands the specific painful experience to the level of being persecuted by the universe (an insurmountable obstacle to coping). For example, the specific painful experience "Lois doesn't like me" generalizes to "Women don't like me".[13]

Generalizing is a widespread practice, for example: "all Orientals are...", "all Mexicans are...", "all politicians are...", "nobody...", "never...", "always..." etc.

The most relevant is to detect that these confinements limit cognition and are usually counterproductive.

The biological tendency toward energy conservation is primarily responsible for falling into simplistic practices that bias our understanding. It requires less effort to generalize than to understand the complexity of diversity.

As for the positive, categorizing in a controlled way can mean an ally for comprehending.

Whatever the case, for psychobiological reasons, we constantly tend to look for patterns that allow us to encompass easily manageable absolutes.

Crucial reflections on this topic are:

---

13 Bandler & Grinder, 2005, p. 80.

1) Identify our own generalizations to broaden our vision and make better decisions.

2) Use generalizations to communicate more forcefully.

Cautionary note: One of the most illustrative examples of the power and danger of generalizations occurred with Nazi party propaganda. Headed by Joseph Goebbels, through repetition, he established general beliefs such as "all Jews are bad" and "the Aryan race is superior." This resulted in an entire country with a compromised faculty of criticism and distinction that supported atrocities in the name of fabricated ideals. Using generalizations to communicate must be done with responsibility and empathy.

Generalization conditioning: for psychobiological efficiency and stability reasons, human beings tend to generalize. It is essential to detect such biases to not limit understanding, make intelligent decisions, and/or communicate more forcefully.

3.4.2 Distortion

Distortion is another frequent cognitive modeling procedure that facilitates the interpretation of perceived reality but can be counterproductive.

It is one thing to adapt thoughts to our individual belief and processing systems and another to drastically change the sense of shared reality. This means distortion is a range and not an absolute value. Essentially, ideas are, *per se*, altered adaptations of experiences that, at a controlled level of inaccuracy, benefit understanding but, in excess, can cause pathologies as serious as schizophrenia.

One of the most common problematic manifestations of distortion occurs with *nominalization* in language. This happens when we transform dynamic processes into definitive nouns.

For example, saying "your perception is wrong" suggests a conclusive and immovable state when, in reality, "perception" is a changing component. The latter limits our understanding and locks us in rigid zones with few options. In this case, we could reverse the final and conflicting statement, making it a fluid concept: "you could perceive more accurately." Technically, we are reversing the nominalization by transforming the noun into a verb, which completely changes the meaning and gives us new possibilities.

Other potentially problematic scenarios examples with their respective restructuring could be:

- Transform "my job *change* is *nasty*" to "*changing* jobs is making me *feel frustrated*."

- Transform "your *decisions bother* me" to "what you are *deciding* is making me *feel* upset."

- Transform "your *job* is *terrible*" to "what you're *working* on *doesn't seem right*."

- Transform "my *intuitions* are *correct*" by "what I am *intuiting seems correct*."

This way, we open the door to change and move away from distorted and apparently unbeatable appreciations. Detect the nominalizations in the language, within yourself and others, to obtain new and better estimation alternatives.

On the other hand, it is crucial to reveal planned distortions in communications seeking to steer us toward favoring other interests. In more colloquial terms, detecting lies that strive to manipulate us.

Again, the essential thoughts on this topic are:

1) Identify our own distortions to broaden our vision and make better decisions.

2) Use distortions to communicate more forcefully (always with responsibility and empathy).

Distortion conditioning: For psychobiological reasons of efficiency and stability, human beings tend to *distort* the perceived reality. It is essential to detect such biases to not limit understanding, make intelligent decisions, and/or communicate more forcefully.

Conditioning of nominalization: In language, it is widespread to transform improvable dynamic processes into definitive nouns (apparently unimprovable); detecting and reversing this practice gives us new and better possibilities.

3.4.3 Deletion

The purpose of recognizing deletions is to assist the client in restoring a fuller representation of his experiences. Deletion is a process which removes portions of the original experience (the world) or full linguistic representation (Deep Structure).[14] - Richard Bandler y John Grinder

---

14 Bandler & Grinder, 2005, p. 59.

Third and last on our list of transformational processes in psychological programming is *deletion*. This is a phenomenon that suppresses perceptions of perceptions to prioritize, which can be beneficial or cause major conflicts.

Bandler and Grinder (2005) propose two primary cognitive levels, the *Surface Structure*, and the *Deep Structure*; a close simile could be Freud's conscious and preconscious. In the case of deletion, we cut out available understanding elements to simplify ideas. On the one hand, when consciously and carefully reduced, this procedure can be beneficial and pragmatic—we will be summarizing—; however, when it is unconscious or the product of a preference for minimal effort, it results in incomplete, incongruent, and problematic interpretations.

Again, this is a necessary dynamic for survival that, in different scenarios, can become self-destructive. Understanding it allows us to take advantage of its benefits and avoid its complications.

A classic inconvenient deletion is when we describe situations that cause us negative feelings without context as:

"I'm confused."
"I'm scared."
"I'm frustrated."
"I'm stressed."

In these cases, the appropriate reaction would be to detect the missing pieces: what specifically confuses, scares, stresses, or frustrates me?

Detecting—and not deleting—the causes of our sentient experiences is a highly liberating and productive exercise.

For example, fear is a negative feeling arising in the face of the possibility of losing or failing to fulfill desires; identifying the latter—present in our Deep Structure—allows mitigating adverse effects and making better decisions

To facilitate the recognition of their psychological root—and mitigate deletions—I have documented in detail, in the book *Creative Intelligence* (*Vol. II, Book 4: Geometry of Feelings*)[15], eighty-five sentient experiences with their prevailing rational origin. Below, find a list of some examples, all of which are the product of fulfilled, preserved, unfulfilled, or lost desires:

Pleasure: partial joy.
Pain: partial sorrow.
Eudemonia: integral joy.
Suffering: integral sorrow.
Love: joy related to a cause.
Hate: sorrow related to a cause.
Confidence: joy for thinking it is possible to obtain desires or lose fears.
Concern: sorrow for thinking it possible to obtain fears or lose joys.
Empathy: joy toward the joys of others and sorrow toward their sorrows.
Evilness: sorrow toward the joys of others and joy toward their sorrows.
Generosity: joy for the joys of others that one does not have.
Envy: sorrow for the joys of others that one does not have.
Benevolence: joy to share joys.
Jealousy: sorrow to share joys.
Praise: joy for the joys caused by the action of others.
Vituperation: sorrow for the sorrows caused by the action of others.
Glory: joy for an action of ours praised by others.
Shame: sorrow for an action of ours vituperated by others.
Tranquility: joy for the presence of what is loved.
Frustration: sorrow for the absence of what is loved.

*Understand joy as a positive feeling and sorrow as a negative feeling.

Figure 7: Examples of feelings and their descriptions based on the Geometry of Feelings.

---

15 J.C. Chávez, 2023, p. 233-362.

Another typical example of deletion occurs when combined with generalizations, for example:

"In my work, my effort is never appreciated."

To this, we could answer: "Can you think of a single time in which your effort has been appreciated in your work?".

If the answer is "Yes." we will have countered an elimination that generates frustration and adverse consequences.

As with the preceding processes, the essential reflections on this topic are:

1) Identify our own eliminations to broaden our vision and make better decisions.

2) Use eliminations to communicate more forcefully (always with responsibility and empathy).

Elimination conditioning: Human beings tend to eliminate perceived reality for psychobiological reasons of efficiency and stability. It is essential to detect such biases to not limit understanding, make intelligent decisions, and/or communicate more forcefully.

3.5 Behavioral Biology

3.5.1 Fixed-Action Patterns and Instinctive Behaviors: programming to act

In his studies on the taxonomy of ducks, O. Heinroth (1910) found that he could use courtship behavior for minute taxonomic classification, just as one does with morphological structures. These patterns proved to be characteristic for each species, and Heinroth called them species-specific instinctive behavior patterns ("arteigene Triebhandlungen"). The patterns were characterized by their constancy in form. They consisted of distinct behavioral sequences that could be homologized within closely related species. These motor adaptations have been investigated more closely since then, and their innate character has been verified. They are known as "fixed-action patterns." Together with orientation movements, they comprise a higher functional unit: instinctive behaviors (K. Lorenz and N. Tinbergen, 1929).[16] - Irenäus Eibl-Eibesfeldt

As Eibl-Eibesfeldt, co-founder of the *International Society for Human Ethology* and whose work represents an important heritage of humanity puts it, all vertebrates share genetically preprogrammed behavioral tendencies that define us as a species

In particular, *fixed action patterns* are consistent and recognizable muscular movement intervals. Neurophysiologically, they are activated by groups of centrally coordinated motor cells (Holst,1939).

---

16 Eibl-Eibesfeldt, 2007, p. 25.

Combined with orienting movements, these *fixed action patterns* lead to *instinctive behaviors*, generating more complex functional units when combined with learning.

As a whole, we colloquially know this latter phenomenological frame as instincts.

For survival, from our birth, we are conditioned to behave in concrete ways. For example, what happens when you put your finger in a newborn baby's hand? That grasping movement corresponds to a fixed action pattern. Other evident conditionings happen when he cries because he is cold or sucks when he is hungry.

As we develop, we juxtapose these muscular intervals with individual recorded experiences (memory and learning), becoming instinctual behavioral tendencies, which allow us to crawl, walk, run, communicate, and much more.

In an economic context, detecting instinctive impulses is an increasingly necessary exercise.

For example, humans tend to relax—suppress our sympathetic system and activate the parasympathetic—in a controlled, temperate, comfortable environment with warm colors and medium-frequency sounds (Porges, 2011). With such a body state, we will want to stay in that environment for longer; this is something *Starbucks* identified and used very well to create its business model. The famous third space, where we spend the most time—besides the home or the office—proposed by Howard Shultz in his book *Onward*, considers the instinctive conditioning factors to configure an offer with the most significant probability of success.

Concerning business, it is imperative to understand that the sense of security and confidence is a primary variable influencing decisions. What is ethologically relevant is that feeling safe is a physiological response triggered by instinctive behavioral tendencies. For example, a suitable negotiating table or sales context can integrate elements that generate trust, such as panoramic views—which provide control—, moderate temperature, a pleasant sound environment without stridency or noise—which avoids "stress"—, ergonomic furniture and decoration *ad hoc* to the values of the company.

Regarding marketing, product development, innovation, and virtually any area involving human interaction, it is vital to consider the instinctive desires that motivate behavior from genetics. We have already addressed this issue previously, but let us remember all *Homo sapiens*, by nature, seek to feel that we: dominate, belong, enjoy, control, discover, protect, learn, can, help, are listened to, transcend, and are recognized. Connect your offer or objective to resolving one of these instinctive desires systematized for survival reasons in all of us.

Instinctive conditioning: Human beings are genetically programmed to behave in specific ways. Identify these conditioning factors to make intelligent decisions and/or motivate actions.

3.5.2 Innate Releasing Mechanisms, Motor Programs, and Phylogenetic Adaptations of Perception: *programming to react and perceive*

The interpretation of stimuli apparently proceeds on the basis of phylogenetic experience. It is certainly advantageous

to avoid objects approaching rapidly without having to un-
dergo the painful personal experience of a previous collision
with them. The necessary "knowledge" for this adaptive re-
sponse is contained in information-processing mechanisms
as a result of phylogenetic adaptation. In this and similar
cases, these adaptations are so structured that specific stim-
uli or stimulus configurations release specific motoric acts,
that is, elicit specific behavioral patterns—in our example,
defensive and avoidance behavior. These mechanisms are
termed innate releasing mechanisms (IRM's; N. Tinbergen,
1951).[17] - Irenäus Eibl-Eibesfeldt

Incredibly, for the rational mind, our behaviors obey genetically configured reaction systems. As Daniel Kahneman—
winner of the Nobel Prize in Economics—calls it, *System*
2 represents the logical and energy-demanding processes in
charge of evaluating the appropriateness of such quick-and-
easy reactions predetermined by *System 1* (reason moderating intuition). Nonetheless, it is crucial to understand the
vast majority of our behaviors go unfiltered on "autopilot."

This phylogenetic programming manifests in specific patterns that can be detected and used to shape perceptions and
decisions.

A simple example of reactive automation occurs when we
exchange facial expressions with a baby, who is programmed
to imitate smiles and other gestures:

---

17 Eibl-Eibesfeldt, 2007, p. 55.

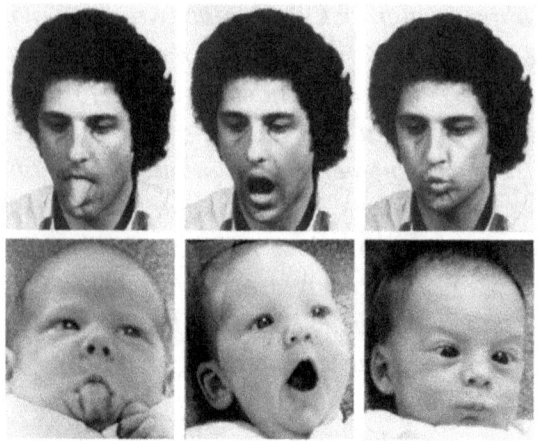

Figure 8: The model and its imitation by a 2- to 3-week-old infant. From A.N. Meltzoff and M.K. Moore (1977).[18]

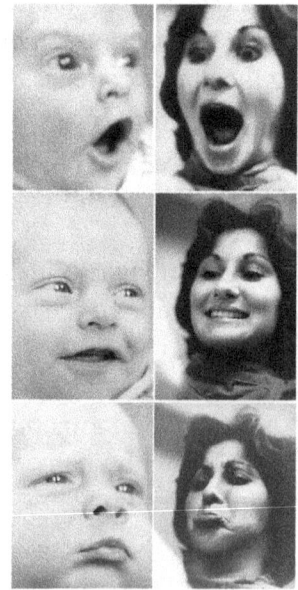

Figure 9: Facial expressions made by T.M. Field and their imitation. From T.M. Field et al. (1982).[19]

---

18 Eibl-Eibesfeldt, 2007, p. 56.
19 Eibl-Eibesfeldt, 2007, p. 58.

Also, an adult will automatically trigger a positive physiological state—on a conscious and unconscious level—upon receiving a smile. This is a necessary interaction to optimize socialization.

Other predefined reactions happen at the psychological level guiding our perceptions. Observe the following image: Which of the three silhouettes is bigger?

Figure 10: Perceptual illusion.

Immediately, our preprogrammed systematization (intuition) tells us that the one on the right is "taller." However, only when we think about it carefully (reason) do we realize all three are the same size.

The intuitive, unconscious, and anticipated conclusions come with everything we experience; sometimes, they work out in our favor, and sometimes they don't. We are conditioned by genes, from deep within, to perceive, process, and react in specific ways; this shapes our system of interpretation and beliefs. It happens because it has meant survival advantages on the evolutionary map.

In an economic context, considering *innate releasing mechanisms, motor programs,* and *phylogenetic adaptations of perception* has direct and practical applications, among others:

- Make better decisions, free of reactive and perceptive biases.

- Align communications to phylogenetic systematization to generate powerful messages.

- Motivate and calculate behaviors and decisions.

- Adjust processes to guide conduct (especially useful in the digital environment, sales experiences, and team motivation).

- Refine economic models integrating biobehavioral variables.

- Configure geopolitical systems in line with human behavior, reaction, and interpretation tendencies.

- Among many others.

We will expose specific applications on this topic in future chapters.

Phylogenetic reaction and perception conditioning: Humans are preprogrammed to react to stimuli with specific innate releasing mechanisms, motor patterns, and phylogenetic adaptations of perception. Consider these conditions to make intelligent decisions and communicate forcefully.

3.5.3 Verbal, Learning and Socialization Dispositions: programming to communicate, learn and socialize

Just as we human beings, for survival reasons, are preprogrammed to act and react in specific ways to the stimuli presented to us, we are also preprogrammed to learn, communicate, and socialize.

On the first aspect, we are designed to learn based on what represents the most significant prevalence benefits. For example, if the sound of a bell means we are going to find food, we will quickly learn to follow it; Gustav Pavlov demonstrated it well. According to classical learning theory, Pavlov's experiment represents a type *1 conditioned reflex* distinguished from *type 2* in that the neutral stimulus (the bell) occurs spontaneously and is not accompanied by a trial-and-error process (Eibl-Eibesfeldt, 2007). This differentiation is relevant because it is not the same for an entity to learn as it experiments arbitrarily as for it to seek to learn actively and voluntarily; it is even a fundamental issue in the development of artificial intelligence.

In the case of *Homo sapiens*, we are phylogenetically wired to learn and seek to learn. In the *Theory of the Multi-Self*, I identify it as an *instinctive desire* to learn.

In synthesis, based on biologically determined physiological reactions, we activate or inhibit behaviors related to emotional and sentient rewards or punishments triggered by spontaneous and/or explored stimuli. Rewards trigger *conditioned appetites* that provoke *conditioned actions*; punishments trigger *conditioned aversions* that cause *conditioned inhibitions* (Hassenstein, 1973).

As Eibl-Eibesfeldt rightly points out: *What is associated with what for reinforcing or extinguishing behavior is programmed by species-specific learning dispositions.*[20]

Modern Marketing knows this conditioning very well—at least empirically. Constantly presenting a brand accompanied by elements that activate *innate releasing mechanisms*, causing positive emotional frames, results in us wanting it close and, therefore, in more sales. For example, associating soft drinks with images of happy families.

Conditioning of learning: the tendency to seek learnings that represent sentient gratifications.

On the other hand, we are predisposed to socialize within specific behaviors. The fact that we can develop cooperative and affective bonds between individuals depends on various factors in different biological layers systematized a *priori*. It is an ability representing a crucial evolutionary advance as a species.

---

20 Eibl-Eibesfeldt, 2007, p. 76.

In the historical timeline, our ability to socialize originated primarily with parental care. This is how Eibl-Eibesfeldt documents it:

Sociability can be seen as having developed in several evolutionary steps. Appetence for partner proximity and compatibility occurs in fishes, which seek protection from predators in schools. But the development of parental care was a prerequisite for more elaborately differentiated forms of social life. With its development, mother-child signals came into existence. Behavioral patterns of affection and infantile appeals were the preadaptations from which adult bonding behaviors were derived. Friendliness evolved with parental care. In a further decisive evolutionary step, came the capability of forming individualized (personal) bonds.[21]

In other words, the mother-child union resulted in a robust relational network that allowed civilizations to be created. Regarding this tie, it is relevant to highlight two fundamental elements, one neurobiological and the other psychological. The first is a neurotransmitter known as oxytocin, the biochemical responsible for procuring emotional states of affective attachment. It is an extraordinary natural "anti-stress" that is released, in significant quantities, in the body of a mother and baby when they see each other. The second is the mental frame, derived from the latter, which we call love; a positive feeling occurring in the face of what brings us joys.

Oxytocin and love are the pioneers of human organizations; they transform into fear, sadness, and aggression when threatened and have given rise to the greatest epics ever told.

---

21 Eibl-Eibesfeldt, 2007, p. 169.

The social phenomenology of *Homo sapiens* is founded on genetically traced shared pillars. For this reason, we can identify ***conditionings of socialization***:

- *Conditioning of reciprocity*: the tendency to give and receive to create affective bonds.

- *Conditioning of family organization*: the tendency to create mother-father-children ties as the nucleus of society.

- *Conditioning of genetic diversity*: the tendency to seek a partner with a broader genetic correlational difference. For example, aversion toward incest and attraction to certain genetic configurations (Wedekind & Füri, 1997).

- *Conditioning of dominance*: the tendency to define relational hierarchies.

- *Conditioning of identity*: the tendency to define meeting points to generate a sense of group.

- *Conditioning of territoriality*: the tendency to assume external elements as "own."

Consequently, these behavior patterns are present in all cultures on the planet, from the most advanced to the most isolated and precarious, as Irenäus Eibl-Eibesfeldt has masterfully documented in his book Human Ethology.

The applications of this information in modern economics and business are countless. Beginning by developing solid value proposals that promote affective ties and a sense of belonging, reciprocity, domination, identity, family, and territoriality.

About the third aspect of this chapter, we are also predisposed to communicate in specific ways.

The prerequisite for communication is to have elements of mutual understanding. Precisely, the phylogenetic adaptations, which we share as a species, endow us with innate signals signifying available familiarities. A clear example is feelings, those unquantifiable neural cartographies that permit unique—but relatable—perceptions to all sentient organisms. Let us remember that sentimental experiences are mental states caused by *innate releasing mechanisms*—present in all human beings—that trigger particular physiological reactions to various stimuli.

In addition to this repertoire of intercommunicating guides, we have the instinctive capacity for language. As Noam Chomsky has cleverly identified, language patterns are genetically determined. We can comprise languages thanks to specific—mainly unconscious—biological conditionings: language is not an essentially rational product. We can know the latter, among other reasons, because of congenital pathologies such as the *specific language impairment* that inhibits said ability.

It is even possible to speak of a *universal behavioral grammar*. That is, body language —non-verbal— is understood by any human being regardless of language. Stephen Porges (1994), an authority in the world of neurophysiology, explains very well, in his Polyvagal Theory (1994), the neural interconnection and intimate correlation between emotions and facial expressions; we transmit feelings—consciously and unconsciously—with the muscles of the face. Countless investigations demonstrate the predominance of kinesic communication, representing the basis of the verbal.

97

Consequently, ***conditionings of communication*** are given, some of them are:

- *Conditioning of concord*: tendency to maintain harmony among members of a group.

- *Conditioning of friendly contact*: the tendency to establish an agreeable initial introduction to other individuals.

- *Conditioning of unity*: the tendency to reinforce social ties through rituals that cultivate shared values and protect against common enemies.

- *Conditioning of imitation*: the tendency to imitate group members to obtain learning.

- *Conditioning of exploration*: the tendency to stretch limits in social norms to restructure them.

- *Conditioning of instruction*: the tendency to teach other members of the group.

- *Conditioning of ranking*: the tendency to place oneself in and protect one's social status.

- *Conditioning of fighting*: the tendency to aggressively defend what is desired.

- *Conditioning of submission*: the tendency to give up in search of reconciliation.

Again, all of them are patterns of behavior with communicative codes shared by all world cultures and with immense practical applications.

Glimpsing the range of influence that learning, social and communicative conditionings have allows us a privileged panorama to understand human decisions.

3.5.4 Motivation Mechanisms, Moods, Impulses, and Biological Rhythms: programming to drive extended behaviors

How does our biology motivate us to behave in pre-established patterns?

All sentient organisms have a complex *motivation mechanism* integrating emotions, feelings, impulses, and moods that induce desires. This systematic view is key to understanding human behavior.

On the one hand, our biological-emotional programming (emotions) is responsible for activating or inhibiting physiological reactions causing phenomena of excitatory charge and abreaction (discharge) with the help of neurotransmitters:

The most important neurotransmitters of the brain are the catecholamines (epinephrine, norepinephrine, and dopamine), the endorphins (endorphin, enkephaline), serotonin, and the amino acids Y-aminobutyric acid (GABA), glycine, and glutamic acid. Some 60 neuro-hormones and neurotransmitters have been identified. (Eibl-Eibesfeldt, 2007)

We find ourselves, once again, facing a *biological dialectic* process of tension-charge-discharge-relaxation, responsible for directing the dynamic states of the body.

Now, in beings with a central nervous system, such bodily movements are perceived by the mind through signals sent by the internal organs to the brain, which are interpreted as feelings. When the vital operation is in or approaches a homeostatic balance, the information is translated into gratifications (positive feelings) and vice versa.

Basically, feelings act like a thermostat regulating the right direction, which is why I refer to them as *homeostatic thoughts*.

In turn, the preference for positive feelings (and dislike for negative ones) evokes desires that cause unconscious (*impulses*) and conscious (decisions) actions.

This is how our own nature moves us.

Sometimes vital objectives are covered quickly, but on other occasions, they extend, channeling lasting *moods*. For example, when we are thirsty, the body will not release a sentient reward until we drink water; it will even command an unpleasant mental sensation—*in crescendo*—until the goal is achieved. Dehydration undoubtedly produces a "bad mood."

So, behavior is not only about reactions to immediate stimuli; it masterfully integrates other temporal planes with the help of memory and neural processing faculties. As with learning, our biological design ensures we not only wait to respond to stimuli that arrive arbitrarily but that we actively seek them out through moods.

Finally, moods are also subordinated to universal factors with biological rhythms corresponding to specific timeframes; for example, to periods of approximately 24 hours, the famous circadian rhythm. As Eibl-Eibesfeldt comments:

Humans also have circadian rhythms for sleeping and wak-
ing, changes in body temperature, potassium excretion, and
many other processes. Physicochemical and psychic states
change during the course of the day.[22]

Bioprocesses are even synchronized with other planetary movements, such as the translation of the moon with the earth (month), the earth with the sun (year), and most probably beyond.

In this way, the harmonic cycle is completed; our mind seeks stimuli (motivates us) coordinated with the existential, vital, genetic, physiological, and psychological operation through feelings that originate perpetual and insatiable desires.

For these reasons, it is so important to know our biological architecture and the desires it engenders; it is such a necessary understanding that our Freedom and prevalence as a species depend on it.

In this book, we have focused on the commercial applications of understanding behavioral biology. However, its benefits transcend much larger planes

Conditioning of moods: We humans are predisposed to behave in specific ways based on our physiological requirements with different durations and deadlines.

---

22 Eibl-Eibesfeldt, 2007, 70.

Conditioning of biological rhythms: vital and physiological requirements are synchronized with universal periods equivalent to planetary movements such as days, months, seasons, and years.

3.5.5 Bases of Behavior

Following, I present a practical overview of behavioral biology, as discussed in previous chapters.

From an ethological point of view, human behavior is founded on three main pillars:

1) *Innate Conditioning*

Genetically pre-established instructions, written for around four billion years based on what has represented the most prominent chances of survival; among other manifestations, we find fixed patterns of action, releasing mechanisms, motor programs, perceptual adaptations, and verbal, socialization and learning dispositions.

2) *Individual Experiences*
(psychological conditioning)

In the case of intelligent organisms (with a central nervous system), innate conditioning are imposed on the mind through feelings channeling desires that cause actions. When genetic specifications are combined with orientation movements and conscious individual experiences—processed and retained with intellect and memory—they result in instinctive acts and voluntary behaviors.

3) *Cultural Constructions*
(cultural conditioning)

Finally, within individual experience, there is non-innate learning transmitted between minds from person to person, group to group, and generation to generation. Which have represented survival advantages and, therefore, are juxtaposed with innate conditioning through sublimated desires: each cultural learning symbolizes the possibility of fulfilled desires. This element complements an instinctive and supra-instinctive prevalence arsenal directing behavior.

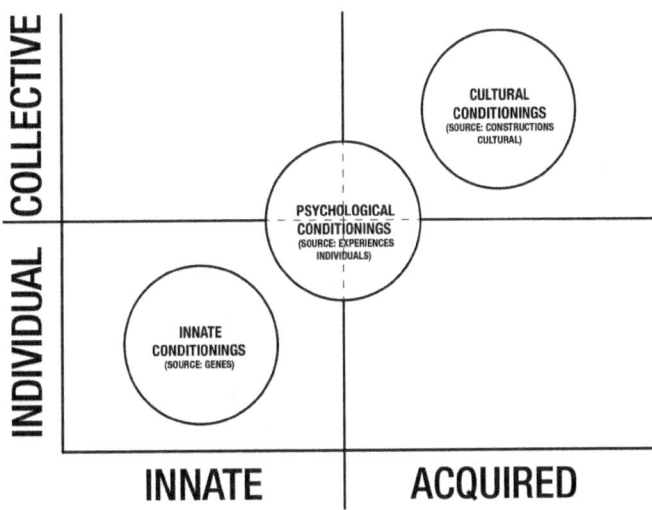

Figure 11: Behavior conditionings based on individual, collective, innate, or acquired character.

In turn, we can differentiate behavior based on its conscious or unconscious nature and its time-frame impact as follows:

1) *Impulses*: automatic and unconscious reactions guided by innate conditionings.

2) *Decisions*: conscious and voluntary movements (although typically influenced by biological conditionings).

3) *Instinctive Acts*: behaviors motivated by unconscious innate conditionings combined with orientation movements and the guidance of individual learning.

4) *Moods*: impulses that last longer (e.g., minutes, hours, or days).

5) *Personalities or Templates*: constant behavior patterns in extended time ranges (e.g., years). In the Western tradition, when they benefit the vital goal of resistance and prevalence, they are referred to as *virtues*, and when they are adverse, as *sins* (see *Creative Intelligence Vol. II* for further reference).

The previous concepts are designed to favor the understanding of the phenomenological framework that we call behavior, which means a crucial instrument to find meaning and make better decisions by revealing their interference. A remarkably beneficial exercise is to analyze one's own choices under the lens of behavioral biology to broaden our vision and obtain many more possibilities.

In the world of Economics, human behavior has predominantly represented a mysterious and unpredictable variable; a fallacious conception that has led to a significant bias of understanding and fundamental flaws in the design of social models. It is not possible to understand how to satisfy human material needs, through the use of scarce goods (economics), without understanding the biological architecture in depth.

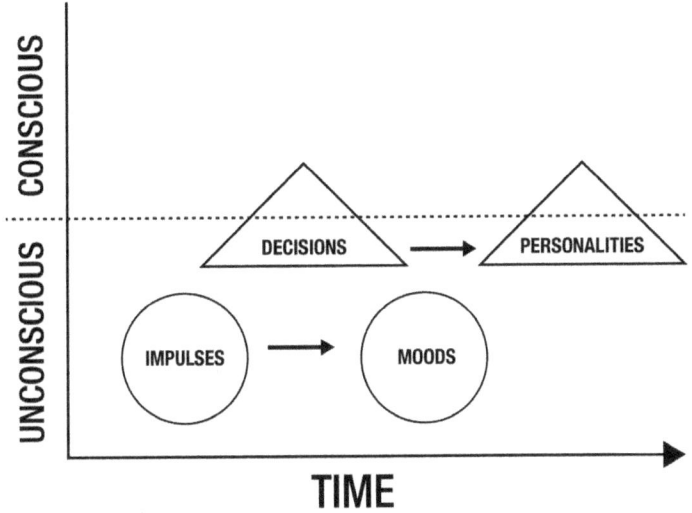

Figure 12: Classification of conduct based on its temporal and conscious or unconscious character.

Let us remember that, far beyond satisfying immediate egotistical desires, the primary biological collective struggle is the resistance and prevalence of Life. Any model, strategy, or tactic benefiting that goal will be favored with consistency, support, power, satisfaction, impetus, and operability.

3.5.6 Cognitive Modes: intuition and reason

Based on the information reviewed so far, a crucial classification for understanding cognitive abilities and behavior is revealed. I am talking about intuition in contrast to reason.

In his famous book *Thinking, Fast and Slow* (2011), Daniel Kahneman (2013) makes a very similar practical distinction and refers to each category as System 1 and System 2. The first is about rapid processes leading to decisions that are little analyzed and taken almost automatically; the second, on the contrary, corresponds to slow and careful reflections. Both culminate at a conscious level but with different ranges of unconscious influence.

On the other hand, Eibl-Eibesfeldt, as part of his research legacy, emphasizes the distinction between drives and conscious self-control, which pinnacles in what he calls the Neuroethology of Human Freedom.

In synthesis, he proposes that human beings can temporarily mitigate instinctive interference—to make decisions different from what is instructed by innate conditionings—through a process he anoints *corticalization*. In other words, as a particular hallmark of the species, we can postpone the satisfaction of impulses and control them consciously, thanks to the cerebral cortex.

However, he also presents another key element that sets us apart and supports self-determination: our ability to combine processes, also understood as *lateralization*. The concept references the differentiated functions of the left and right hemispheres of the brain; for example, as he comments:

People whose left hemisphere is damaged have impaired speech but are emotionally intact. They show sympathy and emotionality and are also musically competent. Those with right hemisphere damage, in contrast, are emotionally disturbed; they have shallow emotions or show atypical euphoria, and lose the ability to empathize with others.[23]

---

23 Eibl-Eibesfeldt, 2007, p. 87.

So, Eibl-Eibesfeldt proposes that *Homo sapiens* can decide because of its conscious capacity to temporarily mitigate instinctive impulses (corticalization) and to integrate emotional with rational processes (lateralization).

Regarding the latter, the simplistic distinction between left-emotional and right-rational is only a didactic tool; it actually has a deep neurobiological specificity that we should not overlook.

With this background, we can summarize and enrich the conceptual proposal of our *Strategic Bio-intelligence* archetype designed with the foundations of the *Creative Intelligence* and *Multi-Self Theory* models.

Human biology is made up of different layers that can be differentiated based on their origin and function:

- It is part of an integral, broad, and complex mechanism we call Life (spiritual stratum).

- Its design is determined by genetic instructions updated over billions of years (instinctive stratum).

- It obeys a system of automated chemical and physiological reactions, conceived based on the most significant chances of survival during the evolutionary map (emotional stratum).

- It can consciously interpret said reactions in the form of feelings, thanks to a central control command we call mind (sentient stratum), with which it can also retain and process information to make different choices from what is automatically instructed (rational stratum).

- Finally, it becomes aware of all of the above and uses it to model new metathoughts impacting inside and outside of the mind toward the future (creative stratum).

We integrate the vital impulse, instincts, emotions, and feelings in a particular cognitive mode I call *intuition* or *homeostatic thoughts* (e.g., System 1; right hemisphere).

On the other hand, I conceptualize processes designed to challenge automated commands, aided by careful retention and processing of perceived information as *reason* or *logical thoughts* (e.g., System 2; corticalization).

Finally, both modes come together exemplary to allow us *creativity* (e.g., lateralization), the most sublime human quality endowing us to unify reason and intuition through thoughts of thoughts to model the future.

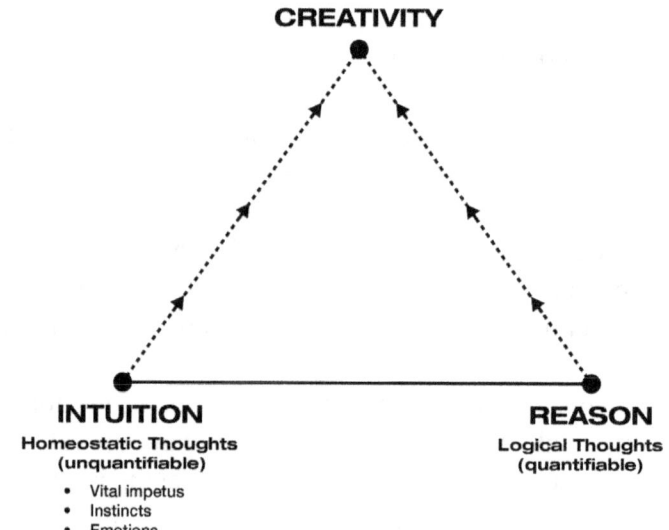

Figure 13: Intuition, Reason and Creativity juxtaposition.

Thus, I would like to emphasize something especially relevant to the contemporary world and to make more intelligent decisions: it is imperative to understand that intuition is a cognitive mode full of extremely valuable and necessary information that must be analyzed and not underestimated; consequently, the correct intention is to ally it with reason leading to creative and truly prosperous destinations.

3.6 Conclusion

We, humans, interpret the environment around us through a powerful interface—we call the mind—in charge of finding meaning as another survival tool.

Such interpretations are causal in nature; they are designed to detect causes. When reaching an inexplicable point, they become axioms (without causes) that we use as cognitive foundations shaping scientific and ideological paradigms.

From this deep point, we begin to find pre-established conditionings that direct our thoughts, actions, and decisions.

We are configured to erect belief systems—individual and collective—helping us detect consistent effects to assemble ideological instruments that support Life's resistance and prevalence.

Identifying this phenomenon, the axioms we use, and the subjective quality of understanding is a first revealing exercise to obtain a broad vision and make intelligent decisions. As a special note, this book is based on critical realism, which allows us to assume there is a reality outside of ourselves that we can access through experiences; however, it would not be correct to take this requirement for granted; it is just a pragmatic element.

Consequently, thanks to this interpretative capacity, we can understand that the environment and our biological architecture are full of instructions and specific conditionings—defined a *priori*—influencing at all levels, from physical "laws" to natural guidelines.

In this chapter, we have identified several of them with the primary objective of allowing us to make decisions free of selfish biases, congruent, and directed toward well-being.

The applications are vast, from the personal to the professional. Considering behavioral biology means understanding ourselves, what motivates us and where we are headed. In the professional sphere, let us remember that the director's competence is a function of synthesis of interrelation in the decision-making processes (Llano Cifuentes, 1996); therefore, without a biological vision, the managerial exercise falls into the absurd.

We find ourselves in the middle of a dialectical existential process loaded with tension and resolution; we are predisposed to value based on biological desires and their availability; our relationship with the whole of Life motivates us to protect it; the genetic coding instructs specific reactions leading us to instinctive behavioral tendencies; the mind is shaped to follow representation patterns limiting and standardizing our vision; memory is a dynamic entity that filters what is frequently present and/or what moves us emotionally; individual experience and cultural constructions are complementary variables; feelings are necessary millenary information; and creativity is the human gift that will set us Free.

In a nutshell, the above summarizes the exciting train of thought from the chapter on cognitive and behavioral phenomenology. Next, we'll integrate it into practical economic tactics.

PROCESSES

1) Intuition
2) Reason

3) Life Connection
4) Instincts
5) Emotions
6) Feelings
7) Reason
8) Creativity

9) Impulses
10) Decisions
11) Moods
12) Personalities

INNATE CONDITIONING
(EXTERNAL)

13) Bio-dialectical conditioning
14) Phylogenetic reaction and perception conditioning
15) Conditioning of learning
16) Conditionings of socialization (reciprocity, family organization, genetic diversity, domination, identity, territoriality)
17) Conditionings of communication (concord, friendly contact, unification, imitation, exploration, instruction, ranking, fight, submission)
18) Mood conditioning
19) Conditioning of biological rhythms
20) Instinctive conditioning

PSYCHOLOGICAL CONDITIONING
(SUBJECTIVE)

21) Axiomatic conditioning
22) Conditioning of subjectivity
23) Memory fragility conditioning
24) Generalization Conditioning
25) Distortion Conditioning
26) Conditioning of nominalization
27) Elimination Conditioning

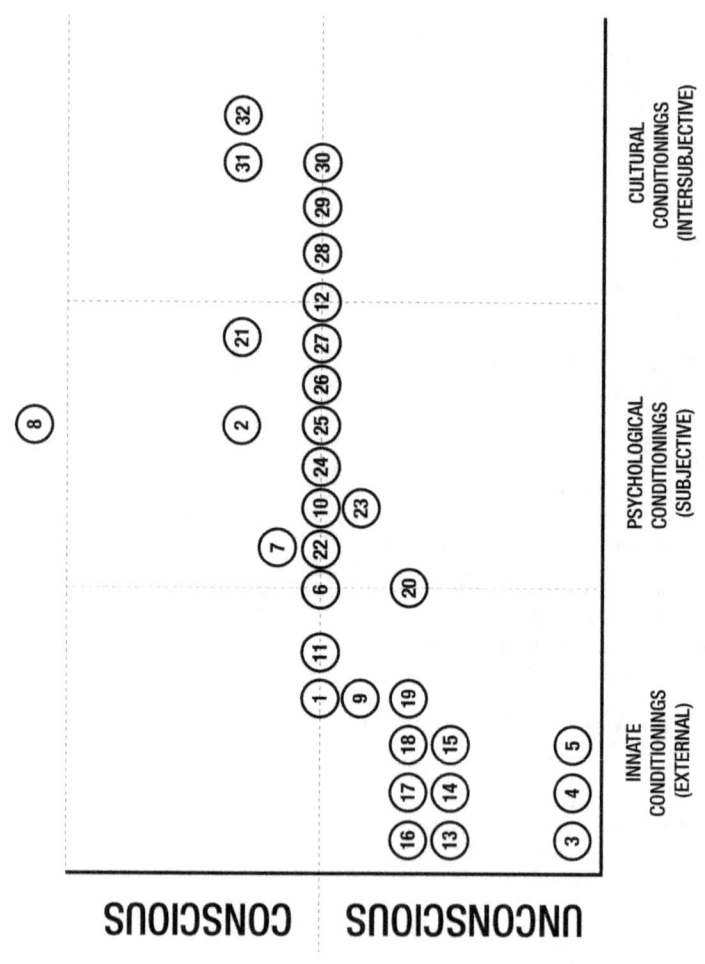

CULTURAL CONDITIONING
(INTERSUBJECTIVE)

28) Language conditionings
29) Conditionings of sublimated codes
30) Conditionings of stereotypes
31) Conditionings of traditions
32) Conditionings of social conventions

Figure 14: Cognitive and Behavioral Phenomenology Processes Matrix.

4.0 INTERSUBJECTIVE MODELING AND BUSINESS POSITIONING TACTICS

Detecting the biological conditionings that drive our thoughts and actions is a double-edged sword. On the one hand, it allows us perspectives full of new possibilities to make better decisions and guide other minds. Yet, on the other hand, in the wrong hands, it is an instrument of mass manipulation. For this last reason, it is so necessary that the majority obtain a broad and conscious vision of the whys of nature and its influence.

The flaws in contemporary economic models are not a systematic problem but a conscious one. We forget about the biological imperative governing every millimeter of our essence: **we are designed to help Life (in all its manifestations) to resist and prevail in the long term**. Selfish impulses are siding elements genetically programmed to promote collective strengths; when they represent the central objective of an economic system, it loses coherence and tends toward self-destruction. Short-term indulgence is one such impulse that, when given preference, causes negative consequences in the future. In other words, the major conflict of modern economies is moving mainly with the energy of selfish, hedonistic, and short-sighted momentums that tend toward self-annihilation.

On the contrary, if we privilege the well-being of Life as a whole and the long term (above immediate individual pleasure), we will find compatibility with our biological architecture and, therefore, prosperity, evolution, and the greatest sentient gratifications; it is really a logical-geometric question.

That said, I emphasize the relevance of beginning any commercial effort with a firm Purpose contributing to vital prevalence. Not only will it contribute to greater odds for success, power of attraction, and motivating coparticipants, but it will also provide sustainability.

Once a reason for being consistent with the vital archetype is established, then we can devise particular tactics allied to individual biological conditionings without providing to the extinction of Life on the Planet.

Next, we will review powerful commercial tools integrating the inertia of our biophysical, genetic, neurobiological, and psychological programming.

4.1 Creativity

Creativity is essential at any time or level of a business endeavor. It is the "ace up your sleeve," allowing us to differentiate—and therefore add value—everything it touches.

Let us remember creativity means developing thoughts of thoughts that impact inside and outside the mind to shape the future.

The first step is considering the types of thoughts available to shape new ideas.

On the one hand, we find the precise-quantifiable data product of our rational capacity. There is no substitute for well-registered and processed measurable information.

Daniel Kahneman (2013) elegantly establishes the strength of statistics with statistics. He remarks that Paul Meehl (1986) —one of his intellectual heroes—, in his controversial text *My Disturbing Little Book*, documents 20 studies proving that algorithmic *clinical predictions* are more accurate than those of trained professional experts. What happens is that opinions are prone to human bias, and data is not.

Ergo, settle all possible variables; the more intelligent information, the better.

Also, despite being counterintuitive, procure regression to the mean. That is, consider the averages as physical laws and align yourself with probability. For example, if your perception is that lately you receive many clients under 25 years of age in your business, but the statistics say in the last 3 months that age range represents only 5%: listen to the data and not your opinion before redefining the segment

No doubt, reason is a compelling cognitive mode that must be a fundamental part of creative practice. It will grant us an imperative causal understanding. However, let's not jump to conclusions; it means only half of the arsenal.

On the other hand, intuition is the second half of the armory and absolutely necessary for a creative outcome; remember that it groups instincts, emotions, and feelings.

Without feeling gratification, there is no motivation and, therefore, no action in the human realm. To move individuals, masses, and ourselves, rewards in the form of positive feelings are needed; they are an immovable variable in the behavioral equation.

Also, despite being unquantifiable, intuition has an immense load of information collected—literally—throughout billions of years. To ally ourselves with this cognitive mode and not fall victim to it, it is necessary to understand its neurophysiological phenomenology and privilege what I call *deep feelings* over immediate ones. I will explain better below.

By nature, we are emotionally designed to blindly follow our intuitions. Within the context they were intended, they are very favorable, but in different environments, they become counterproductive. In this latter situation, it is crucial to consciously understand what our instincts and emotions are telling us and why. To decipher them, we must eliminate the noise generated by immediacy and glimpse the intuitive message in the future (deep feelings); therein lies the key to the biological message. It will not mathematically surpass statistical data, but it will share with us irreplicable and irrational information about our profound essence and its connection with the sublimity of Life as a whole.

The result is explosive when we unite *logical thoughts* (reason) with *homeostatic thoughts* (intuition). This is how the most majestic works of art and the most successful business strategies have been forged.

Consider that creativity is applicable both in interpretative areas such as design or marketing and in more rigorously logical areas such as legal, fiscal, and financial planning. The creative spirit is always beneficial because, in short, it adds quantity and quality of information to find ideological solutions. For this reason, it is not wise to leave out any sources.

Now, it is not just about retention; fine chiseling is essential. The more points we connect—integrating rational and intuitive elements—in a big idea, the greater the power of impact inside and outside the mind. Remember, the creative muscle must be constantly exercised to avoid its atrophy and seek its strength. How? Designing new thoughts of thoughts frequently.

Use this human gift to empower any strategic need.

First positioning tactic: differentiate and add rational and emotional value to the concept of your brand, company, or project using the maximum potential of the creative; faculty; integrate new thoughts with logical and intuitive thoughts that will forcefully impact inside and outside the mind.

4.2 Clarity and Forcefulness

I call positioning efforts intersubjective modeling in this chapter because it is precisely their phenomenological description.

Whether to make better decisions or incentivize behavior, our playing field consists of moldable ideas that we share. Thoughts are what ultimately lead to actions. For this reason, consciously shaping neural mapping activity is a fundamental exercise to sell, motivate teams, or evolve as humanity.

Concerning the managerial field, it is absolutely relevant how other minds perceive people, services, brands, or products; that's what positioning in the market, teams and the social environment is all about.

Therefore, interweaving subjective coincidences between human groups is the responsibility of all executive commands in any area. Defining and procuring positionings is necessary for general management, advertising, marketing, public relations, finance, operations, or any department that includes human interaction.

Positioning involves formulating and integrating ideas shared in many minds. It may seem like an averse enterprise; however, it is something we do all the time with every thought, word, or action. It is not an end but a means; therefore, its positive or negative character is defined by what we use it for.

We shape our ideas and those of others with every small and big decision, from choosing our attire for the day or how we greet others to the career we choose. The essential difference is in the fact of doing it consciously and planned or not.

That said, to meet its goals, intelligent positioning must be creative, clear, and forceful; in other words, well-differentiated, anchoring rational and sentient values with simple and profound constructs.

Yes, simple and profound constructs are not an antinomy but a skillful integration of the conscious with the unconscious. That is why it is so crucial to introduce intuitive variables to the generation of concepts, because they are those that the human mind can process in greater quantity and speed. For example, we can process an image or a feeling with its immense information load in nanoseconds. In counterpart, a logical notion like how much is 13 x 345? is a slow and exhausting task.

Communicating intuitively is a language per se we must consider and procure. We have visual, auditory, gustatory, olfactory, tactile, kinesic, and emotional-sentient elements for this chore.

What phylogenetic, psychological, and cultural values are sublimated in the communicative codes you express? Are they in line with what you are looking for? What instincts, emotions, and feelings do you want to activate with the idea of your brand, product, or service? Do you connect with the bio-universal impetus to protect Life? Do you trigger pre-defined sentient experiences? Do you say what you want to say in a matter of seconds?

All of these, and more, are crucial questions for clarity and forcefulness.

Examples of brands clearly and forcefully positioned with their immediate intuitive connotations are:

- *Volvo*: control, safety, innovation, luxury.

- *Tesla*: discovery, sustainability, wellness, technology.

- *Apple*: learning, belonging, technological evolution, vanguard.

- *Red Bull*: freedom, energy, audacity.

- *SpaceX*: potency, space age, survival, conquest.

Second positioning tactic: communicate with clear concepts including immediate but forceful instinctive significance, connecting in the depth of the unconscious with instinctive, emotional, and sentient values.

4.3 Repetition

A lie said once is a lie, but if told a thousand times, it becomes true. Despite its epistemological imprecision, this phrase attributed to Joseph Goebbels illustrates the impact of repetition very well. However, we could also establish that a truth expressed multiple times permeates the spirit.

Again, repetition is not an end but a means. It is a compelling communication and understanding tool representing cognition's basis.

Without repetition, there is no comprehension, processing, or retention of information. Neural mapping relies on frequent etching to weave strong connections.

Regarding the neuropsychological phenomenology of memory, the number of exposures to a stimulus is one of the primary variables determining what we remember; the second is the sentient intensity. *Transience* in memory condemns memories to disappear if there is no reiteration; without constant commemorations, *misattribution* and *bias* lead reminiscence to a distorted future; *suggestion* favors present ideas, and *persistence* grants memories only based on what we continuously experience. (For further reference, see chapter 3.3 on the phenomenology of memory above) (Schacter, 2001)

Hence, we depend on repetition to position any concept and really connect with other minds. For this reason, a *market positioning* must be repeated in perpetuity (preferably without changes), and an advertising campaign must have an adequate duration (months) to have an impact.

Any message is subordinated to infinite repetition to exist.

How many years has *Coca-Cola* repeated the same state-ment to us? Literally more than a century transmitting "I am the soda that makes you happy." Why do they do this? To sell. Has it worked? Definitely.

The same happens with the reputation we want to build on a personal, professional, and humanity level: it depends on the constant and consistent values in every thought, word, action, and decision we make.

Third positioning tactic: repeat, repeat, and repeat.

4.4 Emotional Intensity

A stimulus will pass the necessary neurobiological filters to transcend memory if it has enough repetition and/or emo-tional intensity.

Emotions and feelings have valence. That is, they present a wide dynamic range determining their impact. It is a survival adaptation designed to prioritize what represents significant advantages or threats.

In the case of emotions, we find subtle or acute somatic re-actions depending on the relevance of the stimulus that trig-gered them. For example, in the face of a life or death threat, the body is configured to fire all possible protective systems to their highest degree: the heart races, blood is routed to the musculoskeletal system, large amounts of norepinephrine are released, and more. On the other hand, if the experience is routinary, it will trigger mild, even imperceptible, emo-tional responses.

These physiological movements (emotions) are translated as feelings with more or less vehemence in the mind

The job of memory is to preserve the information that gives us the highest probability of prevalence, and feeling intensity is a primary value marker for such a task.

We remember for a longer term what generated substantial positive or negative sentimental impacts on us, as events that have caused us great joys or sorrows.

For these reasons, it is highly relevant to trigger intense sentient experiences in established communications to position ideas. In other words, move to the marrow of the message's recipient for them to remember us.

There is nothing more efficient to achieve this latter goal than telling stories. Let us keep in mind the dialectical character of nature; the human Will is encouraged by the search for resolutions to incessant conflicts; a well-structured narrative implies presenting situations with majestic outcomes that inspire the depths of Being. Stories can be long, complex, or even told with a single word:

INSPIRE.

Fourth positioning tactic: strive to detonate high **emotional intensity** with communications to favor remembrance and impact.

4.5 Bandwagon Effect

Human beings are programmed to desire to board the crowded train, not the empty one, no matter where it goes.

Fundamentally, that is what the *bandwagon effect* is all about. It is also known as *herd behavior* and implies the thoughtless following of the majority.

This phylogenetic social conditioning stands out because it has been widely used in communication, politics, propaganda, marketing, and more.

It is approached in advertising phrases such as "we can do it," "who is missing? it's you," "as we all know," and many more.

The central intention of this chapter is to protect our judgment from the impetus of passing trends to devise intelligent decisions.

From an epistemological point of view, the fact that the majority thinks or does something does not mean it is necessarily true or convenient. Regardless, as a group, we are remarkably adept at identifying logical solutions and moderating individual behavior to achieve common goals; after all, many minds are more powerful than one. I consider the latter one of the main reasons we tend to justify collective agreements.

The colossal problem occurs when the majority follows their selfish and decontextualized impulses, finding approval in the (adverse) massive action. The situation this phenomenon has triggered in the contemporary world is so severe that it is destroying humanity's physical, psychological, cultural, and intellectual health. The demand for empty and self-destructive express stimuli multiplies and is promoted by the bandwagon effect. Fast food without nutritional values and loaded with harmful indulgent substances, poor and incoherently sexualized "artistic" expressions, and instantaneous and contextless mental experiences such as those commonly found on social networks, are just a few examples of collectively consented adverse habits.

It goes without saying that such inertia is not sustainable. That is why it is crucial to break this vicious cycle that will end up annihilating the species and the Planet. The antidote? Intelligent information, self-control, creativity, and empathy from the individual.

Using the bandwagon effect to communicate is not something negative *per se*; it is just an instrument mobilized by genetic systematization that we can use to reconcile en masse. It is up to us to allocate it for favoring Life.

Now, efficiently using this effect is very simple: launching a direct message connoting "we are all in" and repeating it an infinite number of times. It will start as an isolated idea connecting with other minds and finally become an intersubjective reality. The effects of these tactics are surprisingly influential.

Fifth positioning tactic: Convey that "the majority is in" regarding your goals to add the potent *bandwagon effect* to your communication efforts.

Practical note: Beware of trends! They are a trap.

4.6 Cognitive Biases

In previous chapters, based on the Creative Intelligence model, we have proposed six fundamental forces that animate the human Will: spirit, instinct, emotions, feelings, reason, and creativity.

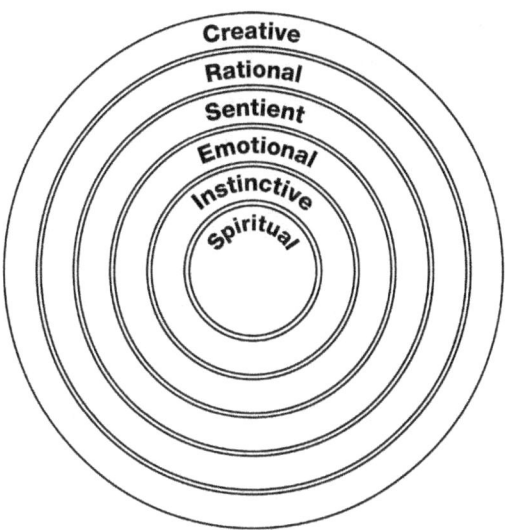

Figure 15: The Circle of Being.

It is essential to note that each force engenders the next one following a nesting principle. The vital impetus originated genes that formed organisms with emotions evolving into beings with minds and feelings that developed rational and creative capacities. The biological procedures and objectives of each layer influence the subsequent one. The forces are superimposed.

This means the psychological phenomenology of *Homo sapiens* is influenced by biophysical (spiritual), instinctive (genetic), emotional (physiological), sentient (interoceptive), rational, and creative processes.

Cognitive or heuristic biases correspond to psychological phenomena influencing decision-making; therefore, based on the latter, they integrate innate conditionings, individual experiences, and cultural constructions. They cannot be fully understood in isolation and coexist in the *Rational Dimension of Being* (Multi-Self Theory,[24] 2021).

Identifying behavioral trends driven by our psychological systematization is especially pragmatic because it provides us with specific elements to guide conduct and seek intelligent decisions.

Next, we will present some mental patterns that cognitive sciences have recognized, accompanied by relevant notes on what is exposed in this book.

4.6.1 Representativeness Heuristic

As we have reviewed in chapters 1.2 and 2.6 on human psychological systematization and cultural motivators, respectively, from birth—and even before—and throughout our lives, we assign sublimated meta-values—representing the possibility (or impossibility) of fulfilled desires—to each stimulus we experience.

An image, sound, smell, taste, or sensation means much more than the stimulus per se (*e.g.*, our mother's voice represents—consciously and unconsciously—a fulfilled desire for protection and much more).

---

24 J.C. Chávez, 2021.

Now, the *representativeness heuristic* attends to the weight we give to meta-values sublimated by genetic instructions, personal experiences, and cultural codes.

For example, when defining the preference for a political candidate, we evaluate their competence—intuitively and unconsciously—with arbitrary elements such as the size and shape of their chin or eyes, the color of their clothing, the frequency of their voice tone, their body movements, their party logo and more. We judge based on the symbols representative to us, such as stereotypes and metaphors that allow us to summarize the information we get from the world to make sense easily and quickly.

However, solely following our intuition to determine logical issues or probabilities is inefficient. Let us consider the following exercise:

Ana is 32 years old, and she is brilliant and outgoing. She has a degree in Philosophy. As a student, she was deeply interested in the issues of justice and social discrimination.

What is Ana most likely to be?

Choose an option:

1) *Accountant*
2) *Accountant and activist*

Undoubtedly, there are elements to think that Ana followed her passions and became a defender of just causes. However, if your answer was 2 (like the vast majority of people), you fell victim to the representativeness heuristic and violated logic. Without further information, mathematically, Ana is more likely to be just an accountant than an accountant and something specific else.

Daniel Kahneman conducted similar experiments with students at some of America's top universities, including PhDs in statistics and decision science. Surprisingly, more than 85% chose the option breaking with the fundamentals of logic.[25]

The most important lesson about this psychological pattern is to contemplate that the qualities of intuitive information differ from the qualities of the rational; they were conceived with parallel functions. *Reason* arose to allow us to detect detailed logical causes; and *intuition* (instincts, emotions, and feelings) to store and rapidly transmit large amounts of information relevant to survival. Both cognitive modes are immensely valuable, and neither should be underestimated.

Sixth positioning tactic: detect how intuition influences decisions and consider the **sublimated meta-values** of each element used in the communication pieces.

4.6.2 Availability Heuristic

On the one hand, we only remember what has had an adequate frequency and/or emotional intensity. On the other hand, when thinking, we only make conscious nearest experiences and a minimal part of what is stored in memory. It seems obvious, but we rarely consider it: the vast majority

---

25 Kahneman, 2013, p. 158.

of decisions are made based on that tiny fraction of filtered information immediately available in the mind.

Within the range of data retained in memory to choose from, our present and aware thoughts integrate solely relevant elements concerning the current context. In other words, our ideas at a given moment are formed with what we remember easier according to what we are experiencing.

The *availability heuristic* corresponds to judgments influenced by easy-to-process-and-remember stimuli.

For example, if someone has recently been robbed, that person, in general, will consider the city much less safe than someone who has never been burgled. Crime statistics and the actual probability of being the victim of an attack in a specific city is a single number, but the recent experience of each person will strongly predispose their appreciation.

In particular, the *availability cascade* effect (Kahneman, 2013) accurately illustrates the issue; it is a potent communication tool the media knows very well. Usually, it happens when the same piece of news (idea) is transmitted many times in mass communication channels, which structurally transforms collective beliefs and opinions. If the main story of the week is about insecurity in the country, it will be much more likely that the government's approval ratings will drop; in contrast, if it deals with the optimum performance of the economy, the opposite effect will occur. Current neural processes are shaped by information accessible in the short term.

For another example, consider the following exercise:

1) Name 3 countries in the world with their capitals.

Give yourself a moment to do so.

2) Rate your knowledge of geography from 1 to 10.

Rapidly choose a number.

Most probably, the answers came relatively quickly to your mind, and your rating was generous.

Now, name 10 African countries with their capitals.

Really try.

The reply is no longer so simple.

After the latter, would you rate your knowledge in the same way?

The fact of remembering easily or difficultly influences our perceptions.

Like most cognitive biases, the availability heuristic substitutes one question for another to promote swift insight. In the previous example, to answer "how would you rate your knowledge of geography?" we subconsciously replaced that question with "how much geographic data can I easily remember?".

To benefit intelligent decision-making, it is essential to maintain focus on the central issues and avoid the excessive influence of passing and prevailing elements at the given moment.

Seventh positioning tactic: Consider whether your perceptions and decisions are biased by available and fleeting data. On the other hand, ensure the constant presence of the positioning you want to establish by turning the *availability heuristic* and the *availability cascade* into strategic allies.

4.6.3 Affect Heuristic

The psychologist Paul Slovik presented in the year 2000 an *Affect Heuristic* emphasizing the interference of emotions on apparently rational decisions.

On this point, we must be very clear. In the case of the *Homo sapiens* (or any *sentient organism*[26]), there is no single thought, action, or decision that does not involve superpositioning emotions and feelings. Which is not a good or bad fact by itself.

Processing exclusively rational ideas is a biological impossibility in the human mind. All brain activity is accompanied by energetic and physiological oscillations deriving in emotions interpreted as feelings. In other words, thinking (interconnecting neural cartographies) is a dynamic exercise that necessarily implies **motion**.

Etymologically and biologically, **emotion** assumes movement, which is triggered in the body in predefined manners with each experienced stimulus. By nature, with each thought, we are designed to unleash—automatically—somatic frames (emotions) translated as feelings in the mind.

---

26 J.C. Chávez, 2023, p. 131.

Therefore, absolutely all ideas are influenced by emotions. What varies is the level of impact and awareness of such interference.

Furthermore, let us consider we only remember what is frequent and/or emotionally impactful enough. The intimate fibers of the conscious and preconscious mind, individually and collectively, are interwoven with essentially sentient information. Even the cold digital universe (internet) is full of human emotional connotations; Elon Musk—interestingly—refers to this attribute as *limbic resonance.*

Slovik did not discover anything new. We have known this as humanity for millennia; however, he coined a practical conceptualization of the phenomenon.

The affect heuristic highlights the biases derived from likes and dislikes in our belief systems and decisions.

The warning regarding this issue occurs when the affects lead us to irrationality with adverse consequences moving us away from the—hypothetical—Truth.

For example, our individual emotional response to issues such as vaccines, nuclear energy, and animal consumption dissembles the "objective" view of their problems and benefits. Commonly, except in cases of life or death, the rational system works to justify what instincts and emotions favor.

This is one of the main reasons why it is crucial to validate information and decisions collectively; hence, the source of the convenience of democracy and open systems. Many minds partially mitigate *individual affective biases.*

I emphasize "partially" because there are also *collective affective biases* that are even more dangerous since they are ratified and reinforced by their popular nature: as happens with the great crises of contemporary humanity. For example, self-destructive eating habits, vital, ecosystemic and planetary devastation, excessive consumerism and hedonism, racial, ideological and cultural polarization, and many more. Ironically, the antidote to this dangerous march is more minds that, from their individuality, radiate the collective path with intelligent luminosity.

Eighth positioning tactic: Be smartly wary of detecting the unconscious biases that likes and dislikes exert on your beliefs and decisions. On the other hand, align the positioning and value proposition to individual and collective emotional preferences to multiply its strength.

4.6.4 Personal Overestimation

The vast majority of us tend to think we are better than average at everyday tasks like driving; mathematically, this could not be true. We are facing a case of *personal overestimation*.

From another perspective, consider the following experiment. Psychologist Craig Fox recruited NBA followers and asked their opinion on the odds of winning the tournament of 8 different teams. With every assignation, the focal event would change; for example, to calculate the probability of winning for the specific case of the Chicago Bulls, the participant would imagine that scenario, confirm them as the winner in his mind, and draw attention away from the other seven competitors. This would happen with the probabilistic estimate per team. Adding up the probabilities given to each of the 8 squads separately, the number rose to 240%! An absurd number, more than double the 100% that should result. This means that by imagining team by team as a winner, their individual chances were overestimated.[27]

When we vividly focus on some imaginary scenario seeking to confirm its viability, we tend to overestimate it.

In another famous experiment, a prize was offered to participants who drew a red marble from one of the following two options:

1) Urn with 10 white marbles and 1 red.

2) Urn with 100 white marbles and 8 red.

This should be a straightforward selection, as the first option has a 10% chance of winning and the second only 8%. But, the result was by no means homogeneous: between 30% and 40% chose the urn with the most number of red marbles (the option with the slightest chance of winning). Imagining eight winning marbles against just one skewed the proper rational perspective and resulted in an *overestimation*.[28]

If we contemplate this phenomenon applied to everyday life, we commonly overweight the possibility of unlikely events happening when we actually imagine them. If the figurative situation is favorable (e.g., winning the lottery or tripling realistic sales goals), we tend to fall into the so-called *planning fallacy*. The latter explains why casinos are a lucrative business. Conversely, we also tend to overestimate risks—

27 Kahneman, 2013, p. 325.
28 Kahneman, 2013, p. 328.

and on a larger scale, according to *loss aversion*—when we carefully imagine particular negative scenarios.

In summary, overestimation occurs along with cognitive processes such as:

- *Focused attention*: when representing specific scenarios in detail.

- *Confirmation bias*: by devising scenarios confirming a situation.

- *Cognitive ease*: by seeking the lowest consumption of mental energy.

Regarding the neurobiology of memory, as we reviewed in chapter 3.3, we tend to remember what is most convenient for us. Therefore, overestimation occurs in the processing but also in the retention of neural information.

The antidote to this bias is constantly measuring the patterns observed, keeping an eye on statistical data, and detecting whether our considerations are influenced by "ego" and personal interests.

Ninth positioning tactic: Detail situations that are easy to imagine vividly to convert the *overestimation* bias into a strategic ally and, on the other hand, privilege statistical data so as not to fall into decision biases.

4.6.5 Framing Effect

The inertia of the moment strongly infers when making a decision. At that moment, our body and brain mobilize many physiological and psychological processes to favor the most convenient choice based on biological objectives.

Something imperatively relevant—that we must always consider—is that our survival has depended mainly on quick selections within the evolutionary chronological map. Taking the time to deliberate by carefully analyzing the available data is a rare luxury. Intuitive interference has been the protagonist in the actions of sentient organisms for billions of years, literally, due to a matter of life or death. Therefore, the strong influence of instincts, emotions, feelings, and immediate rational data, happens automatically in the human mind and is inevitable. What we can do is invest an additional effort to reveal the possible biases that this phenomenon generates; nevertheless, it is not sustainable to multiply the consumption of valuable energy with each of the decisions we make; we must prioritize. Consequently, we are predisposed to think and act unconsciously, intuitively, and automatically in most situations we experience.

The latter is something evident but slightly considered in everyday contexts, as in science and philosophy. The fact of temporarily being able to choose against our instinctive impulse has caused us to overrate our capabilities as a species in ordinary acting. For this reason, it turns out surprising to detect covert psychological conditioning affecting the apparently-controlled consciousness. The heuristics that the so-called *behavioral economics* has pointed out are more natural than they first appear.

Having said this, it will be consistent for us to understand that the way a question or situation is presented directly intervenes in our decisions. That's what the *framing effect* is all about.

For example, the percentage of people in a country who agree to donate organs when they die strongly depends on how the issue is presented. An article published in 2003 noted that this proportion was close to 100% in Austria, 86% in Sweden, only 12% in Germany, and 4% in Denmark.[29] Could some cultures be more prone to empathy? The answer is much simpler. The high donation rates were due to the request format: they would become automatic donors if the opt-out option was not explicitly checked. On the contrary, in cases with low rates, one had to "make an effort" to check the option to become a donor. It is a fascinating phenomenon not due to the physical effort of putting a cross on a piece of paper but to the mental effort of reflecting on the matter and responding directly. The majority chose not to actively participate in the election and joined the automatic option (*cognitive ease*).

A classic pattern of the framing effect occurs when a consideration is requested with a focus on something positive or negative. For example, if we were asked about the advisability of a vaccine that can save 90% of the population, this option would be much more desirable than another that poses the potential to kill 10% (even if it were the same case presented differently). The first data will instantly trigger a positive emotional response, and the second *vice versa*. Unfortunately, in the medical industry, this bias is widespread; serious adverse effects are ignored and overshadowed by highlighted advantages.

---

29 Kahneman, 2013, p. 373.

The automatic bodily responses (emotions) triggered by a question or situation—interpreted as feelings in the mind—predispose the action we will decide to take accordingly.

There is always a framing effect in all human thoughts and behaviors; the big difference will come from expanding—or not—the pre-established limits of our vision in each circumstance.

Tenth positioning tactic: Carefully configure the context framing the moment of decision aiming for positive emotional reactions and *cognitive ease* supporting the objective pursued. Likewise, stop to reflect on the momentum and analyze the junctures with a broad vision to avoid the biases of the *framing effect*.

4.6.6 Loss Aversion

What is more emotionally impactful? The chance to win $1,500 or lose $1,000.

Because of *loss aversion*, most people would consider the worry of losing stronger than the hope of winning.

From another perspective, how much would you be willing to bet for the opportunity to win $1,000 with a probability of 50%? Various studies have shown that the response is typically given in a ratio of between 1.5 and 2.5[30]. In this case, it would be $1,500 to $2,500.

In other words, we value not-losing more than winning. For survival, humans are predisposed to pay more attention to

---

30 Kahneman, 2013, p. 284.

dangers than opportunities. It is an inevitable phylogenetic conditioning affecting some more than others.

This trend reveals something very interesting. The *triphasic syllogism* of the *Creative Intelligence* model establishes that **positive feelings** are the product of preserved or fulfilled desires and, proportionally, **negative feelings** of lost or unfulfilled desires. Based on *loss aversion*, the relationship seems to become asymmetric, giving more strength to the negative.

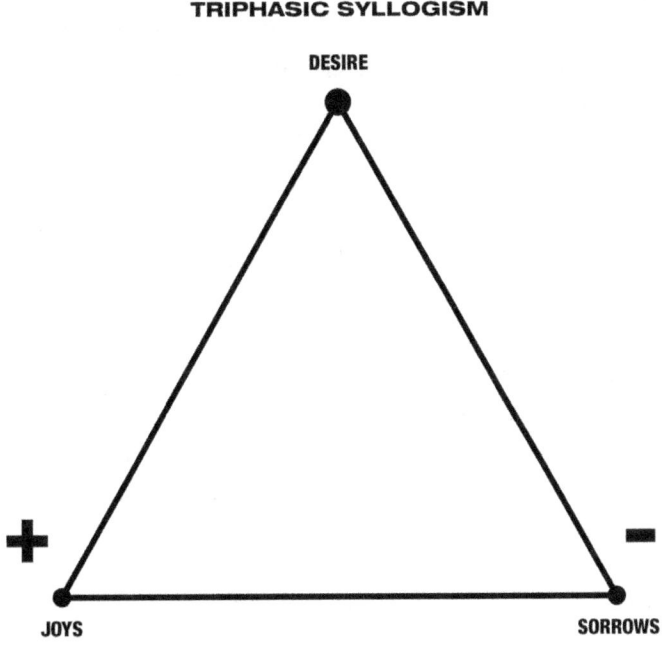

Figure 16: Triphasic Sylogism (Creative Intelligence, 2022).

The rational solution to this paradox is relatively simple. The intuitive impact of the loss occurs rapidly condensing in time; on the other hand, that of "possession" or conservation fades into the future. If we unify the plane of time, the relation of the syllogism is harmonized again. The positive is proportional to the negative because one does not exist without the other; by definition, they will always keep their correlation intact.

Consequently, the phenomenon of loss aversion occurs, in large part, due to immediate intuitive considerations. It even explains part of why—against elementary logic—it is so challenging for contemporary human beings to make decisions that represent small losses in the short term but much more significant benefits in medium and long periods.

After this brief parenthesis, I present the *endowment effect* derived from loss aversion. As we saw in chapter 3.5.3, with the *conditioning of territoriality*, *Homo sapiens* are designed to build consensus determining the right of something as "own." Of course, it is a cognitive illusion: if we cannot identify the "I" as a specific isolated element, much less can we assume something is exclusive; in the reality we experience, nothing exists by itself. However, it is a powerful psychological mirage that manifests in directly utilitarian social conventions.

We not only assume as "our own" material goods but also ideas, spaces, and times. The case of "timeshare" is a very didactic illustration of the latter.

The assumed "properties" mark a reference point with which the mind determines profit or loss. The famous *status quo* or the amount shown in a bank account are benchmarks to which we cling rationally, instinctively, and emotionally.

For example, if they inform you that your salary will now be 1 million dollars a month, it will surely mean excellent news; but it won't be like that for someone who made 10 million before that.

The point of reference is crucial to understanding "retained" or "lost" desires. For this reason, desires are relative to the individual and the moment. With this, for example, it is inferred why real estate owners tend to overvalue their property with respect to market value.

The *endowment effect* consists of the overvaluation of what we consider "own" and is given because of the resistance to losing it.

And I insist on never losing sight of the individual **reference point** to understand behavior based on "gains" or "losses" that correspond to wishes fulfilled, conserved, lost, or unfulfilled.

On the other hand, if you manage to channel a sense of belonging, you will add value sheltered by loss aversion.

Eleventh positioning tactic: Generate a sense of belonging concerning your offer to create human ties well protected by *loss aversion* (*e.g.*, loyalty programs). Also, consider the long term so as not to fall into biases derived from fear of immediate loss.

4.6.7 Escalation of Commitment

Does investing time and effort guarantee success?

The simple answer is no. An effort is required for conquest but could be channeled in the wrong direction.

However, our instinctive, emotional, and psychological systematization encourages us to protect what we have dedicated energy to without making further differentiation.

On the instinctive level, as a species, we are conditioned to protect the sources that grant well-being. Access to them or even their very existence has involved effort, and our own nature is their avid defender. For genes, what has represented invested vitality is a potential supplier.

In the psychological realm, the mind interprets unconsummated effort as a loss and is consciously despicable because it is the antithesis of what is longed for.

In the emotional layer, the mere possibility of loss triggers a defensive and—undesired—physiological reaction prepared to face dangers.

The biological pieces are ordered to encourage the continuation of a previous physical or ideological endeavor. For example, our individual and collective belief systems are castles in the air, protected by the desire to sustain what they have built regardless of their validity, and we will defend them tenaciously.

This phenomenon has undoubtedly been mainly favorable to survival; however, it entails a problem referred to as the *es-*

calation of commitment or *sunk cost fallacy*. It occurs when we assume something will improve simply because of what was previously invested. This can cause us to continue allocating resources to a practically lost cause.

In this case, careful-rational analysis is critical since continuing or discarding an explored path always carries both risks and opportunities. What is relevant is to be very attentive to the unconscious impulse that clings to what we have dedicated effort to and, without attention, can cause bad decisions.

From a contrary point of view, derived from this pattern at the psychosocial level, it happens that when a company manages to get the potential buyer to dedicate time and energy to considering its offer, the possibilities of purchase are multiplied. The greater the involvement, the greater the commitment. For example, in a sales process, connecting with the customer, asking questions, making calls, inviting them to events, or anything requiring an investment of time will increase the chances of buying.

Twelfth positioning tactic: We humans tend to commit to what we have invested effort into. Strive for involvement and time invested from other minds in your positioning to encourage affiliation and demand. Also, be aware of the bad decisions that *escalation of commitment* and *sunk cost fallacy* can cause.

4.6.8 Anchoring Effect

The *anchoring effect* essentially consists of positioning a specific reference point in a mind.

The illusion of control our conscious simulates makes us think our decisions are free of influences beyond our desires and considerations. The reality is different.

Let us remember—although it may not seem like it—the conscious plane is only a tiny piece of the robust neural gear. We in no way control everything going in, out, or being processed.

When processing, since commencing a thought, the mind starts from a primary state that adjusts in different ways to determine judgments and beliefs.

The starting point is crucial to mark the ranges determining "too much" or "too little."

Hence, a compelling way of directing psychological processes is by establishing a starting position representing the center for making corrections. This way, the balance can be strongly tilted to favor decisions and determinations.

In experimental psychology, this is a well-validated phenomenon. For example, in an investigation by Daniel Kahneman and Amos Tversky[31] (1974), students at the University of Oregon were shown a number determined by a rigged wheel of fortune that could be either 10 or 65 and were subsequently asked:

Is the percentage of African nations in the UN higher or lower than the number you just saw?

31 Kahneman, 2013, p. 119.

What percentage do you think African nations have in the UN?

The results were unquestionable. Those who saw the number 10 before on the arbitrary wheel estimated 25% of African nations at the UN on average, and those who saw the number 65 averaged 45% on their response.

Incredibly, something utterly unrelated to the data in question dramatically affected the calculations because it placed a different unconscious adjustment point.

Other famous references on this topic are the Ariely experiment (2008) and the Knutson and Grether experiment (1996).

The anchoring effect is crucial in a negotiation, referring to "negotiation" as any human interaction seeking a consensual reaction, whether or not numerical or commercial. We are talking about a tactic used since *Homo sapiens* managed to organize en masse to conquer collective desires. Motivating an individual or group implies setting conceptual reference points to establish improvement objectives. A simple primitive trading algorithm would be:

We have X; if you follow me, we will have X + 1.

And so human civilization began.

Now, in a capitalist context, the initial terms to be negotiated set the tone for tuning agreements. Not only is it meaningful to predetermine the initial numerical variables, but the conceptual configurations are also just as relevant. Among other non-quantifiable and pivotal concepts in a negotiation, we find instinctive (sense of domination, belonging, control, freedom, trust, learning, power, transcendence, recognition, etc.), sentient, spiritual, and rational forces. For example:

The proposal provides unique qualitative specifications (instinctive/domination), inclusion in a privileged group (instinctive/belonging), and adequate monitoring to control the main parameters (instinctive/control). It also protects the ecology (spiritual), and 98% of users say they experience a deep sense of well-being (sentient). The cost is X (rational).

In this imaginary sales exercise, we established an invisible fence (Klaff, 2019) that works as a starting point to compare not only quantities but also valuable constructs.

We speak of the *anchoring effect* when the referential centers mainly impact rational processes and *priming* when they act primarily on intuitive sequences. We will review the latter in the next chapter.

Thirteenth Positioning Tactic: Determine the starting mental reference points in advance to limit the range of behavioral responses you seek. Consider if there is a preset value for the *anchoring effect* dissembling your decisions unconsciously.

4.6.9 Priming

When a mind processes information, there is a starting point with which it adjusts and shapes consequent ideas that, in turn, influence new thoughts and actions.

Determining an initial signal can have a logical impact (reason) but also a spiritual, instinctive, emotional, and sentient one (intuition). For example, suggesting a numerical reference value prior to a consideration operates in the world of reason and, on the other hand, channeling moods in the emotional stratum.

The *priming* effect occurs when a pre-established stimulus unconsciously affects subsequent ideas, behaviors, and decisions, mainly at an intuitive level.

In a very curious experiment, psychologist John Bargh and his collaborators asked young students at New York University to form sentences with a set of 4 words. For one of the groups, these words corresponded to a theme related to advanced age (*e.g.*, wrinkles, forgetfulness, Florida, baldness, etc.). Subsequently, they were asked to move to another room. The experiment consisted of measuring the time it took each group to move from one place to another. Surprisingly, the group exposed to connotations related to old age walked significantly slower on average.[32]

The concepts positioned in the young people's minds directly impacted their behavior quality.

Integrating constructs loaded with sublimated meta-values into the mix of available neural mappings at decision-making is evidently compelling.

To moderate a neural pattern with the priming effect, the crucial question is to identify the symbolic charge behind the stimuli corresponding to spiritual, instinctive, emotional, sentient, and rational desires.

---

32 Kahneman, 2013, p. 53.

The key is found in predisposing mental states through codes with signifiers aligned with the response we seek to obtain.

For example, an adorable puppy will channel empathy, warm colors: comfort, intellectual conversations: focus, inspirational words: confidence, and images of food: hunger. It is all in the symbols and the order in which they are given.

At a point of sale, the entrance and façade are highly relevant. In a piece of communication, the first second is essential. At a negotiating table, the attributes of the environment at the beginning and the first theme will dictate the course of the agreements. Everything adds up to the outcome, but the first impression has much more potency because it determines the starting point.

Fourteenth positioning tactic: Intelligently use codes with controlled sublimated values to generate a first impression leading to the response you are looking for. Consider the symbolic elements that unconsciously influence your decisions due to the *priming* effect.

4.6.10 Halo Effect

To understand a situation as quickly as possible, the mind interconnects the signifiers readily available and, based on them, builds judgments, beliefs, opinions, and decisions.

The *halo effect* occurs due to the magnified influence of the notions preceding an idea.

As we reviewed in chapter 3.3 on the phenomenology of memory, our ability to retain information is highly limited.

Cognitive processing depends on 1) the items available at the moment (short-term memory) and 2) the abstract pre-judgments prioritized and recorded as memories (long-term memory).

These neural conditions set the stage for the halo effect to flow. For example, when the first impression of a person is positive, we will tend to agree with him or her much more frequently and vice versa: a short- or long-term prejudice is amplified and affects future considerations.

We clearly observe this pattern when a mother enhances the virtues of her children and minimizes their defects; we do the same with our favorite politicians or collaborators. In these cases, the *affect heuristic*, *priming* and the *halo effect* come together in an evident mix of psychological biases.

In synthesis, we correlate errors or validities derived from subjective perceptions and use them as foundations that impregnate new notions, which are born conditioned. In the negative cases, they result in false or adverse ideas, and in the positive scenarios, they result in correct or favorable conceptions.

The antidote to counteract the negative consequences of the halo effect is to decorrelate error. That is, detecting the conditioning that limits adequate vision and disconnecting its influence.

The latter implies, at the individual level, an exceptional self-control effort and, at the collective level, team collaboration.

Regarding the former, when it comes to deep imprints, identifying the interference of spiritual, instinctive, and emotional desires on our rational deliberations is an act that requires a lot of mental discipline and virtuosity, but it leads to a port full of well-being. On the other hand, when the source of a psychological bias is superficial, just detecting it will have immediate beneficial effects.

Concerning the latter, a group front acting in unison admits the correction of mistakes very efficiently. This was demonstrated by James Surowiecki in his book *The Wisdom of Crowds*, where he documents the ability of many minds to estimate values that, on an individual level, are very complicated to determine. Surowiecki backs up his theory with several experiments and stories, including the famous exercise in which a group of individuals made predictions about the weight of a bull, and the mean of their estimates turned out to be more accurate than the answer of any single individual. That is the convenience of decentralization.

From another perspective, the halo effect may be significantly favorable for driving behavioral responses. A very effective way to ally with this phenomenon is through loyalty programs, pursuing a consistent positive perception of the group, product, or service we represent.

Fifteenth positioning tactic: Team up with the *halo effect* by detonating and maintaining a positive perception of what you represent. Regarding individual decisions, identify those cumulative biases present in the foundations of your judgments, beliefs, opinions, and decisions.

4.6.11 Judgement Heuristic

The rational faculty of *Homo sapiens* is structured to detect causation. Judgments are, precisely, the interpretation of the correlation of thoughts in the mind.

With an Aristotelian spirit, we can categorize them as follows:

- *Identity judgments:* marking something is. For example, "Aristotle is Aristotle."

- *Judgments of non-identity:* marking something is not. For example, "Aristotle is not Plato."

- *Judgments of relationship:* marking the relationship of one concept with another. For example, "Elephants are bigger than ants."

- *Judgments of mode:* describing how something is. For example, "Memory is fragile."

On the other hand, Immanuel Kant also makes a transcendental contribution regarding this notion. He defines judgment as a mental process that allows us to classify, signifying a bridge between perception and true knowledge. He makes a distinction between *synthetic judgments* (which add information), *analytical judgments* (which describe logically), subjective judgments (which attend to individual perceptions), and *objective judgments* (which coincide with universal maxims).

In other words, we compute the information received through our proprioceptive, interoceptive (feelings), and exteroceptive (senses) channels in the form of judgments.

This range of rational possibilities directly affects all our thoughts, actions, and decisions.

The *judgment heuristic* occurs when we conclude about causes and effects biased by conceptual interpretations that are not directly related to each other: for simplicity, we exchange one question for another.

A prevalent example would be attributing good or bad abilities to a person based on his or her facial features. In this case, a generalization charged with sublimated meta-values in the form of a synthetic, subjective judgment of mode regarding a person's appearance responds to another question about his or her competence. For example, various studies, such as those by Alexander Todorov[33], have well documented that the perception of a politician's strength and honesty are directly related to the shape of his or her chin and expressions.

These cognitive shortcuts are part of our intuitive machinery and are very useful in contexts where quick decisions are required; however, they can often lead us to fallacious and self-defeating conclusions.

Once again, to inter-communicate efficiently, I highlight the relevance of pursuing a positive intuitive impression in the messages and in all the elements—directly related or not—that comprise them.

Finally, to prevent negative biases in perceptions and decisions derived from judgment heuristics, I insist on 1) practicing critical thinking, 2) being aware of common biases, 3)

---

33 Odorov, 2017.

considering different perspectives, 4) seeking more information, and 5) reading or consulting experts.

Sixteenth positioning tactic: Pay close attention to the causal constructs you form and validate them with critical thinking to prevent *judgment heuristics* from adversely biasing. In communication, understand the phenomenology of such heuristics to guide perceptions and decisions.

4.6.12 Hindsight Bias

"I knew it all along" is a widespread psychological effect when analyzing the past. The rational stratum of the human being acts as a magnet connecting everything that seems plausible compatibility with the highly valued personal and collective belief systems. It is a necessary adaptation for survival: designing representational models of what we experience and pursuing logical validations complementing them over time. Undoubtedly, this correlation effort is instrumental and allows us control over existence, but it is still an illusion with errors and anomalies that can lead to incorrect and adverse interpretations.

The *hindsight bias* is given by inconsistent conclusions about our past beliefs once we know the result. Baruch Fischoff and Ruth Beyth demonstrated this pattern with a survey where people exaggerated the probabilities they previously assigned to an event when it did happen and minimized them when it did not.

For example, if the event they predicted occurred, they would assume a position of "I always knew it," and when it did not, of "I knew it was difficult."[34]

The desire to defend what we assume to be true or highly probable is an impetus that can be very productive or destructive. Thanks to this trend, we *Homo sapiens* have built astonishingly pragmatic models like the sciences, but it has also locked us in rigid structures with limited vision ranges. The resistance is such that the great thinkers who have dared to challenge the prevailing paradigms have suffered from violent social condemnation. At the time, this was the case with Socrates, Galileo, Darwin, Spinoza, Tesla, and, more recently, Willhelm Reich, to name just a few.

Challenging one's convictions—against our biological design—is an exercise requiring harsh open-mindedness and self-control, but it can be colossally revealing and beneficial. Beginning by detecting retrospective biases that distort the perceived reality about our cognitive successes and errors.

At this point in history, we have a lot of knowledge demonstrating consistency and practicality, but there is much more that we don't know yet. Only by daring to leave our control zone can we discover new and astonishing ideas that bring us closer to the much-coveted truth.

Seventeenth positioning tactic: model intersubjective thoughts with the help of current belief systems to facilitate their impact. On a personal level, reflect on whether you really knew what you think you knew to avoid the adverse effects of *hindsight bias*.

---

34 Kahneman, 2013, p. 201.

4.6.13 Confirmation Bias

Psychologically speaking, to understand, we must first believe. This pattern is relevant because it implies we are intuitively designed to assume any idea as true before rationally invalidating it.

When we are presented with an assertion, the first thing the mind does is imagine it; afterward, the logical analysis—which signifies an additional effort—will determine its possibility of being true or false. For example, if we are told: "atoms are mostly empty space," our intuitive mode will quickly try to connect images illustrating the idea; if we can visualize it, we will initially believe in it. However, if we invest additional energy in questioning it logically, we will find reasons to invalidate it, starting with detecting that "emptiness," by definition, could not exist.

This means that without reflection, there is pathological credulity. The alarms about this phenomenon go off when we realize contemplation is an increasingly less common exercise in contemporary society. Technological advances and economic systems that promote extreme consumerism without questioning are taking away the ability to unbelieve from human beings. The adverse effects occur when ideological oligarchies impose notions—convenient for a few in the short term—threatening the joint possibilities of Life to resist and prevail. Unfortunately, this is an increasingly prevalent situation instrumentalized to capitalize with votes, money or power.

The only way to protect ourselves against such a tsunami of harmful information is by individually assuming the effort involved in connecting critical thoughts; the antitoxin is found in our creative faculty.

Confirmation bias occurs when we do not question and integrate false or unfavorable information into our belief systems. From a psychophysical perspective, it is much easier to believe because it requires less energy than unbelieving; that is the mechanical source of the problem.

We find these types of frames in a wide range of situations, especially in political warfare and modern health issues. The misinformation is such that humanity has never been so manipulated; even the conflict worsens and becomes a vicious cycle due to our neuropsychological tendency to defend what we originally believed.

The good news is an expressly planned lie will usually be exposed over time when processed in a group. However, short-term damage is often difficult to repair.

For more reference on believing and unbelieving processes, psychologist Daniel Gilbert documented an entire theory on the subject in his book How *Mental Systems Believe*.

Eighteenth Positioning tactic: Before assuming something is true, question it rationally to avoid negative effects due to *confirmation bias*. In communication, always consider the immense power of the first intuitive impression; the mind tends to believe anything; use that pattern responsibly.

4.6.14 Multi-Self Heuristics

Let's recap.

From an etymological perspective, the word heuristic comes from the Greek "heurisken," which means "find" or "discover." Essentially, it implies problem-solving strategies.

The human mind uses these heuristics to make judgments and decisions, integrating its entire biological arsenal to obtain answers.

For this task, we have two fascinating fundamental cognitive modes, reason, and intuition, which process the information they receive from the perceptual channels.

Reason builds quantifiable neural maps of slow, difficult, and detailed processing that I refer to as *logical thoughts*[35].

On the other hand, intuition is easy and fast to process and builds synaptic maps with non-quantifiable *homeostatic thoughts*[36] (designed to regulate behavior with agility).

As we explained at the beginning of this section, cognitive sciences have popularized the term heuristics, referring mainly to psychological patterns; the previous subchapters correspond to a collection of the most cited, accompanied by special notes related to the *Multi-Self Theory*[37] and *Creative Intelligence* models.

However, it is essential to consider that such processes derive from our entire biological structure and cannot be fully understood through psychological phenomenology alone. This is where a broad vision endows us with new possibilities.

35 J.C. Chávez, 2023, p. 61.
36 J.C. Chávez, 2023, p. 64.
37 J.C. Chávez, 2021.

With this integral spirit, I propose the following unprecedented tools within the framework of behavioral economics, established based on the ideological model of this book that we call *Strategic Biointelligence.*

Spiritual heuristics: we human beings, due to our germinal and biophysical interconnection with Life as a whole, tend to protect it in all its manifestations. When choosing between options—especially when they are very similar—we are conditioned to prefer those defending vital prevalence and resistance. For example, a product that takes care of the Planet will be more attractive to us than one that does not.

Instinctive Heuristics: Homo sapiens follow genetically defined innate behavioral tendencies that have represented a survival advantage on the evolutionary map. When we decide, we will be inclined to opt for what satisfies our instinctive—egotistical—desires. For example, a luxurious watch that provokes admiration will be attractive due to our innate predisposition for domination and territoriality. As a side note, we might as well propose a specific heuristic for each identifiable instinctual conduct tendency.

Emotional heuristics: emotions are automated physiological reactions aiming to regulate their organisms' optimal functioning and behavior. When looking for answers, we are prone to privilege those eliciting body frames interpreted as positive mental states. For example, a food that, due to its ingredients, causes the release of dopamine—such as chocolate—will be more appetizing. The same happens with concepts loaded with sublimated meanings; likewise, they increase—on a greater or lesser scale—the levels of specific biomolecules that trigger emotions.

Sentient heuristics: the mind translates emotions into feelings. Human judgments and decisions are heavily charged with limbic resonance; that is, they tend to be defined based on what produces positive sentient experiences. For example, we will prefer the drink that, due to its brand architecture, connotes a longed-for feeling over another that simply highlights its formula.

Rational heuristics: reason is the biological collaborator in charge of determining the convenience of innate conditionings based on a present context. In other words, it has the primary function of temporarily mitigating behavioral tendencies driven by instincts and emotions when they become out of context and self-destructive. For this, its main tactic is the identification of congruent causes and effects. The human being tends to prefer what logically supports his or her convenience. For example, we will be more willing to buy a real estate asset—which we already instinctively desire—if we are told of its particular financial benefits.

All these patterns or heuristics have meant survival advantages as they help us to make intelligent decisions. Nevertheless, they can also create biases leading us to make adverse choices and judgments. Identifying their strengths and weaknesses is a necessary exercise for evolution.

In the case of spiritual, instinctual, emotional, and sentient heuristics, intuition is the dominant processing mode; they allow us to think broadly and fast, fueled by evolutionary learning collected over four billion years. It is very similar to what Daniel Kahneman refers to as *System 1.*

In contrast, rational heuristics use reason—or System 2—, which requires additional effort and represents slow, limited, and specific thoughts.

Finally, I allow myself to note the existence of "System 3", the cognitive mode endorsed by creativity. It is about the fusion between intuition and reason that enables us the creation of new hybrid thoughts: the source of art and the most intelligent decisions.

So, let us exalt our creative capacity, be careful about the weaknesses of our cognitive abilities, and together model a fruitful and intelligent future with a penetrating vision.

5.0 BIOETHICS

5.1 Purpose, Biological Morality and Future Vision

The fundamental mission of ethics is to identify the appropriateness or inappropriateness of our thoughts, actions, and decisions. It is a complex task that requires objectives as a reference point. We cannot determine if something is "good" or "bad" if we do not analyze it in relation to a goal. For this reason, the first task of ethics is to define a purpose.

But what is the correct purpose? Is it predetermined, or do we have to create it?

It is possible to detect an answer within the framework of observable biological mechanics. We can access it through our senses and thoughts and partially validate it by correlating its consistency with other minds.

Following this impetus, contemplating our biological architecture, we find an imperative in all vital manifestations: Life is designed to maintain order, resist and prevail in the face of a chaotic existence full of entropy that condemns everything to dispersion and freezing.

Living beings fight against a destructive force—referred to in science as the second law of thermodynamics—pushing us to lose energy and disappear. To protect us from it, nature has equipped us with powerful weapons that have been very effective; as a germinal force (*spirit*) defending Life as a whole, *instincts* allowing the transmission of learnings, *emotions* automating convenient reactions, *feelings* guiding behavior, *reason* letting to evaluate causes and effects, and *creativity* enabling to form new thoughts impacting in and out of the mind to shape the future.

They are six primary forces working together to resist and prevail.

With this maxim, we can detect a guiding biological meta-Purpose deriving in modes or sub-purposes: apparently independent functions that, in equilibrium, feed an integral harmonic system. Life depends on an appropriate balance; based on it, we find bioethical answers. For further reference, I have documented the phenomenology about Purposes and biological meta-causality in more prominent detail in the book *Creative Intelligence*.

For example, is it correct to follow our egotistical instinctual impulses? When they act at the service of the prevalence of Life as a whole, we could consider it a bioethical fact, and vice versa. Across the evolutionary map, such individualistic behavioral tendencies, genetically programmed to increase the gene's chances of surviving and reproducing, have generated collective strongholds in a kind of altruistic selfishness. The problem is that, out of the context for which they were designed, they tend to become self-destructive; in that case, they will lead to inappropriate behaviors.

Consequently, we can rank biological morality based on the positive or negative character and intensity of impact concerning the central objective of resisting and prevailing.

The great challenge is to discern if a fact is really favorable or adverse for the prevalence of Life as a whole in the present and future tense; it is certainly a very complex exercise. And, the great danger is falling into rhetorical illusions created by malicious and selfish minds claiming to protect a greater good. For all this, critical thinking, collective information processing, empathy, intelligent information, and unrestrained creativity are more necessary than ever in the history of humanity.

Finally, the central bioethic objectives of this book are, precisely, 1) to promote critical thinking for taming and understanding the individual forces that threaten our prevalence, 2) to pursue empathetic and conscious markets that demand bioethical products and services, 3) to promote intelligent decisions, and 4) to establish tools allowing us to interconnect minds to act in synchronicity aiming a fertile and bright future.

STRATEGIC INTELLIGENCE

PART 2

STRATEGIC INTELLIGENCE

PART 2

INTRODUCTION

After our journey through the depths of behavioral biology in the first part of this book, the time has come to interconnect ideas with practical tools for strategic and managerial exercise. For this objective, we have configured the *Business Model Generator* integrated with fundamental conceptual frameworks to accompany us from research and data collection to the profitability of a product, project, or company.

This model will facilitate the processing through *Strategic Intelligence* that can be interpreted as the transformation of data to favorable decisions in an economic context.

When making a decision, it is essential to consider both rational and intuitive data to avoid counterproductive effects. On the one hand, quantifiable data must flow in abundance, accompanied by patient and careful scrutiny. But, the quick intuitive data that limbic resonance transmits to us through feelings must also be taken into account to 1) integrate its invaluable messages, 2) avoid own subjective biases and 3) ponder its behavioral effects in work teams and potential customers.

Both cognitive modes, reason and intuition, are the primary variables influencing the decision-making process with their respective strengths and weaknesses. Sometimes, the slowness caused by scrutiny is criticized with the phrase "analysis paralysis"; however, the good judgment of a director will determine when a situation deserves more time to consider or when intuition allows being agile to take advantage of particular opportunities. However, it is crucial to emphasize that correct intuition is complemented by a set of experiences and knowledge accumulated through years of work and hours of research.

It is evident that a strategy lacking in study and research is risky; still, making decisions with a lot of information but no clarity can also result in disaster. We will illustrate this last scenario with two examples; one of them historical, and the other derived from technological advances.

Professor Robert Dolan of Harvard Business School documented one of the most discussed decisions in the world of Marketing when *New Coke* was launched, replacing the original *Coca-Cola* with its classic flavor and trajectory since 1886[1]. This happened in response to the well-known *Pepsi Challenge* that demonstrated supremacy in taste tests. When this decision was made, the strategic rationale seemed congruent: renew the formula to win the tasting competition. After much research, it was possible to validate that *New Coke*, with its new flavor, would surpass Pepsi, and they were pre-

1 Christen, 2001.

paring to celebrate the great success. What they lost sight of was the emotional impact this maneuver would have. Company president Donald Keough summed it up this way in a speech in 1985:

The reality is that all the time, money, and skills invested in studying consumers could not measure or reveal the deep and lasting emotional attachment that so many people had with the original Coca-Cola.[2]

The famous decision was a resounding failure for failing to consider the unconscious sublimated values of the product and what customers were actually buying—definitely not flavor.

The other case is that of the GAP[3] stores in the midst of the Internet 4.0 era. Faced with a sustained drop in sales, the CEO thinks their designs are the cause and decides to replace three designers with algorithms that compute new fashion trends. Again, this a costly unfruitful decision because of not understanding the origin of the problem: what happened was a typical case of inadequate positioning. They weren't cheap, nor were they a designer brand that justified a high price tag. In the low-cost range, they were flanked by *H&M, Zara*, and their own *Old Navy* brand, and in the high-priced scope, they competed with *Armani, Ralph Lauren*, and Abercrombie, among others. GAP was left in the middle of a market vacuum, a problem of concept and strategy, not of design.

A broad vision is essential to make more accurate and efficient decisions. Next, we will expose the variables of the

---

2 Keough, 1985.
3 Ayelet, 2017.

Business Model Generator that, in combination with the fundamentals of behavioral biology, will represent an extraordinary ally for the management exercise.

Note on the financial impact of decision analysis:

Some managers find it unhelpful to perform qualitative and behavioral analysis because they need to clearly see the financial outcome of the business. A key objective of this second part of the book is to understand the relationship of these efforts with the return on investment, which we will present with the support of documented cases in important academic institutions to obtain financial, strategic, and pragmatic tools.

6.0 © STRATEGIC BUSINESS MODEL GENERATOR

We have designed the *Strategic Business Model Generator* by combining the value scheme taught at the Harvard Business School (*Figure 1*), the Canvas[4] model, our consulting experience, and the previously exposed fundamentals of Economic Ethology. It represents a well-structured practical guide for the directive exercise.

In this development, traditional strategic pillars serve as a basis for integrating fundamentals of the biology of human behavior in an economic context. It is an exercise allowing us to delve into the main variables that influence the possibility of obtaining commercial assertiveness but also promote the creation of products and services that protect human well-being and the prevalence of Life. Ultimately, in a market

---
4 Osterwalder, 2017.

like the current one, the potency of an offer and the sustainability of its profits, the emergence of conscious economies with the vital impetus, and the very transcendence of *Homo sapiens* depend on the latter.

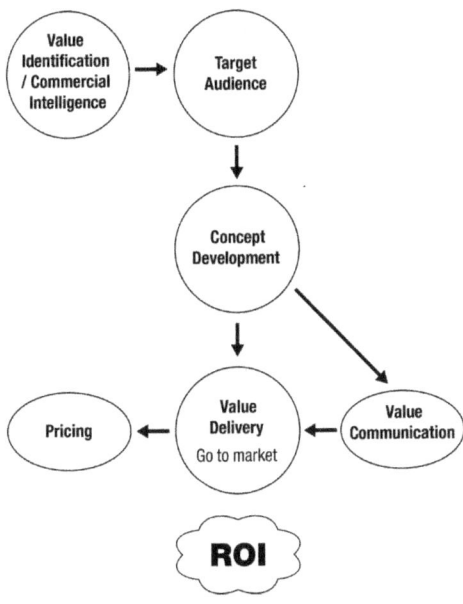

Figure 1: Harvard Business School Value Scheme.

To achieve all this, it is crucial to configure rigorous and rationally congruent tactics that, at the same time, consider the most influential human cognitive modes in decision-making, such as instincts, emotions, and feelings.

Thus, the purpose of *Strategic Biointelligence* and the derived *Business Model Strategic Generator* is to provide potent biologically intelligent strategic tools to positively impact the future.

Let us now review its core elements as shown integrated into the full map in *Figure 2*.

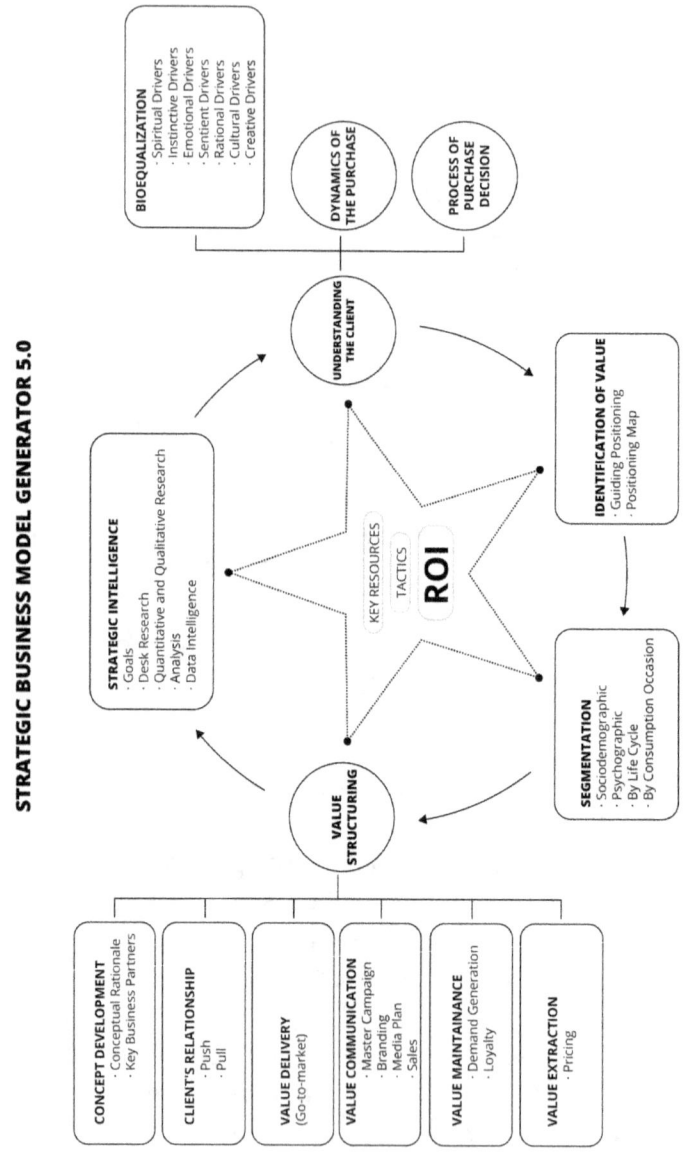

Figure 2: © Strategic Business Model Generator (C. Chávez & J.C. Chávez, 2023).

6.1 Strategic Intelligence

The various modes of intelligence in the *Homo sapiens* depend on its ability to process the information it receives from its perceptual channels. The same happens with a collective project. **We define Strategic Intelligence as an organization's ability to turn data into solutions.**

To choose between options adequately—or, in other words, intelligently—like a living being with a central nervous system, a company requires efficient processes for input, retention, processing, and output of information.

Continuing with the analogy, we can identify the following similes with a general perspective:

1) *Input* - resources to receive information.

<u>Living being</u>
Exteroceptive channels: five senses
Interoceptive channels: internal organs
Proprioceptive channels: body

<u>Company</u>
Exteroceptive channels: market research
Interoceptive channels: internal monitoring
Proprioceptive channels: positioning

2) *Retention* - resources to retain information.

<u>Living being</u>
Memory

<u>Company</u>
Databases

3) **Processing** - resources to process information and deliberate.

<u>Living being</u>
Brain with mind
Intuitive analysis
Rational analysis

<u>Company</u>
Strategic Intelligence
Intuitive analysis
Rational analysis
Digital Algorithms

4) **Exit** - resources to influence the outside.

<u>Living being</u>
Faculties of communication and action

<u>Company</u>
Communication Strategy
Communication systems
Operation systems

The primary task of Strategic Intelligence is deep scrutiny of the information to conclude optimal determinations. Therefore, it must weigh all the parts.

For this objective, it is necessary to consider the market, competition, and customer trends and detect opportunities to optimize efficiency, expand the business, reduce costs, and improve profitability, among other relevant factors. Likewise, it is essential to take into account the particular situation of the company contemplating its purpose, objectives, human capacities, material resources, and financial possibilities; this way, we will be able to delimit the scope and establish real opportunities. From the above, development can be planned in the short, medium, and long term.

One company that has been successful in using Strategic Intelligence, and with it, has even managed to change the market's momentum, is *Amazon*. Undoubtedly, it has been capable of executing well-structured tactics based on a broad vision integrating the variables mentioned above. This has allowed them, among other things, to design disruptive and personalized offers, improve the shopping experience and obtain sustainable revenue growth.

A frequent problem in companies occurs when the Strategic Intelligence function is not well defined; hence, there is no person in charge, and it ends up being resolved by the board of directors without the necessary information, mainly intuitively. This creates a dangerous vacuum in the process that drives gaps between data and decisions.

Recently, these activities have commonly been commissioned to the commercial department, which has the advantage of integrating market signals but leaves out fundamental fields such as operations, control, and finance.

For example, a common mistake occurs when market research is done, and the recommendations are established uniquely by the agency carrying it out; this case can lead to uncertain conclusions due to not incorporating the internal context and learning curve.

The risk of not having a specialized area in Strategic Intelligence is losing vision, control, and direction, as happened, for example, to the *Blockbuster*[5] company when it succumbed to a changing market that passed them by.

Instead, understanding the importance of Strategic Intelligence allows us to exponentially increase the chances of meeting goals. Next, let's punctually evaluate its fundamental pillars.

6.1.1 Research Methods

Input channels are key to providing the information to be processed. Strategic Intelligence will be incorrect and even impossible without the right raw material.

To be more certain about the reliability of the received data, we propose the following main steps:

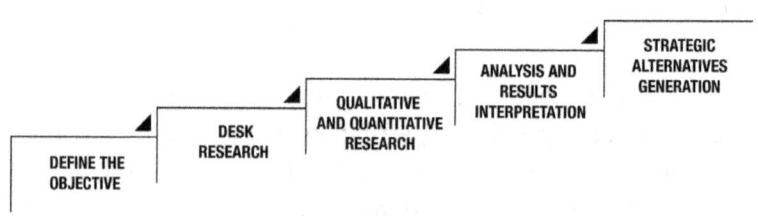

Figure 3: Main steps of Market Research.

1) *Define the objective*

In any dynamic process, an objective is necessary to synchronize the efforts in the same direction. Without a com-

5 Moss, 2019.

mon goal, the parties—rather than allies—will represent obstacles to one another.

Strategic Intelligence is a process, just like a company and even a living being; absolutely all their elements are in an incessantly constant movement.

For these reasons, identifying a purpose is imperative to an intelligent exercise.

In the case of a business project, as a first step in market research, the questions to be answered must be specified to justify the decisions that lead to a central objective. Based on this primary goal, key subgoals can be derived.

Intelligence, due to its etymological root, implies choosing between options. The function of market research is to present alternatives to choose appropriately based on a core purpose.

Therefore, this starting point will set the tone for the following actions. With a clear mandate, experts can begin to collect and interpret useful data; for example, inquire about consumer behavior, brand perception, market size, participation percentages, future trends, and much more.

With a well-defined line, it is possible to determine the type of investigation and the most qualified persons or agencies. For example, in an investment project, a finance expert should be summoned to coordinate with the marketing department's sales projections. Ultimately, **the processing work to derive intelligent decisions depends on identifying probabilities**; the more specific we are, the more accurate we can integrate efforts and experienced teams.

2) *Desk Research*

Currently, an enormous amount of information is available on any subject on the Internet. Also, with the latest advances in Artificial Intelligence, the data is automatically sorted to receive direct and practical answers.

Desktop research provides us with what we call secondary data, accessible from any computer without major investment or specialized efforts; they are quick to obtain, but one should be very cautious about their reliability and up-to-dateness.

Among other sources, we have government statistics, chambers of commerce, online surveys, social networks, specialized blogs, and research databases. It is important to complement these efforts with several sources to improve their validation and obtain a more complete perspective.

3) *Qualitative and quantitative research*

Qualitative and quantitative research is part of the so-called primary data; they are specific and can be classified as shown in the following table:

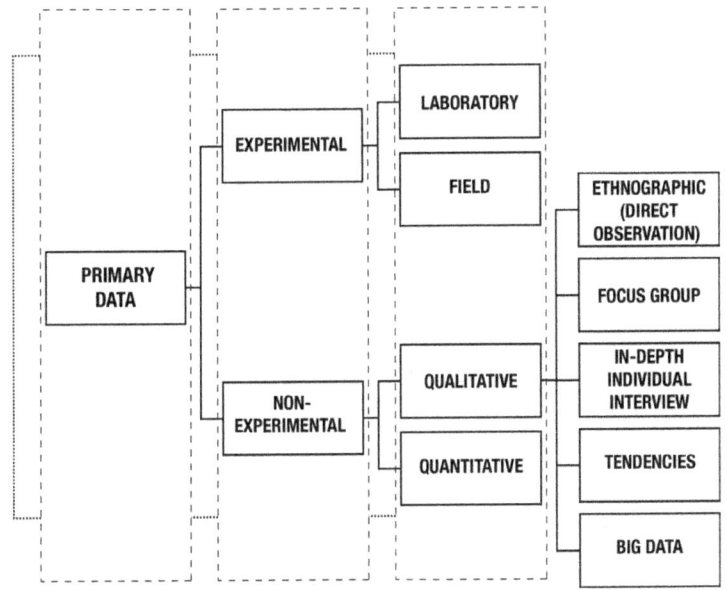

Figure 4: Method classification for obtaining primary data.

In *experimental* methods, the researcher alters the setting and structures a design to compare results between test and control groups—also known as A/B tests.

On the other hand, *non-experimental* research is categorized based on its approach to 1) higher quality (qualitative), commonly involving in-depth individual interviews, focus groups, and direct observation, or 2) higher quantity (quantitative), primarily involving surveys.

Regarding the **qualitative** lines:

The *in-depth individual interview* consists of a free and detailed one-on-one conversation.

The *focus group* depends on unrestricted collective interaction; it is regulated by a moderator who will mark the issues but seek to have as little interference as possible to avoid bias. Typically, 10 people with the target audience's characteristics are summoned and comment for approximately 2 hours. The revelations of this type of exercise, well carried out, are usually very valuable and counterintuitive.

Direct observation contemplates—without intervention—behavior in different contexts, such as purchasing or while using a product or service. This practice can be very pragmatic for validating hypotheses and detecting new relevant considerations.

Otherwise, in the **quantitative** field, numerical data is collected with a non-experimental approach for statistical analysis. Experts often do this through surveys administered online, in person, by phone, or by mail.

Starting with qualitative research and, from the results, generating conjectures that can be validated with quantitative efforts is a convenient combination.

Another productive practice is to define psychographic segments from the information collected in the focus groups and validate them statistically. For example, in the *Palacio de Hierro* Case[6], which uses the sociocultural dynamics of women and their relationship with purchases as a basis, the following categories were detected:

6 C. Chávez, 2000.

Evolution of psychographic segmentation of women in Mexico.		
Year	2000	2020
Sophisticated	19%	35%
Self-Sacrificing	12%	3%
Materialists	16%	10%
Very Traditional Mothers	30%	31%
Dreamers	19%	21%

Figure 5: Psychographic segmentation in the Palacio de Hierro Case.[7]

With this vision, *Palacio de Hierro*, a well-known department store in Mexico, managed to reactivate its sales considerably: it reoriented its communication—with the campaign *Soy Totalmente Palacio* (I'm totally Palacio)—towards modern and growing sub-segments such as the "sophisticated" or "alpha" woman, characterized by having a dominant influence on decision-making, contributing the most significant portion of the family income, and being involved in roles traditionally considered as masculine.

This last example illustrates well how qualitative research can result in extraordinary returns. The aforementioned campaign is still valid after more than twenty years and led the company from financial statements in a tailspin to being one of the world's most advanced department store models.

Finally, as a crucial consideration, quantitative and especially qualitative research are essential partners to detect the unconscious desires that actually motivate a purchase or any behavior.

7 C. Chávez, 2000.

4) *Analysis and interpretation of the results*

Analysis and interpretation are the fundamental processes in the transition from market research to Strategic Intelligence; data is transformed into specific alternatives to make decisions—with short or long-term impact—that are well aligned with the objectives, purpose, and capabilities of the project or company.

At this point, the options to choose from for an intelligent exercise are determined; in other words, points are joined with an effort to synthesize interrelationships that provide a broad and orderly vision.

It is an exercise of conceptual architecture integrating rational and intuitive thoughts to find solutions that have a future impact inside and outside the mind. That is, it is a creative act.

Currently, input, retention, processing, and output of information operations usually depend on human minds but are exponentially reinforced with digital tools.

Very recently, the development of Artificial Intelligence has reached such a specialized level that we could say it has become creative. Therefore, in the analysis and interpretation, it means a powerful ally. Nevertheless, we must be very aware of the limitations of these technological associates: since they do not have a biological body, they do not have emotions and, hence, they do not have homeostatic thoughts (feelings) that regulate their behavior to protect Life. The latter entails a severe danger to humanity and vital continuity; likewise, it implies their intuitive correlation performance will be insufficient in the strategic exercise. Even with current advances (February 2023), Strategic Intelligence still requires human beings to control digital instruments and efficiently integrate intuitive variables (instinctive, emotional, sentient, and spiritual). For example, a human perspective is still needed to detect the sublimated values in a product or service—manifested in the form of feelings—that trigger a purchase; ultimately, what we are doing, is using these algorithms to comprehend our own behavior as a species. With a purely rational or digital analysis, the *Coca-Cola Company* would not have understood why improving the taste of its product did not generate positive results when it launched its *New Coke*[8]. In any case, we must closely follow technological developments as new applications are increasingly efficient in computing information related to human emotions.

6.1.2 Data Intelligence

The use of new technologies to collect and process data is so assertive and prevalent today that it has a specific field: *Data Intelligence*. It is one of the greatest analytical innovations in history that has exponentially improved obtaining, retaining, processing, and outputting of information.

Technological advances in human civilizations are based on what is most valued. Some of the most coveted goods from ancient times have been gold, silver, salt, spices, silk, and sugar; more recently, oil and real estate; today, victor is the data.

World leaders and business people are well aware of this situation, which is why we are witnessing astonishingly rapid progress in new tools that enable Data Intelligence.

---

8 Markus, 2001.

Currently, these digital automations allow describing, prescribing, diagnosing, predicting, and even deciding on fictitious and real situations.

Data intelligence includes the use of big data to obtain and record large amounts of information, *artificial intelligence* to correlate it, and *machine learning* to make decisions based on previous experiences. A complete artificial ecosystem that possesses the deepest essence of the faculty of intellection.

In business, one of the first examples of success in integrating modern technologies for Strategic Intelligence is *Harrah's* Case[9]. What this casino did was document the actions of its customers in a CRM (*customer relationship management*) system with the help of a loyalty program to set up efficient tactics taking into account what was most valuable: not what they said, but what consumers did. This allowed it great precision to detect the users' real segments and motivators, optimize their actions and become the most profitable casino in the United States.

Going deeper into the subject, we find the central axis of Data Intelligence is the so-called algorithms, a set of digital instructions used to perform a task or solve a problem. These arboreal rules can be as simple as "if x, then y" and as complex as multivariable equations that allow simulating a creative and informed human conversation—as is the case with the famous ChatGPT. If now we can accomplish this latter impressive task with traditional systems, we cannot even imagine how potent such processes powered by quantum computing will be in the near future.

---

9 Lal, 2004.

An interesting consideration is that algorithms are not a human innovation; they are at least as old as the beginning of life more than four billion years ago: the genetic code is an extraordinarily complex and efficient biological algorithm. The elementary indication "if x, then y" is notoriously prevalent in vital processes, not only for the synthesis of proteins and the creation of organisms but also for regulating their behaviors.

The basic steps for creating an algorithm are:

1) Define the problem to be solved.

2) Establish the input and output data's characteristics, configurations, and sources.

3) Design a solution with flowcharts.

4) Implement the algorithm with code.

5) Evaluate if it is correct, efficient, and scalable.

6) Optimize.

For example, *Garmin* watches set out to offer tools to improve heart endurance with their devices. To this end, they 1) integrated information collected with global positioning systems (GPS) and movement sensors, 2) processed it to determine distance, speed, and the user's heart rate, and 3) managed to present guides determining if an effort when training is optimum. Thanks to these sorts of functions, their products have been very successful and preferred by athletes worldwide.

Another classic example is *Netflix*. Thanks to the use of algorithms that stand out for their individualized learning, this application recommends to its users, in a highly accurate way, content that will most likely interest them based on their previous actions. The objective of engaging and retaining audiences was achieved 1) by collecting data on the content they actually consume—again, facts, not words—2) by correlating it with the characteristics of other series and similar user interactions, and 3) in consequence, suggesting entertainment options that connect directly with personal preferences.

In 2022, *Netflix* reported having more than 279 million subscribers who—thanks to the use of big data—provide feedback on the processes with each use. Contemporary social networks follow the same fundamental process to attract and engage billions of people daily.

In conclusion, Data Intelligence is indisposable to complement and model Strategic Intelligence.

6.1.3 Financial Risks without Market Research

The probabilities of making correct decisions to mitigate financial risks are directly proportional to the quantity and quality of available information collected and its proper interpretation by market research.

Kodak[10] bankruptcy in 2012 is a didactic event to understand the devastating impact that a limited vision derived from mishandling information can cause. In the first instance, we

---

10 Gavetti, 2004.

might think the failure of this company was because of not knowing how to adapt to technological advances; however, the irony is that they developed what would eventually spell their own downfall. *Kodak*, understanding the value of investing in innovation—well, the success of its traditional model was due to it—invented the digital sensor in the year 2000. The fundamental problem was not the inability to develop technology but an incorrect reading of the behavior and direction of the market; it had the resources and the information but could not process and derive it into appropriate decisions.

This case has been subject to multiple analyzes, and the consensus indicates that market signals were ignored. Still, we believe the critical issue was the mistake of holding on to its production, distribution, and sales strengths. That is, against the odds, the directives wanted the market to adapt to their business model rather than the other way around. One of their attempts to try to change the course of the inevitable was to digitize the photographic film on a CD. In this way,— according to their expectations—the film and the vast number of businesses dedicated to developing it would continue to be valid. The reality is that this option was a curious added value but not very practical since it meant unnecessary steps such as 1) buying a film, 2) installing it in the camera to take the pictures, and 3) taking it to a development center for digitization in a compact disc. On the other hand, the new digital cameras of the time would allow obtaining the same results saving steps 1, 2, and 3 with a click; furthermore, the photographer could take infinite pictures and delete the ones he wanted. By 2008, there were already clear indications of these functional trends, and *Kodak* chose to ignore the risk; if they had generated alternative scenarios and detected their probabilities, they might have made different determinations.

Kodak became king when it succeeded en masse in satisfying our *instinctive desire for transcendence* with immortalized moments on a piece of paper. But, it lost its throne by not considering that the *instinctive desire for control and organization* in the human being is equally assertive; the new options offered it all.

With this information, we can better understand the relevance of integrating predictive models in Strategic Intelligence; using tools that set feasibility parameters based on probability is a very profitable endeavor. We can detect important risks and opportunities by responding to controlled prefactual thoughts like:" what if…".

Below, we present a methodology allowing us to project scenarios to quantify the average financial impact based on probabilities:

1. Collect as much historical data as possible.

2. Detect the causal relationship between variables and make projections aided by regression methods to visualize scenarios with mathematical curves. These techniques allow us to distinguish trends with the available facts. An expert data analyst can support using these types of procedures, including linear, logistic, polynomial, nearest neighbor, decision tree, and neural network regressions.

3. Evaluate the probability of each scenario happening using a random number generator such as *Monte Carlo* or *Python*. These are statistical simulators that, based on the principle

of randomness, estimate the behavior of a system. It will be very profitable to feed the process with variables such as the product life cycle and those related to the biology of human behavior.

4. Simulate income statements with each scenario to determine the return on investment or possible losses.

5. Make decisions based on the new vision.

For example, in the case of *Kodak*, this methodology could have marked the imminent risk of not restructuring its products and business model. Had they considered regression methods, probability simulators, and the product life cycle (*Figure 6*) describing changes in demand within its stages of development, growth, maturity, and decline, they could have estimated the time frame of sales fall. With this perspective, their decisions would surely have been different, and they would have avoided the loss of 10,000 million dollars in the period 2000 to 2012 before declaring their bankruptcy.

We can see this same phenomenon in action with what happened later between digital cameras and smartphones *(Figure 7)*.

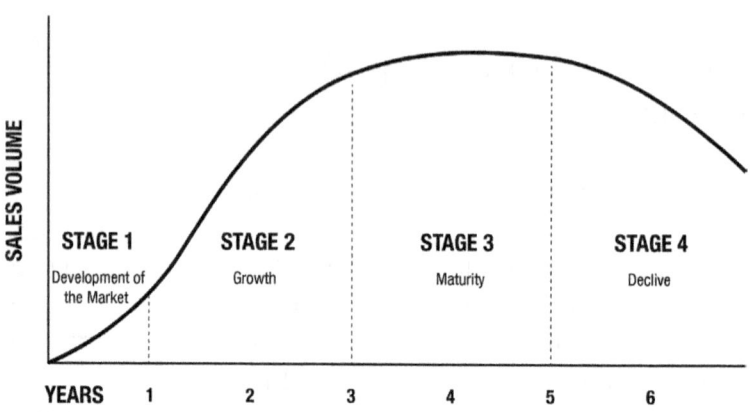

Figure 6: Product life cycle with the Sigmoid curve.[11]

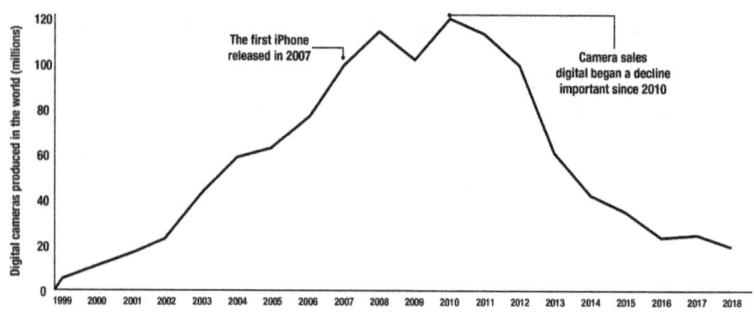

Figure 7: Product life cycle of digital cameras.[12]

---

11 Iveson, 2022.
12 Statista, 2023.

6.2 Understanding the Client

6.2.1 Bio-equalization

Understanding who we are going to address and what moves them is an essential exercise before establishing another parameter in a business model. How could we sell something if we don't know what they want?

Chapter 2.0 reviews commercial bio-equalization, marking how to align an offer to diverse biological conditionings representing collective conscious and unconscious desires. Considering spiritual, genetic, neurobiological, psychological, rational, cultural, and creative drivers is essential to understanding the consumer. Commonly, the value proposition is built contemplating the rational variables mainly; the latter is a strategic error since, although they are relevant, other non-rational factors are much more influential in decision-making. Consequently, an intelligent intention must integrate the human Will's wide range of elements.

In summary, based on our own characteristics and strengths, we suggest identifying and defining the following bases:

1) Determine a Purpose
Spiritual Drivers

How does the project, company, product, or service contribute a greater good—beyond the sale—that protects Life's well-being and prevalence?

Is it potent enough?

Example: Tesla is defined as an entity whose primary purpose is accelerating the world's transition to sustainable energy.

2) Choose an instinctual trigger
Instinctive Drivers

What phylogenetic conditioning (instinctive desire) can we best satisfy?

In the *Psyche-Marketin* model (J.C. Chávez, 2020), we propose 12 of them to streamline the selection process:

Desire for:
Domination / Belonging / Pleasure / Control / Discovery / Protection and Family / Learning / Power / Cooperative Altruism / Being Heard / Transcendence / Recognition

Example: Rolex does not sell watches; it sells a desire for domination fulfilled.

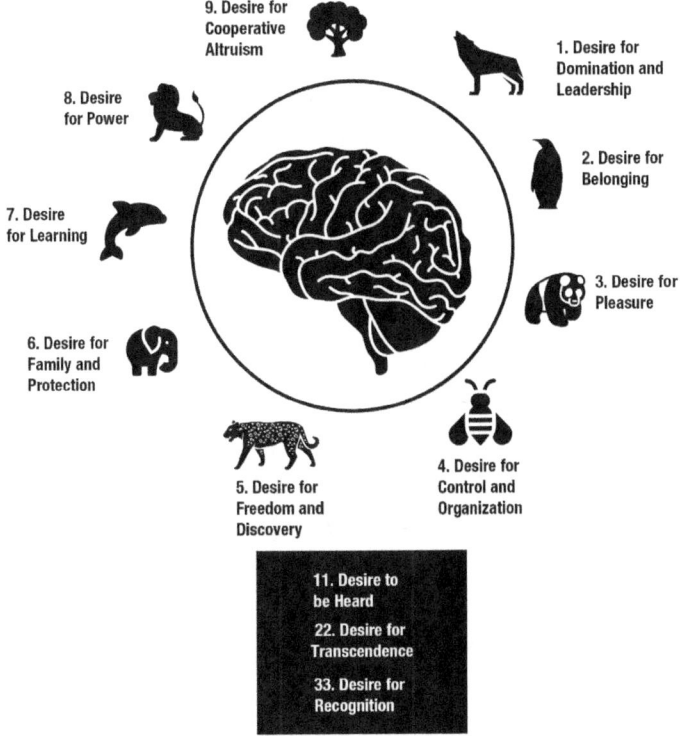

9. Desire for Cooperative Altruism

1. Desire for Domination and Leadership

8. Desire for Power

2. Desire for Belonging

7. Desire for Learning

3. Desire for Pleasure

6. Desire for Family and Protection

5. Desire for Freedom and Discovery

4. Desire for Control and Organization

11. Desire to be Heard

22. Desire for Transcendence

33. Desire for Recognition

Figure 8: The 12 Instinctive Triggers of the ©Psyche-Marketing model.

3) Select a neurotransmitter
Emotional Drivers

What emotional reward can I offer?

Recognize which biomolecule is most representative concerning its physiological effect to anchor it with your brand, product, service, offer, etc.

We propose six main ones to consider:

Norepinephrine / Dopamine / Acetylcholine / Oxytocin /
Endorphins / Serotonin

*Example: Red Bull is consistent with communications that
connote strong emotions to turn its brand into a norepinephrine anchor.*

4) Choose a feeling
Sentient Drivers

What do we want people to feel every time they hear from
us?

How attractive is the sentient gratification I offer? To choose, we suggest reviewing the more than eighty sentient experiences we have rationally decoded in the book *Creative
Intelligenc* (J.C. Chávez 2022, p. 233).

*Example: Volvo has chosen to anchor a feeling of "safety"
with its brand.*

5) Associate cultural codes
Cultural Drivers

What existing symbols best convey the intuitive and rational
values we want to project?

There are visuals, sounds, smells, flavors, and sensations—
representing *consensus maps* (Zaltman, 2003)—integrating
the same group connotations in each culture; select some of
them and use their symbolic charge to communicate forcefully.

Example: McDonald's chose two arches for its logo, acknowledging its cultural connotations of triumph, conquest, and might.

6) Document rational benefits
Rational Drivers

What rational advantages do we have?

With logical argumentation, list specific attributes.

Example: Sealy argues that they have a patented functional system, making their mattresses adapt to the body and not the body to it.

7) Consider a creative differentiator
Creative Driver

How do we uniquely contribute and inspire for a better future?

Configuring an artistic idea, fusing intuitive and rational thoughts that impact inside and outside the mind to model a better hereafter, is deeply attractive and rewarding on all levels.

Example: SpaceX has decided to bring life to other planets as quickly as possible.

Example 2: John Lennon masterfully combined ideas and feelings, manifested in songs that continue to sell, changing the course of humanity and inspiring to treasure empathy.

Next, we will review the nuances arising in various contexts of the purchase process for a more detailed understanding of the client or consumer.

6.2.2 Sales Dynamic

If we pay close attention, we can confirm no uniquely rational thoughts exist in the human mind. Kant would say that although pure reason allows us to achieve objective knowledge about the world, our cognitive abilities and experiences will always limit this knowledge. In this sense, pure reason in a human mind necessarily entails subjectivity.

In other words, those rational justifications we assign to a purchase are always accompanied by the influence of non-rational processes such as instincts and emotions.

However, the weight we give to logical argumentation to make a decision is proportional to the level of mental effort during the process.

Consequently, it is practical to differentiate an interaction concerning the level of involvement it typically presents. In this way, we can deliberate how much we communicate through the intuitive or rational channels of the receiver.

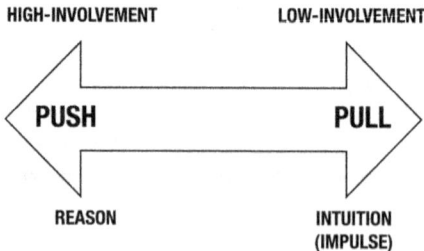

Figure 9: Purchasing dynamics based on involvement in the process.

Low-involvement purchases are fast because there is often a perceived low risk of making a wrong decision. In this dynamic, we must communicate almost entirely through intuitive modes; talk to System 1—Daniel Kahneman would say. Also, a *pull-type* sale will be the most recommended: attract the customer without additional insistence or persuasion, looking for an automatic impulse purchase. For example, this happens markedly when purchasing a snack or soft drink at a convenience store.

On the other hand, *high-involvement* decision-making requires a special effort because more significant potentially derived risks are estimated. In this case, we must reconcile with rational forces; they rarely become the main factor but will acquire greater weight. For example, when choosing a computer, wedding dress, car, or house, we tend to look carefully at its quantifiable features. However, it is crucial to understand that, even in these cases, instincts, emotions, feelings, and more intuitive elements - fast and not quantifiable - represent the predominant influence of the final selection. In this scenario, a *push-type* insistent sale is generally adequate.

Identify at what point in the range of the purchasing dynamics is the product or service you offer located to establish the most convenient type of sale and rational or intuitive levels. It is imperative to emphasize this tool corresponds to a range and not to absolute values. There will always be a level of involvement X regardless of whether it is low or high; that is, we could well place ourselves in the middle of the line.

6.2.3 Purchase Decision Process

Everything changes all the time. What we specifically want right now is different from hours, days, months, or years later; neither is it in other contexts.

To achieve order, it is very useful to standardize consistent situations in the purchase path to identify particular motivators and participants.

When we consider the steps composing a sale, attention is regularly focused on the immediate moment of the transaction; however, there is a very relevant interactive load before and after.

The *purchase decision process* presents six fundamental phases: felt desires, pre-purchase activities, purchase, user experience, and post-purchase feelings.

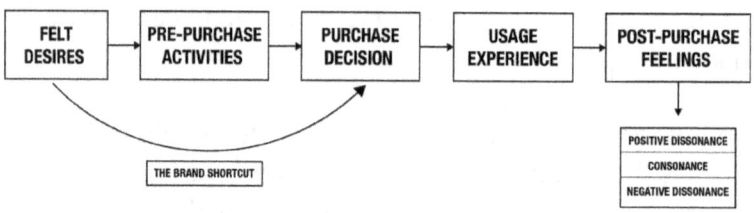

Figure 10: Purchase decision process.

Desires are forces existing by themselves that animate us in every way; they have predefined biological origins and are involuntary. Collectively, we refer to them as Will, and they influence every human thought, action, and decision. When they manifest in the conscious processes of the psyche, they become *felt desires* or *needs*. In other words, we sublimate these longings into specific things or situations and recognize that "we want something."

Based on this initial point, if a clearly preferred option has not been chosen, a stage of *pre-purchase activities* can begin, where available possibilities are explored by comparing their features, accessibility, costs, benefits, and more. The choice will depend on how well each concept connects with what is consciously and unconsciously sought. A brand may even be so well established in the mind—thanks to positioning efforts—that it eliminates consideration of alternatives (*brand shortcut*); behold a reflection of the importance of *branding*. It is relevant to mention that within the previous activities, there is the frequency and emotional intensity of the communicative impacts: the more reminders and emotional impact, the greater the chances of leading to sales.

The next stage is the purchase decision when the transaction is intended to be executed. At this time, the potential client approaches, and offering the appropriate attention is decisive.

But, the road does not end with the purchase. The user experience and what happens afterward are equally important for the profitability of a project. Meeting or, preferably, exceeding customer expectations is crucial to generating a much-needed recommendation supporting repurchases and new takers. In the current market, the testimonial of an unknown user is more valuable than that of the company. This is especially relevant in the context of social networks, which is a key element for a brand and its results.

Immediately after, we find the ***post-purchase feelings***. When the user experience does not meet functional and emotional expectations, *negative dissonance* occurs with dangerously adverse effects; instead, when they are satisfied, we obtain a *consonance*. In the ideal scenario, if they are exceeded, we find a *positive dissonance*; a client receiving more than he or she expects leads to a particularly valuable and profitable sentient experience: <u>gratitude</u>. However, if the positive dissonance is very high, it implies we are not conveying the virtues of our offer well enough, and we face a possible communication problem; the optimal is to find a balance where the expected desire is slightly exceeded.

In the last stretch, with ***post-purchase activities***, one of the most transcendent brand assets can be nurtured: loyalty. Any contact commemorating a positive dissonance closes the cycle, and the path begins anew.

If it is planned and executed correctly, a well-consolidated strategy concerning the decision process means a dialectical swing with cumulative potential, a circle that feeds itself exponentially.

The differentiated participation of various actors during the process stands out: the one who uses or consumes the product or service, the one who receives the benefits, the one who pays, the one who decides, the one who influences, and the one who evaluates. Ideally, for each one, we should implement different communications well aligned to the various motivators they present.

Some key components to consider in each phase are:

Stage: Felt desires.

Key Element: Creative positioning communications well aligned to conscious and unconscious motivators—correct bio-equalization, creativity, and representation.

Stage: Pre-purchase activities.

Key element: Frequency and emotional intensity of communications.

Stage: Purchase decision.

Key element: Careful detailing of the buying experience, including the attention provided and the sensory characteristics of the environment, whether digital or on-site.

Stage: User experience.

Key element: Product and/or service design that meets and exceeds the customer's functional and emotional expectations when using it.

Stage: Post-purchase feelings.

Key element: consider unexpected features allowing you to exceed expectations to generate positive dissonance and, therefore, gratefulness.

Stage: Post-purchase activities.

Key element: Ongoing communication campaigns designed to remind the customer of their experience, build loyalty, and encourage repurchases and referrals.

6.3 Value Identification

6.3.1 Guiding Positioning

After considering Data Intelligence, bio-equalization, and dynamic attributes in the purchase, we have the foundation to identify our offer's potential value and establish a *guiding positioning*.

In our *Strategic Bio-Intelligence* model, (guiding) positioning as a noun is a concept. On the other hand, as a verb, it represents the actions to share said conceptual design with other minds. We will now talk about the former.

At this point, based on the strengths of our offer, we define a strong phrase that summarizes, integrates, and connects with biological motivators, which—with the appropriate tactics—we will seek to place in the mind of the target audience, forming consensus neural maps.

Here, we must sublimate the physiological and psychological factors that influence decision-making, so the ability to synthesize is crucial. In other words, taking into account the biological architecture of the human being—which we have extensively reviewed in the first part of this book—we must align biophysical, instinctive, emotional, sentient, rational, and creative conditionings in one idea.

Defining a thought with the force of attraction forcefully is a creative act of the highest sophistication; it requires penetrating vision and all possible intuitive and rational potential.

Some examples of a guiding positioning that have permeated the global collective psyche and generated high financial returns are:

Apple: tools for the mind that allow advances in humanity.

Coca-Cola: the sparkling drink that makes you happy.

Google: digital services to find everything you want to know.

OpenAI: Artificial Intelligence to benefit all humanity.

Volvo: the safest cars in the world.

Facebook: technologies to connect people.

Disney: stories to inspire people around the world.

Intel: processing power.

Tesla: innovation to accelerate the world's transition to sustainable energy.

SpaceX: technologies to bring life to other planets.

As a practical tool to configure a guiding positioning, estimate the deep human desires, define those you can satisfy better than anyone else, and, based on that, answer the question: how do I want to be known? Or: who am I?

From a correct guiding positioning approach, a sequence of determining effects will be derived—or not—marking positive or negative inertia for the impact and profitability in the short and long term. It is essential to give it the due estimate. In previous chapters, we have exposed fundamental considerations both to define the central concept and locate it in the audience's mind.

So, who are you?

6.3.2 Positioning Map

Since we have a defined positioning idea, what happens when the competition occupies the target territory?

Ries and Trout[13], pioneers in the study of positioning, introduced the concept of *orientation to the competition*, which is logical since the number of brands fighting for recall and communication impacts we receive daily is such that it is necessary to find a place in the cartography of the market.

We must detect the concentration of the offer so as not to fall into difficult-to-integrate saturated points, as is done with the equalization of sound frequencies in the production of a song.

A *positioning map* interrelates two strategic variables and locates the competition's spots. For example, we can analyze price against quality, brand strength against investment in communication, price against benefits, etc. In our professional practice, we have found it helpful to combine some typical marketing variables with *instinctive triggers* (J.C. Chávez, 2020), as shown in *Figure 11*.

---

13 Trout & Ries, 2006.

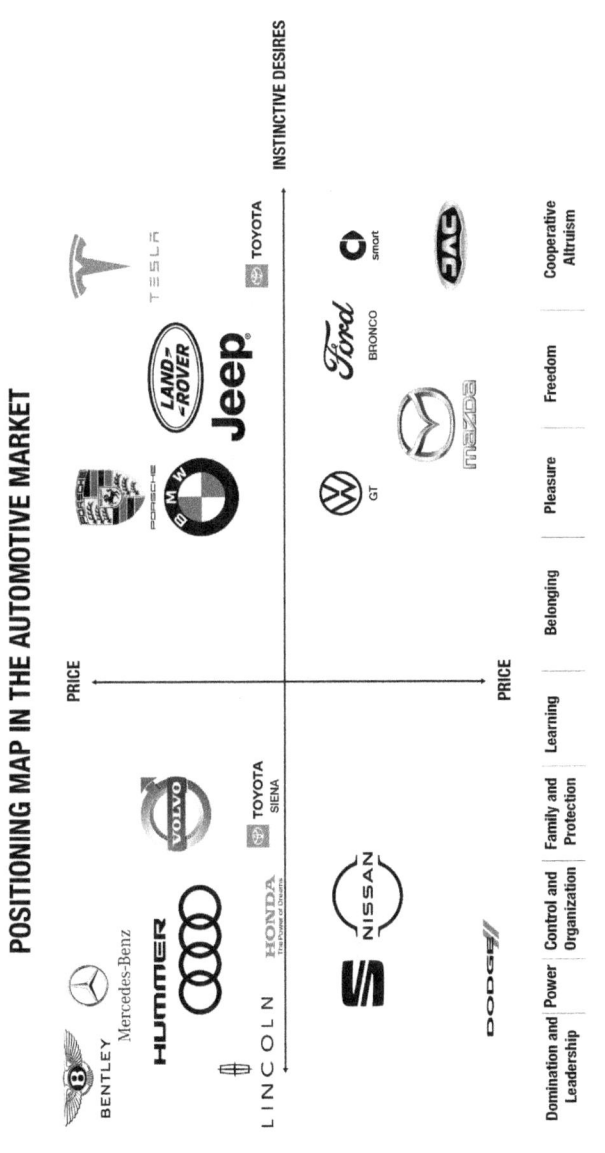

Figure 11: Positioning Map, instinctive desires against price in the automotive market.

On the map, we see empty spaces representing unfulfilled desires and, therefore, opportunities. For example, no car brand has connected with the *desire to belong* like Harley Davidson has in the motorcycle category.

In a recent consultancy with the sausage brand *Johnsonville*, one of the leaders in the United States, we found that correlating the consumption occasion against the price is a relevant tactic in the category. What was detected is *Johnsonville* has a prime, high-priced space for special occasions. The latter led to the recommendation to stay in the premium category and extend its brand to other elements consumed in those events where the host is empowered as the connoisseur and great chef.

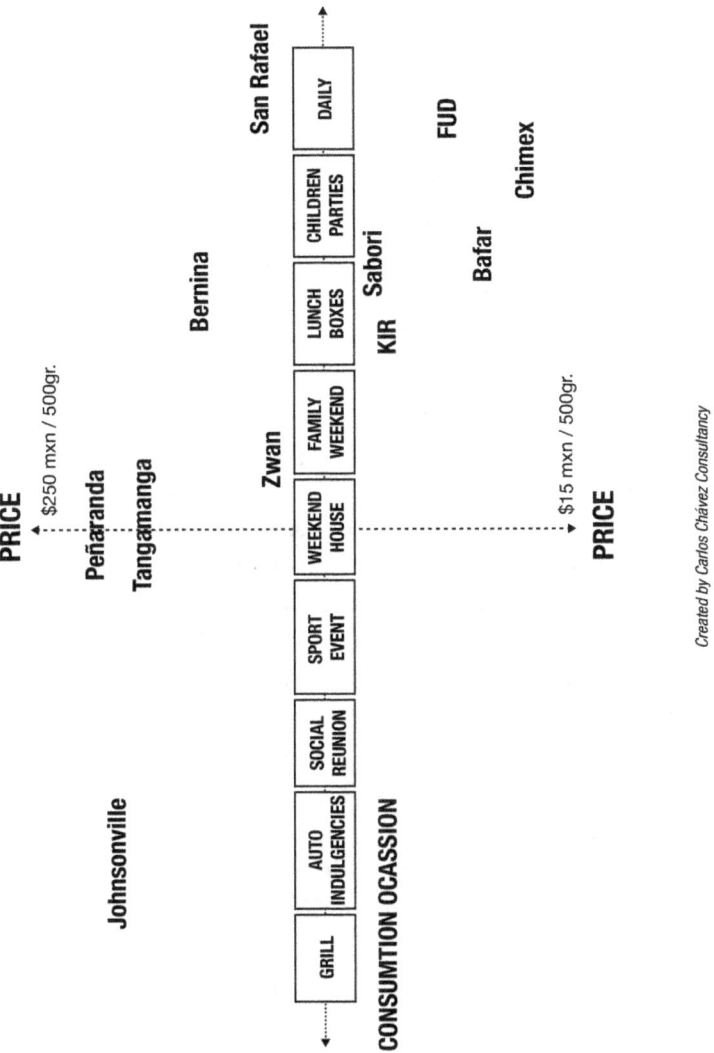

Figure 12: Positioning Map, instinctive desires against price in the automotive market.

On the other hand, if we made a map of protecting the planet and living beings against price, we would realize there is a colossal opportunity for these brands to become the *"Tesla"* of animal products. Not only is it an urgently needed responsibility, but it also means an ample business opportunity—just like it did with *Tesla*. The killing of more than fifty billion animals a year for human consumption is an unnecessary cruelty representing one of the most significant damages to the Planet due to the consumption of resources it needs, such as water, food, territory, waste management, energy, and more. New brands like *Beyond Meat* have already capitalized on this space in the market. In this sense, traditional players will have to act soon to avoid becoming obsolete in the near future—as happened with *Kodak*. The grand opportunity for *Johnsonville*, contemplating this strategic mapping, is to take advantage of its symbolic charge and offer premium products, free of animal cruelty, for barbecues and special events where the host is the dominant protagonist. To achieve this, there are already available techniques that enable replicating a sausage with vegetable raw material and even biological technologies to grow products of animal origin in laboratories from stem cells. Remember, we do not sell products or services but the opportunity of fulfilled wishes; with this maxim, the possibilities of developing more efficient business options aligned with our desire to protect Life and well-being on Earth are multiplied.

With these examples, we realize Trout and Ries were right to see the competition as a war front and the consumer's mind as the strategic objective. To stay relevant and thriving in the marketplace, brands must adapt to changing consumer demands and be aware of the opportunities in the competitive environment.

6.4 Segmentation

Segmentation is a fundamental concept in any marketing strategy. Although digital data now allows us an impressively detailed level of personalization, we have to consider groups with similar characteristics for the purposes of a business model. The individualized offer is not at odds with grouping; their combination is an effective and widely used tactic.

If we do not classify the market, we can get lost in a sea of confusion; the latter is well illustrated by the phrase, "we cannot be everything to everyone because we end up being nothing to anyone."

Even large mass consumption companies, such as *Bimbo*—with the vast majority of participation within the bread market in Mexico[14]—carry out categorization actions to maintain their acceptance. This Mexican brand has products such as toasted, white, wholemeal, and even flourless sprout bread; that is, it segments the market. It also does so with its sales structure, diversifying its means of distribution; it sells to modern channels, traditional channels, and price clubs with different forms of service, prices, and payment conditions.

To be efficient, a target audience must be measurable, accessible by distribution and/or communication, profitable and defendable.

In order to facilitate the process, it is convenient to answer the following questions about the defined segment:

---

14 C. Chávez, 2014.

Can it be identified and measured?

For example, when doing a qualitative study, it is common to identify well-defined psychographic segments but without the possibility of knowing their volume, location, and other characteristics. We must validate we have access to sufficient data for its proper measurement.

Is it big enough to be profitable?

In this topic, it is necessary to delve into aspects of price sensitivity, competition, and distribution channels to identify possible profit margins.

Is it achievable?

It often happens we define a segment that can be very large and profitable but difficult to access. For example, seeking to sell a product in China as a foreign company will present significant cultural, legal, and communication constraints. It also happens when we target segments in very high socioeconomic levels surrounded by entry barriers that can only be overcome with specific public relations.

Is it sensitive to our product or service?

The chosen group may not have a history of our brand or product, which implies allocating significant resources for its launch and awareness. This commonly happens with technological developments.

Is it stable?

We can find very volatile or fleeting segments, as is the case with the fashion world; in this case, short life cycles and frequent innovative developments must be considered.

Can it be defended?

Considering how vulnerable our position is regarding the segment is substantial. For example, the fierce competition between beers has led to hyper-segmentation in recent years; the *Indio* brand in Mexico was very successful by conquering people related to the national culture with creative campaigns on traditions and a low budget. It wasn't long before the *Victoria* brand was contending for the same position with very similar tactics; the latter implies, for both brands, defending the segment with a higher budget and innovation, which should have been considered from the beginning.

As a complementary note, it should be noted that a segmentation effort corresponds to identifying probabilities. That is, we are choosing the typical characteristics of the group of people **most likely** to purchase our offer. It is a "bet" of time and resources that should consider a map of possibilities. The primary tools we have to diagnose them are information gathering, market research, use of big data, statistical processing, and correlation of behaviors and biological motivators.

6.4.1 Segmentation Methods

Why segment the market?

The gain is mutual; both companies and customers can benefit from products or services tailored to their desires and expectations. It is a symbiosis. However, for it to really lead to the collective good, it is urgent the consumer is much more aware of his or her desires and how they operate biologically; we have already set an essential guideline for it in this book.

About executive tactics, different categories allow us to differentiate market preferences to find an appropriate strategy:

Sociodemographic segmentation
Psychographic segmentation
Segmentation by consumption occasion
Segmentation by person's life cycle
Segmentation by product's life cycle
Segmentation by value appreciation

Figure 13: Market segmentation modes.

Sociodemographic segmentation

Social and economic classification is standard and indispensable; although it is not enough, it implies only the beginning of the appropriate process. This data allow us to calculate the size of the market and potential value for the company; it includes age, sex, educational level, place of birth, place of residence, socioeconomic class, religion, and nationality, among others.

The personal or family income variable helps ratify access to our offer by price and the number of people represented by each range.

For this definition, it is usual to use statistics calculated by data and measurement agencies, as in *Figure 14* of *Nielsen AMAI*[15] on socioeconomic levels in Mexico.

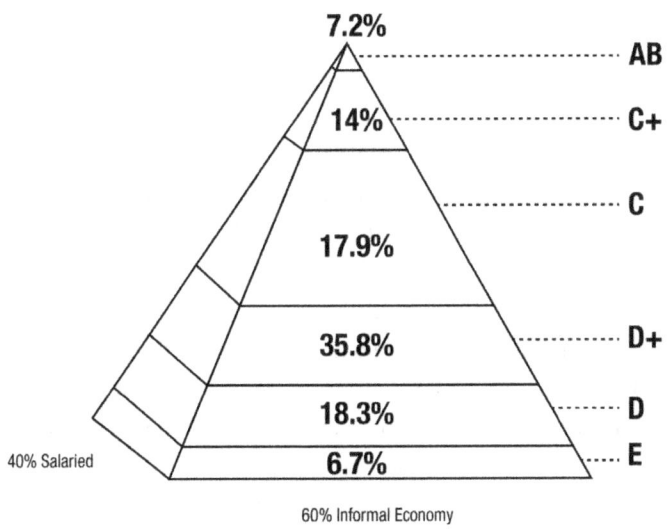

Figure 14: Socioeconomic levels in Mexico according to NIELSEN, 2020.

Likewise, it is important to consider that any statistic presents error ranges and inaccuracies. Regarding the *AMAI* format, although it has the advantage of standardizing various investigations, its methodology uses variables that may differ from reality; for example, one of its parameters to determine socioeconomic levels is the number of lamps in

---

15 *AMAI, 2020.*

the respondent's house; however, this indicator is not always representative of household income.

Understanding the research criteria is necessary to use the tools and the available data.

Therefore, this type of information contains a high referential value but should not be used as a source of exact input.

Psychographic segmentation

Identifying notes on the psychological profile of the target audience is the unavoidable complement of demography. This exercise involves grouping based on lifestyle, opinions, habits, interests, and more.

Establishing hypotheses with qualitative research through Focus Groups or In-depth Interviews and validating them with quantitative studies will allow us to detect the existence and size of psychographic groups.

For example, collaborating on the creation of *Sport City's*[16], concept, we identified five interesting classifications:

1) *Competitive*: they train intensely to compete at an amateur or professional level; their goal is to break their own records and accomplish being in an award ceremony.

2) *Healthy*: they exercise to improve or maintain their well-being; they are not concerned with performance registers, and their goal is to improve their health indicators (mainly weight).

---

16 C. Chávez, 2008.

3) *Fitness*: they seek to look good and be admired for their body.

4) *Social*: they attend a sports club to socialize or find a partner in a safe and comfortable environment. It takes them longer to talk than to exercise.

5) *Of good intentions*: : they reappear every January intending to reduce the weight and health damage derived from the holidays. It is a very profitable segment for gyms since they usually only attend a few times even though they have contracted for the whole year.

With this type of indicators, the strategy will be more efficient when defining specific tactics for each segment in relation to sales, communication, price, and more.

The most relevant point is to contemplate that each group presents a particular hierarchy of motivators, understanding it is essential to predict and promote behavioral phenomena.

Segmentation by consumption occasion

The moment in which the consumption or use of the product or service is carried out is decisive for the commercial strategy since the environment guides significant differences. For example, people are willing to pay more or less in certain circumstances; also, the presentation of the product, packaging, and functionalities may vary depending on the context.

Among other cases, a bottle of water can cost 8 pesos when bought in a supermarket and up to 40 pesos in a hotel minibar. In this last situation, factors such as comfort, fatigue, or difficulty acquiring the bottle outside the hotel are determining factors.

Likewise, the consumption occasion is related to the distribution channel used and, therefore, to the ideal commercial configuration, including the profit margins that can be achieved. For example, serving the supermarket channel implies tighter margins, a specialized sales force, and promotions. On the other hand, selling to hotels and restaurants could have a higher margin but requires different tactics, such as negotiating exclusivities.

It is always very didactic to observe how the dynamics of desires change according to time and space, revealing the multiple nature of our essence. The particular moments and locations are leading factors in the story that mark the impulses to act; it is crucial to consider them to define the strategy.

Segmentation by people's life cycle

Until a few years ago, we were used to very limiting parameters in people's way of life according to their age. For example, at 35, they were expected to be married with two children, divorces were not as common, and the activities of older adults focused on a life of retirement and rest.

Today, things have radically changed. Some people marry at an older age, others live as a couple without getting married, prefer not to have children, or marry individuals of the same sex. Divorces have increased exponentially, and in Mexico, 30% of couples who marry in the civil registry divorce in the first 3 years. Life expectancy has increased recently, from 65 to around 75 years in Mexico, 76 in the United States, and

81 in Europe; for the new generations, their life expectancy can reach 100 years. This implies the lifestyle of the elderly is changing, many perform sports and social activities that were not common in past decades, and their preference for supplements and medical services associated with aging control has increased. Also, it is common to see second marriages and families with two fathers and mothers.

This explains the opportunity to segment the market according to the stage of life, as shown in the scenario of *Figure 15*.

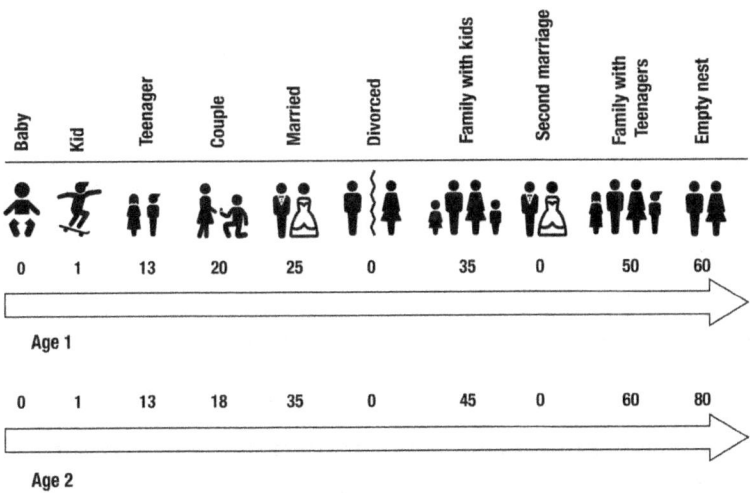

Figure 15: Segmentation by family life cycle.

Age 1 refers to the traditional concept, while *age 2* integrates the changes described in the previous paragraph.

Pets deserve special mention. Although they have always been considered part of the family, today, they are replacing children in the segments of singles and young couples. They are called "fur babies" since they are treated like human be-ings. Consequently, the pet food and product industry has grown by double digits in the last decade, generating busi-nesses with products and services such as spas, hotels, bou-tiques, strollers, premium food, and more.

One of the uses of this form of segmentation is to find new opportunities in the market. Additionally, it allows us to re-flect on how desires evolve and change with age and family circumstances.

Within this topic, we note the forceful inference that cultu-ral constructions have in generational psychodynamics and their juxtaposition with individual experiences and innate conditioning.

6.5 Value Structuring

Up to this point, we have researched the market, transfor-med the data into strategic alternatives, explored the mind through bio-equalization, and identified buying behaviors and decision processes. By understanding the customer, we have laid the foundations for the strategy, starting with seg-mentation and leading to the definition of positioning—with its corresponding differentiation based on what that group really values.

It is time to specify the strategy through value structuring, which is integrated with the elements of *Figure 16* that we will review below.

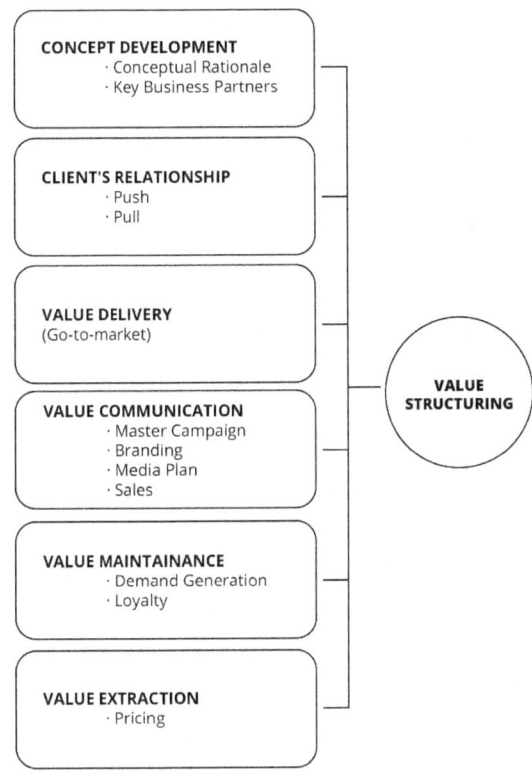

Figure 16: Elements of the Value Structuring.

6.5.1 Concept Development

The *guiding positioning* sets the tone for the *concept development*; it is about bringing the basic idea to intersubjective reality by connecting the predefined meta-values with the notion of the brand, product, or service in the mind of the segment through predefined experiences.

6.5.1.1 Conceptual Rationale and Value Proposition

The conceptual rationale specifies the strategy, establishing the "what" we will do to create value and differentiate ourselves from the competition with a strong proposal. It is one of the most creative moments in elaborating the business model, where the strategic alternatives must be synthesized and defined with a clear path. For this task, it is essential to take into account the defined Purpose that has permeated the guiding positioning based on what we reviewed previously.

For example, *Starbucks'* published mission statement is:

"To inspire and nurture the human spirit - one person, one cup, and one neighborhood at a time."[17]

Which has been documented that it procures by:

"... offering its customers a coffee experience of the highest quality, promoting a welcoming and positive environment for all. In addition, the company is committed to serving as a world leader in the coffee sector, respecting the environment, and offering its customers a wide variety of products"[18].

With this background, the conceptual rationale of the *Starbucks* strategy is based on 3 pillars: the quality of the coffee, the atmosphere, and the philosophy of service. We can illustrate it as seen in *Figure 17*.

---

17 Starbucks Corporation, 2023.
18 Starbucks Corporation, 2023.

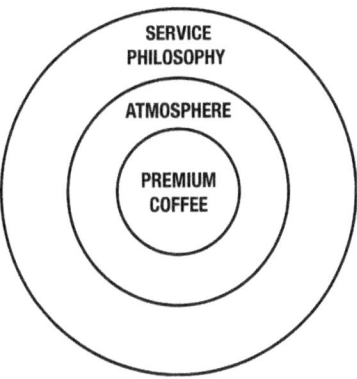

Figure 17: Key elements of the Starbucks Value Proposition.

Based on the value structuring, during the company's evolution, *Starbucks* coined the concept of *third space*, which proposes its cafeterias as a place of tranquility, relaxation, and pleasure that is not your home (*first space*) or office (*second space*).

Arriving at this idea meant years of work and reflection for its creator. With the help of business intelligence, Howard Schultz found a vacant spot on the industry positioning map. Until the 1970s, coffee in the United States was considered an essential product; it was consumed with breakfast, using the percolation method in homes or offices. When mixed with food, the quality of the coffee was not identified, but it was important because it generated feelings of enthusiasm for work. An alternative to percolated coffee was instant coffee, but it also did not meet the expectations of enjoying its flavor and comprehensive experience (as Italians did for centuries). Consequently, *Starbucks* began a tactical process that shaped its conceptual rationale and continues to evolve to date; we summarize and relate it to the *instinctive triggers* they have managed to satisfy in the following table:

Tactic	Instinctive Trigger
Positioned as roasting experts and discussing coffee with customers at the first store in Seattle.	*Desire to Be Heard.* *Desire for Belonging.* *Desire for Learning.*
Cafeterias located near workplaces, decorated, comfortable, and with fast service.	*Desire for Control and Organization.*
Baristas who know your name and talk to you.	*Desire for Recognition*
Individualized drinks by choosing unique components and quantities.	*Desire for Freedom and Discovery.*
Premium coffee prepared with the best machines.	*Desire for Pleasure and Desire for Domination.*
No pressure; you can stay as long as you want, even without consuming.	*Desire for Belonging.*
To be one of the first to offer biodegradable packaging and the disposal of straws.	*Desire for Cooperative Altruism.*

In synthesis, the **conceptual rationale** will give life to the **guiding positioning** by condensing and justifying strategic tactics representing together the **value proposition**.

A lot of intelligent information, a broad vision, creativity, and an understanding of behavioral biology are essential allies to accurately shape the collection of meta-values we want to place in the minds of the target audience concerning our commercial offer. The secret is to cover conscious and unconscious desires with well-structured coordinated tactics in line with the perception we want to achieve.

6.5.1.2 Key Business Partners

Nowadays, proposing a business model with a high degree of vertical integration is difficult since the specialization in products and services of companies dedicated to specific activities is challenging to achieve or implies high costs. This situation is aggravated by the speed of technological changes and innovation in all fields.

For example, at some point, many companies purchased and operated their own servers, which took up large spaces and required low temperatures to function efficiently. Shortly after that, the size of these servers was reduced as memory and processing capabilities advanced with the development of microchips for cell phones, tablets, and laptops. However, this quickly changed again with the appearance of the cloud, whose capacity to handle huge volumes of information and high speeds in processing left owned servers aside.

Therefore, a business model not only admits external service providers, but these are becoming a condition of efficiency for the model's profitability.

When talking about *key business partners*, we refer specifically to those who will allow us to comply with the conceptual rationale that comprises the value proposition. On the other side, in the daily operation, there will be providers that can be easily replaced or whose failure in their services will not alter the strategy.

For example, the *Asdeporte* company, a leader in organizing sporting events such as marathons, races, triathlons, cycling, etc., has a key partner: the *Times and Results* (TYR) company, which, as its name indicates, is dedicated to measuring the times of the competitors in a precise and punctual manner through chips and specialized software. The competitor's experience largely depends on the result he achieves. *Asdeporte* could integrate this function into its own structure, but they prefer to direct the investment towards improving its value proposition.

The key partners in the business are not only providers of products or services but also specific distribution channels, both physical and digital. For example, despite negotiating with Walmart or Amazon being complex, sometimes it is necessary to consider these channels not as distributors but as business partners and, therefore, consider the cost they imply to guarantee the model's profitability.

As an illustrative case, it is common to see entrepreneurs with a good idea regarding their product or service who have followed adequate business intelligence and concept development processes but fail because they do not assess the need for key business partners. In Mexico, a frequent case is the appearance of mezcal brands that, with a lot of creativity, have selected the suppliers and created a bottle that could be an award-winning design; they could even have a good platform and digital strategy. However, this market is governed by large supermarkets and distributors specializing in wines and spirits. If these channels are not associated, aspiring to a reasonable volume that generates enough critical mass to cover expenses will be complicated.

If the **guiding positioning**, **conceptual rationale**, and **value proposition** are well-defined, based on the conscious and unconscious desires of the potential customer, it is possible to complement the *concept development* by marking the *key business partners*. The latter can be integrated into the business model through cost analysis as long as they pass the corresponding profitability test.

6.5.2 Client Relationship

The importance of relating to the client is indisputable. When procuring a relationship, it is crucial to differentiate it from a simple transaction, consider it must have long-term objectives, and orient it on generating satisfaction by exceeding expectations. The latter interconnects to product quality, good service, ease of access, and other tactical business variables. The relationship with the client is strategic since the repurchase, recommendation, and permanence will depend on it.

The most common ways of relating to the customer are 1) the *push*, where the seller, distributor, or retailer significantly influences the purchase decision, and 2) the *pull*, where mass communication, digital communication, public relations, and promotions generate a significant trademark for the minds of the target audience—better known as *Branding*. For academic purposes, we consider both extremes, but most companies use a combination with an emphasis on one or the other.

It's important to note that *push* can also build powerful brands; the difference lies in the business structure needed and the time it takes to achieve it. If you have the proper budget, the *pull* will have results in a shorter period.

Both modes can be used in effective polarizing ways even within the same industry and segment. For example, in the detergents category, the two giants in Mexico are *Procter & Gamble* and *Fábrica de Jabón La Corona*. The first is characterized by a substantial advertising investment (15% of revenue[19]) in its brands and distribution, emphasizing the modern channel. On the other hand, *La Corona* has practically not advertised in its 80 years of existence and has managed to lead the market through a *push* strategy, with more than 600,000[20] small stores existing in the country as business partners. They have achieved this by offering an interesting margin for shopkeepers to encourage them to promote their brands *Roma*, *Soap Zote*, and *Foca*, among others, at socioeconomic levels C-, D, and E. Also, they include in their value proposition the sale of reduced quantities of detergents aligned to the weekly spending capacity of its consumers. Thanks to product quality and strategic consistency, *La Corona* brands have equally become present in the modern channel, offering competitive prices and accompanying large chains and wholesalers in opening their own small stores in cities and small communities.

Two contrasting cases demonstrating the potency of totally different customer's relationship tactics. Let us review them with more detail next.

6.5.2.1 Pull Mode

Business academics have evaluated *push* and *pull* modes from different approaches to systematize processes, but traditional maps have significant limitations.

---

19 Deloitte, 2019.
20 INEGI, 2016.

The first approach is focused on results: it is proposed that *pull* corresponds to what generates demand or brand value. However, from this perspective, *push* can also generate demand, as happens in the so-called activations; furthermore, strictly speaking, all of a company's actions add to or subtract from the perceived value of a brand.

The second approach focuses on media: it is said mass media correspond to a *pull-type* effort and the sales force to *push*. The foregoing is partially true if the content of the campaigns is mainly branding-oriented, but mass media communications about discounts or offers could well be launched to push the product.

Finally, the approach closest to our proposal focuses on the psychological effect, placing *pull* as a cause of bonding with the client (engagement) and *push* with the mission of calling to action to close the sale.

In the map of human psychological systematization (J.C. Chávez, 2022) that we presented in chapter 1.2, we can see *pull* coincides with the first three steps (*see figure 18*); in other words, attracting people to our brand implies correlating desired values to the perception that our communications, products, and services form in the mind. As we have previously reviewed, the above is achieved by connecting with biological conditionings—manifested in desires—triggering positive emotions and feelings in the face of the possibility of being satisfied by our differentiated value proposition. In this way, the client will look for the brand on his or her own initiative and will be convinced before purchasing. Starting from this reflection helps us determine an adequate budget to integrate enough scope and frequency to permeate the psychodynamics of the target audience.

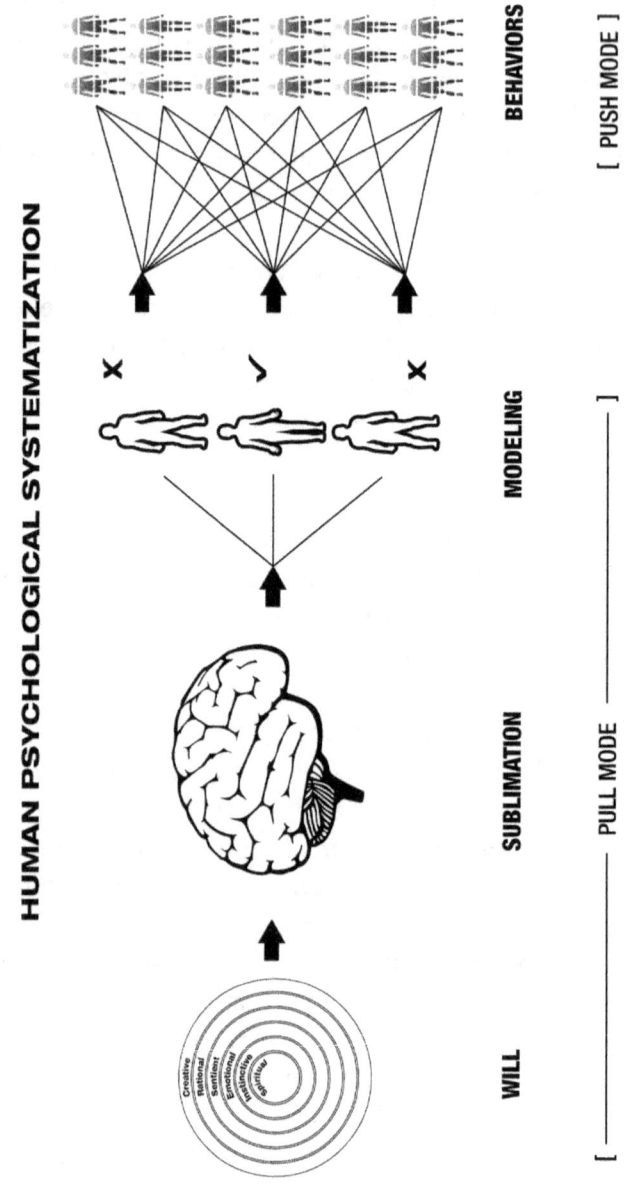

Figure 18: Influence of pull and push marketing modes with respect to the Human Psychological Systematization Map (J.C. Chávez, 2022).

6.5.2.2 Push Mode

On the other hand, *the push* will be the final impulse to close a sale; that is where the rational elements, such as the logical arguments of a seller, discounts, and promotions driving the conclusive action, mainly operate.

The *push* in the *psychological systematization map* influences the last step corresponding to the behaviors.

The context we design around the purchase decision is essential for the results. In the *push*, we must integrate tactics leading to short-term behavioral effects such as logical justifications, interactive and convincing sales scripts, communicative pieces alluding to a sense of urgency, arguments allied to cognitive biases and heuristics, and more.

There has been a debate about whether digital communication is an ideal medium primarily for *push* or *pull* mode. To answer this question, if we value the previous reflections, we find following both paths can be fruitful in this environment. Without a doubt, we are not limited to one or the other, much less after the exponential growth of e-commerce during and after the Covid19 pandemic in 2019.

As an essential reference, the terms *awareness campaigns* for efforts in *pull* mode and conversion campaigns in *push* mode are popular in the digital marketing industry. Regarding the first, it is crucial to understand "awareness" (being known) is only one variable in the positioning process; it would also be necessary to define forcefully "how we are known," so the term *positioning campaigns* is much more appropriate. Other widely employed models refer to levels within a funnel divided into upper, middle, and lower. The top corresponds to efforts to attract the masses, get followers, and position brands; the middle to engage and maintain interest with people; and the bottom to close transactions. In the latter case, *pull* mode would be at the middle and upper levels and push at the bottom.

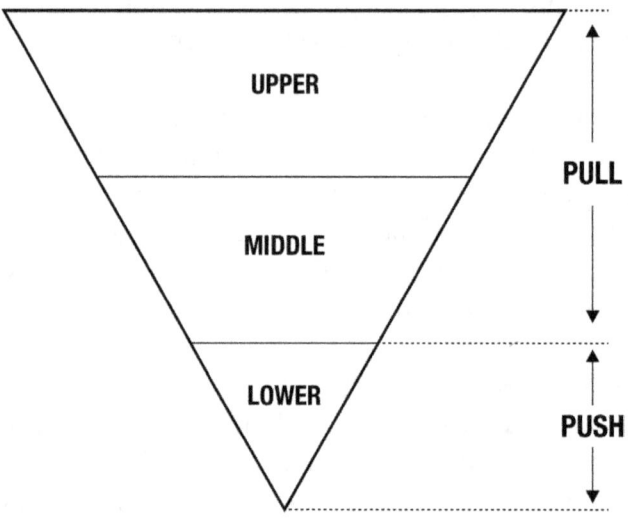

Figure 19: Digital Communication Funnel regarding push and pull marketing modes.

Considering *push* and *pull* marketing modes is a key need for the structuring of value and profitability of a project, none should be underestimated, and it is crucial to constantly feed and update them.

6.5.3 Value Delivery (Go-to-market)

The new technologies forced the integration of new digital channels in value delivery; thus, the term multichannel arose a few years ago.

In the first attempts, the incipient digital transformation of companies caused the various channels to work independently, which provided more options but complicated the customer experience because they had to interact with multiple service points as if they were different companies. To date, the latter still happens in some companies, such as banks restricting certain procedures to one channel; for example, activating a credit card in some institutions can only be done by telephone and not in a branch. As a result of similar situations, which make the service difficult, the *omnichannel* initiative arose.

According to Erik Brynjolfsson[21], an omnichannel marketing strategy focuses on providing a consistent experience across all communication and sales channels. This means customers can coherently interact with a brand through its website, text messages, mobile applications, phone, email, social networks, physical stores, and other mediums. Omnichannel seeks to offer diversity, uniformity, and consistency with integrated systems that interact on the same platform and complement each other to generate superior value. For example, *Walmart*[22] seeks this path by connecting its e-commerce systems with the strength of its physical stores, which even operate as delivery points with special spaces in the parking area for online orders; this adaptation gives *Walmart*

21 Brynjolfsson, 2013.
22 Casadesus-Masanell, 2019.

an advantage over the robust competition *Amazon* represents.

In summary, the channel's relevance lies in how it adds value to the process by helping to satisfy customers' desires.

Below, we present some examples of tactics to add value through the delivery channels—which sometimes become the central axis of the strategy—based on the *instinctive desires* of our behavioral biologic model.

Desire for Domination
The age-old tactic in delivery channels.

The local markets in Mexico originate in the "tianguis" of the pre-Hispanic period. The most representative is Tlatelolco[23], where more than 250,000 people met negotiating goods from all over the Aztec territory through barter. In these spaces, merchants honored royalty and, with the arrival of the Spanish, treated wealthy conquerors with submission and respect. These practices continue to this day; sellers in both traditional and modern channels understand that making the customer feel dominant is useful. For example, in current Mexican markets, attention calls to potential buyers with honorific nouns such as "don," "doña," "señor," "güerita" and "patrón" stand out.

Consumers find such an approach attractive because they feel empowered; the same happens with tactics of large companies such as the classic "the customer is always right," which results in greater profitability.

---

23 Rees, 1970.

Desire for Belonging
Exclusivity and feeling as part of in delivery channels.

Palacio de Hierro created an innovative campaign aimed at the generational change of women, recognizing their independence and love for shopping. We can synthesize it with its slogan, "I am Totally Palace." After more than 20 years of using this phrase, the general perception is *Palacio de Hierro* is an exclusive place and that buying there includes you in a select group of people with refined tastes and a preference for prestigious brands.

Alternatively, *Sam's Club* used a different tactic by offering a financial benefit for joining their community. Being a member only requires an annual payment granting access to the store, which represents a significant income for the company. In return, the customer receives half-wholesale prices and is willing to purchase higher quantities of products. The *Sam's Club* customer desires and appreciates being part of a group with business privileges.

Desire for (sensory) Pleasure
Entertainment and enjoyment in the delivery channels.

Shopping malls—crucial outlets—have evolved alongside the market. Initially, they comprised 2 or 3 department stores considered anchor stores and small complementary specialized stores. The large footfall in these spaces has attracted major brands now competing for locations and paying high rents. Mall expansions included movie theaters, gyms, and restaurants, turning them into places of entertainment more related to weekend outings than specific or necessary purchases. These walks lead customers to purchase desirable, though not essential, items that constitute indulgences and offer a pleasurable experience.

The most recent stage of shopping centers has integrated a more prominent gastronomic offer and more pleasant architectural designs. In 2022, *BAL Group* and other investors inaugurated the *Mitikah* shopping center, which has become a star attraction point in Mexico City. The value for the client is based on a comprehensive experience of sensory pleasure by observing, listening, tasting, eating, and, secondarily, buying. *Mitikah* bet this reason has enough weight to keep the business profitable in the face of the potency of digital purchases.

Desire for Control and Organization
Excellence in delivery channels.

In digital channels, process efficiency has become an essential expectation. More than 330 million customers shop on *Amazon*[24] because they find control and organization over their time, spending, market insight, the possibility of returns, tracking their purchases, delivery schedules, and more.

In addition, thanks to automation, *Amazon's* algorithms allow users to offer very accurate recommendations for products that will surely interest them, which it detects based on their actions. In an environment so full of commercial proposals, the consumer gains control over their time and the offers they receive through this channel.

---

24 Statista, 2021.

Finally, through this impeccably systematized platform, you can easily find the most valuable reference for a buyer today: other people's recommendations—representing control and organization over the parameters of confidence.

All human beings —instinctively— appreciate feeling in control of the situation; adapting this perception to the delivery channels is a highly productive addition.

Desire for Freedom and Discovery
New experiences in delivery channels.

Napa and Guadalupe Valley vineyards have become important communication channels for wine brands like *Duckhorn* and *Monte Xanic*. The vineyards represent a dream for stressed-out city people, promising a peaceful and pleasant retirement; this is where the possibility of discovering a charming lifestyle and the processes allowing its treasured products becomes a unique attraction.

We *Homo sapiens* are programmed to incessantly seek new experiences; this longing is a core attribute of evolution. Integrating the possibility of obtaining extraordinary experiences through a delivery channel will automatically make it more attractive and profitable.

Desire for Family and Protection
Well-being in delivery channels.

Protecting family and what is considered "self" is a potent automated conditioning; it is a behavior compelled by the innate tendency of territoriality present in the human species since its origins. Satisfying this desire in delivery channels results in a crucial asset for any commercial endeavor: trust.

For example, hospitals and insurance companies directly offer the necessary care to ensure the well-being of the family and the protection of their assets, resulting in very profitable businesses.

Hospitals such as *ABC* and *Ángeles* in Mexico have stood out for facilitating check-ups in dedicated facilities, separating themselves from the critical activities of the hospital, and offering preventive medicine activities that seek to inspire tranquility and confidence. These specialized centers are "distribution channels" since they become a showcase and point of sale for subsequent treatments.

On the other hand, what *Geico* insurer has achieved with its mobile application has been relevant; it facilitates any customer requirement not only at the time of the claim but also for payments, changes in the policy, repurchase, cross-selling of other insurance, follow-up on the recovery of expenses due to accident or illness and even purchase and sale service of cars as an extension of the business. Said environment is designed to generate a sense of protection, allowing problems to be mitigated most easily and efficiently as possible. *Geico*'s business model is based on digitizing all its services, concentrating them on its *Geico Mobile* application. Thus, it eliminates the dependence on agents and allows them a greater margin to carry out massive communication campaigns—it's common to see *Geico* commercials at the *Super Bowl* every year, which can cost anywhere from $3 million to $5 million for a 30-second ad. In this way, *Geico* has turned its application into its sales, communication, and operation channel.

Desire for Learning
Education in delivery channels.

Learning is a primarily rational process, but *desiring to learn* is an instinctive command.

Since the COVID-19 pandemic in 2020, digital channels have become an essential source of income for all universities. Faced with the impossibility of giving face-to-face courses, they continued their programs by developing online learning platforms. This allowed them to offer continuing education courses which, during the lockdown, became an attractive offer. At the end of the pandemic, the platforms were consolidated, and the participants developed the necessary adaptation to learn through the network.

The convenience of not commuting, managing time for other activities, and the global reach have meant excellent benefits for the education industry. Even the most prestigious universities offer options in virtual mode. For example, by 2020, Harvard Business School had obtained 10% of its income through online programs, representing 60 million dollars[25]. They also detected a growing interest in web-based programs, reaching 52% of their target audience.

In this case, learning became multi-modal; the participant acquired knowledge of the product's contents but was also instructed regarding new interactive ways of apprenticeship.

Other interesting examples of learning related to delivery channels are the restaurant chains *Hard Rock Café* and *Planet Hollywood*, which have integrated a museum-like format into their locations. Offering experiences that allowed lear-

---

25 Gupta, 2022.

ning and admiring interesting items in the delivery channels meant crucial added value for the success of such projects.

Desire for Social Responsibility
Awareness and cooperation in delivery channels.

All human beings are conditioned to help in order to help themselves; without this instinctive symbiotic impetus, collaboration would not be possible.

For the groups defending the Planet, the *Whole Foods* supermarket chain has been very well accepted despite its high prices and not having the most representative mass brands of unhealthy food. There you can find organic, vegan, vegetarian, and other foods contributing to environmental care. The company understands the clientele is still in a transition stage; for this reason, for the most demanding concerning the characteristics of the products, it still does not comply 100%. However, it is interesting that the chain's potential was recognized by none other than *Amazon*, which acquired it to complement its offer of perishables and integrate its great digital experience into a traditional channel. *Amazon* acknowledged the trend towards healthy food but also the continued preference for the physical point of sale, which, in this case, favorably impacts the brand as it is considered socially responsible.

Desire to be heard
Interaction in delivery channels.

The neurophysiological channels for collecting, retaining, and processing information would not be of much use without means of output. Communicating our ideas is a necessary genetic guideline for human evolution that, like any instinct, leads to sentient rewards when satisfied.

In 2017, the *Doritos*[26] snack brand launched a series of communication campaigns in which its segment, comprised of adolescents, was widely involved. First, it summoned them through digital and traditional channels and points of sale to qualify musical projects associated with various products; 462,000 evaluations were received, resulting in rock concerts organized based on public comments. A year later, *Doritos* asked them to create a campaign in a contest, and, in addition to winning a cash prize, the idea would be taken to the media; 6,000 proposals were registered. Giving a voice to its consumers was the reason for its success.

On the other hand, the sales channel of the cosmetics and skin care brands *Nu Skin* and *Mary Kay* incorporates a structure of representatives who are motivated to undertake under a pyramid scheme. The possibility of influencing and being heard is given to promoters and clients. The training these brands give to the representatives—who are mainly women—makes them experts not only in the products but in the subject of beauty, allowing them to establish contact with potential clients as experts in the field. This changes the lives of many of them accustomed to routine tasks at home; reps become personal advisors to buyers who can call them for advice—serving the need to be heard. This process makes the direct sales channel much more valuable than a cold digital purchase.

---

26 C. Chávez, 2017.

Desire for Transcendence
The future is already present in the delivery channels.

Leaving a legacy, thinking that our passage through life had an impact, deeply motivates us collectively and individually as a species.

The *metaverse*—already a "reality"—is a suitable example of human efforts to transcend. Mark Zuckerberg and other major investors have bet heavily on this virtual delivery and experimentation channel that exists independently of the laws of physics; the possibilities are fascinatingly vast. This environment is not only a fact but a wide range of products and services are already marketed within it. Without a doubt, the go-to-market in the realm of virtual and augmented reality should be seriously considered in our value delivery strategy.

Another prominent example of the human drive to transcend is *SpaceX*, a germinated project to bring life to other planets. One of its most important missions is to colonize Mars, including a series of developments such as establishing space bases and raising funds with civilian travel to space. This means an exo-terrestrial extension to be considered within business models, as is already the case with the installation of satellites allowing diverse functions, commercial and military services, and more. Participating in any way in these innovations implies captivating our deepest desires for transcendence.

Desire for Recognition
Collaborative motivation in delivery channels.

The social reward manifesting itself in recognition is an asset intensely and incessantly sought by the human spirit. This happens when we seek appreciation from our mother at birth and continues as we seek acceptance from others and ourselves throughout life.

An illustrative example of this motivator regarding delivery channels is *Strava*[27], a social network for athletes whose main medium is an application reaching more than 70 million users. Unlike other digital services that also record training, competition, and bodily function data during sports activity, *Strava* understood the emotional value of recognition by integrating communities of athletes who cheer each other on by celebrating their achievements through *kudos*. The latter interactions are equivalent to *likes*, but they are given not only because something was liked but also because of showing appreciation to another community member. In this way, the delivery of value bathes in a sea of mutual recognition.

6.5.4 Communication of Value

In the value structuring process, communication plays a fundamental role. No matter how potentially valuable our product or service is, the strategy will not work if the customer does not know the value exists or does not identify it.

Communication is the key to adding desirability to our concept and modeling its perception. Transmitting the correct

---

27 Lassiter III et al., 2016.

information appropriately is an essential foundation to motivate purchase decisions and involvement and generate loyalty and satisfaction in the short, medium, and long term. For a commercial endeavor, the function is evident; sales, positioning, and economic results depend on the expression and interrelation of ideas with other minds.

In short, communication is the guiding principle in any exercise of human interaction.

In *Figure 20*, based on our *Strategic Bio-intelligence* model, we have updated the *6 Ms* proposed by Robert J. Dolan at *Harvard Business School* as essential variables to consider before starting any communication effort.

Mission:	What are the communication objectives?
Market:	Who is the communication aimed at?
Motivators:	What does the market consciously and unconsciously want and motivate?
Message:	What is the idea to be communicated?
Media:	Where, how, and with what budget will the message be communicated?
Measurement:	How will the impact be assessed?

Figure 20: 6Ms proposed by Robert J. Dolan. (1996) updated by Carlos and Juan Carlos Chávez based on Economic Ethology.

As a note on adaptation, we integrated the *Motivators* variable since it is impossible to connect with the human psyche—and establish the appropriate Message—if we do not understand what drives it. Also, for practicality, we join *Money* with *Media* as it is traditionally integrated into a *Media Plan*.

Regarding the *Mission*, it refers to the strategic role specifically communication has in the business model, which represents the most critical variable to position a brand in the market; therefore, the resources allocated must be consistent with the objectives. However, it is relevant to consider that the greater the differentiation of the offer *per se* (unmatched products or services), the less need for investment in communication will be required to achieve the goals, and *vice versa*.

Only on rare occasions does communication become less important in products that, due to their significantly differentiated nature, can position by themselves.

Next, for practical purposes, we will define the essential variables for a communication campaign to obtain results. Once the message to be communicated has been determined, based on the *Guiding Positioning* of the strategy, the following elements must be considered:

1) Reach

You must invest what is necessary to reach the adequate number of people, at least hundreds of thousands of impacts per month —preferably millions—for a mass communication effort. In traditional advertising, this is known as *rating*. In the modern digital context, it is referred to as *impressions* or *reach*.

2) Frequency

In the book's first part, we have established the importance of repetition; the correct frequency in communication is essential to position an idea in the target audience's mind that leads to actions. It is not enough to connect with many people; we must do it many times; otherwise, the message will be quickly forgotten. The latter is especially relevant in our so-mediated society saturated with information fighting for individual and collective attention. Increasing the frequency of intercommunication impacts means exponentially increasing the chances of achieving business objectives.

3) Communication Strength

This factor depends on the creativity and quality of the production. For greater depth and understanding of the creative faculty, we suggest reviewing the books *Creative Intelligence* and *Creativity* (J.C. Chávez, 2022): *the Most Powerful Weapon in the World* (J.C. Chávez, 2019).

Concerning favoring the creative process in a commercial communication context, we propose to consider the following guidelines:

a. *Originality*

It is based on using new and surprising elements, things out of the ordinary. For example, *Librerías Gandhi* has launched very successful campaigns using billboards as the primary medium with designs that stand out for only integrating a yellow background with a peculiar phrase.

b. *Elaboration*

It is achieved when a simple idea is detailed to generate something more complex. For example, the *Evian* ad showing computer-simulated babies dancing with great charisma and prowess on skates requires a lot of production and creative elaboration.

c. *Synthesis*

The French writer Blaise Pascal wrote in 1956:

I am very sorry for writing you such a long letter, but I did not have time to write a shorter one.

Enrique Gibert, one of the most creative Latin American publicists, was an expert on this subject. He created well-remembered slogans such as.

- *Raleigh es el cigarro.*

- *Everyone has a Jetta, at least in their head.*

- *IPADE, inspiring people, perfecting leaders.*

d. *Artistic Value*

The artistic inspiration and adequate execution in a video, photograph, jingle, or phrase permeate the mind deeply. We refer to *artistic value* as the ability to tell short or long narratives that masterfully combine sensory, rational, and emotional elements, creating a unit in harmony with multiple symbolic layers. A great work of art fuses visuals, sounds, smells, flavors, and/or sensations with rational ideas and feelings connecting with the being at all its cognitive levels.

There are many examples; we just need to think of our favorite symphony or painting.

e. *Generation of Emotions*

In the subjective world of creativity, the best indicator of a good communication piece is its emotional charge. From a neurophysiological point of view, what happens is that a stimulus—or message—represents the possibility of fulfilling, failing to fulfill, keeping, or losing conscious or unconscious desires, which will trigger the release of biomolecules (such as neurotransmitters), causing an internal bodily reaction that the mind experiences as feelings.

It is then pragmatic to identify the *feelings* (mental response) and *emotions* (physiological response) related to a neurotransmitter that a communication triggers or tries to trigger. For a better understanding of the dynamics, we present below some examples with the option to view the referred video online with a QR code.

1. In the ***Discover the Pleasure of Magnum*** video, an indulgent experience is shown aimed at creating a solid craving triggering the release of ***dopamine*** and the feeling of ***pleasure***.

Figure 21: QR code directed to the video "Discover the Pleasure of Magnum.[28]"

_____

28 Magnum, 2023.

2. In the video ***The Best of Andre Rieu***, from the conductor generating the most income in the world[29], a part of his famous concerts is shown that adapt popular songs with classical arrangements and a curated production with a world of musicians and dancers immersed in an extraordinary setting. With this communication, ***acetylcholine*** is immediately presented in the bloodstream; a biomolecule involved in attention, learning, and motivation processes that can result in the so-called *goosebumps*. The feeling of ***amazement*** could well be the product of a mix of visual and sound stimuli like this.

Figure 22: QR code directed to the video "The Best of Andre Rieu.[30]"

3. Nike's ***You Without Limits*** video showcases a collection of impressive feats that encourage you to think big and overcome fear at all costs, no matter your current condition. With this communication, it is inevitable to produce ***norepinephrine***, typical of an adequate body state designed to face dangers or obstacles, and receive a sentient reward in the form of ***empowerment***.

29 Mi, 2017.
30 Rieu, 2023.

Figure 23: QR code directed to Nike's "You Without Limits" video.[31]

4. In the video ***The Clydesdales Brotherhood*** by *Budweiser* presented at the Super Bowl, a story of loyalty and friendship is shown between a rider and his Clydesdale[32], horse, separated after many years of shared happiness, to emotionally reunite in the final scene. It is a love story, not in the traditional format of a couple but in the sense of seeking closeness and protecting the one who means a source of joy. This feeling is usually accompanied by the release of ***serotonin***, a neurotransmitter related to well-being and plenitude.

Figure 24: QR code directed to Budweiser's "The Clydesdales Brotherhood" video.[33]

We conclude the chapter by suggesting the following neurotransmitters as a strategic guide for communications: norepinephrine, dopamine, acetylcholine, oxytocin, endorphins,

31 Nike, 2023.
32 Budweiser, 2023.
33 Reichheld, 2001.

and serotonin. Regarding feelings, we recommend consulting the *Geometry of Feelings* section of the book *Creative Intelligence* (J.C. Chávez, 2022) with a list and description of sentient experiences.

6.5.4.1 Master Campaign

The Master Campaign is a fundamental method and concept that we have named to reflect its relevance and function; it is about the *guiding positioning* (or *Message* in the *6 Ms* model) landed in a tactical communication execution. In other words, to make it permeate correctly in other minds, it materializes the answer to how I want my brand, product, or service to be perceived.

For example, based on its strategy, how has *Coca-Cola* repeatedly told us that it *is the soft drink that makes you happy?*

Such execution can derive in audio, video, and even olfactory and sensory formats; however, we suggest starting with a visual that vehemently sets the tone.

In other words, the Master Campaign is the main message ready to be communicated; it is designed to achieve proper positioning by connecting with strategically defined conscious and unconscious desires to maximize profitability. To comply with these attributes, it is essential to transmit the rationally defined *guiding positioning* with proper synthesis and creativity that integrates high precision in the message, stands out for its originality, and conveys the idea in nanoseconds. Let us remember our human decision-making processes in everyday life are characterized by being mainly intuitive—typical of *system 1*, Daniel Kahneman would say. Therefore, the Master Campaign must speak loud and clear to the intuitive mode of cognition: triggering emotions by presenting the possibility of fulfilled spiritual and instinctual desires. And on the other hand, it can be complemented with rational justifications as the next priority. Many times one falls into the error of doing the latter in reverse; in communication, using logic as the main element and neglecting the emotional impact is a highly inefficient effort.

Once we achieve a robust implementation through an image—as if it were a design for a billboard—then we can use it as a compass to creating all kinds of adaptations consistent with each other and well standardized, such as radio and television spots, sales materials, content for social networks, packaging designs and many more.

Finally, with a well-achieved message, it is imperative to communicate with the appropriate reach and frequency. The incessant repetition of the same message is a crucial requirement of the Master Campaign method that we have systematized. We recommend updating it quarterly by evaluating its most and least successful elements but always following the same fundamental idea strategically marked by the defined guiding positioning.

6.5.4.2 Branding

Within the value structuring process, the brand plays a very relevant role.

For the client, it is a potential symbol of trust, tranquility, belonging, certainty, satisfaction, and all kinds of possible fulfilled desires, among other connotations.

For the company, it can mean efficiency in communication, generation of loyalty, a contribution of perceived value, greater demand, higher margins, bargaining power with channels, competitive differentiation, a major financial asset, pride in work teams, and more.

The brand is the container of positive and negative thoughts. Over time, significations accumulate, and a *brand culture* is created with its own values, perceptions, and behaviors reinforced with stories from the company, influential profiles, customers, and even popular culture. For example, *Corona* is one of the most recognized Mexican brands worldwide and the protagonist of endless narratives. It started as a traditional product in canteens where people played dominoes on tables labeled with their logo. Later, an extensive campaign associated with Mexican pride made it known as the best-selling beer in the world. More recently, a new communication burst into the minds of international markets, successfully sublimating ideas of freedom, pleasure, and exotic experiences—characteristic of a paradisiacal vacation setting—that, for example, transport the imagination to the white beaches of the Caribbean with the communication elements that have made the brand characteristic, such as the transparent bottle and a piece of lemon on the spout.

If the strategy is correct, a brand has a generally longer life cycle than the products that provide it with long-term value. A product, whether due to technology, market changes, competition, or fashion, can decline rapidly, but if you have invested in the brand, it becomes the company's survival vehicle. Consider the case of *Apple*. The design and functionality of those early *Macintosh* systems that created a significant differentiation, representing the rise of the personal computer and inspiring pride in its users, were just the beginning of a grand story. At that time, their legendary bitten apple logo was introduced. As time passed, the *Macintosh* declined but then came the launch of the *iPod*, which led to the *iPhone*, *iPad*, and *Mac* computers that now represent a cult brand. Regarding the previous mention of popular culture, in this case, we can remember the scene in the movie *Forrest Gump* where the protagonist acquires shares of *Apple*. Actually, the *iPhone* is present in many series and films as an essential part of contemporary life.

In short, endless stories guided by strategic communications and the offer's qualities comprise a perception full of meta-values that make great brands a symbol of fulfilled desires and an extremely valuable intangible.

The brand-building process is essential for any company. Therefore, numerous books and resources address the topic. One of the most influential is David Aaker's *Building Strong Brands*, where he establishes five assets that integrate brand value, which we present and complement with important notes related to our biobehavioral model:

1) Brand recognition: depends on persevering exposure derived from a media plan with adequate reach, frequency, and investment.

2) Perceived quality: it is developed around the possibility of delivering what the market wants based on the material and ideological attributes of the brand, products, and services. The perceived quality and value are directly proportional to the spiritual, instinctive, emotional, sentient, and creative desires they manage to satisfy consciously and unconsciously.

3) Brand associations: this element is about the correlation with individual experiences and, therefore, with their respective positive or negative connotations. In long-term episodic memory, happenings that have caused some impact are recorded in the mind, either because they are repetitive or emotionally intense; those related to the brand will add or subtract from its perceived value. For example, when you have a positive first impression using a product or service, it will permeate your memory and provide desirability. On the other hand, negatively transcendent examples have been when benzene was found in the water in *Perrier* bottles, when *Tylenol* was attacked by a psychopath who poisoned pills, and when *Firestone* fought with *Ford* to disclaim responsibility for blowout tires.

4) Loyalty: represents a key asset for profitability that depends on forging emotionally positive relationships with potential customers. In his book *The Loyalty Effect*, Frederick Reichheld researched such impact. He found that in various categories, the increase in profitability (referenced with the net present value), with respect to loyalty, ranges between 35% and 95% (see *Figure 25*).

According to Reichheld, the following five indicators explain why loyalty can double margins.[34]

---

34 Reichheld, 2001.

a. Optimizing the cost of acquiring new customers.

b. The curve of the customer's experience leading them to feel "at home" and to know better how a company works—building trust.

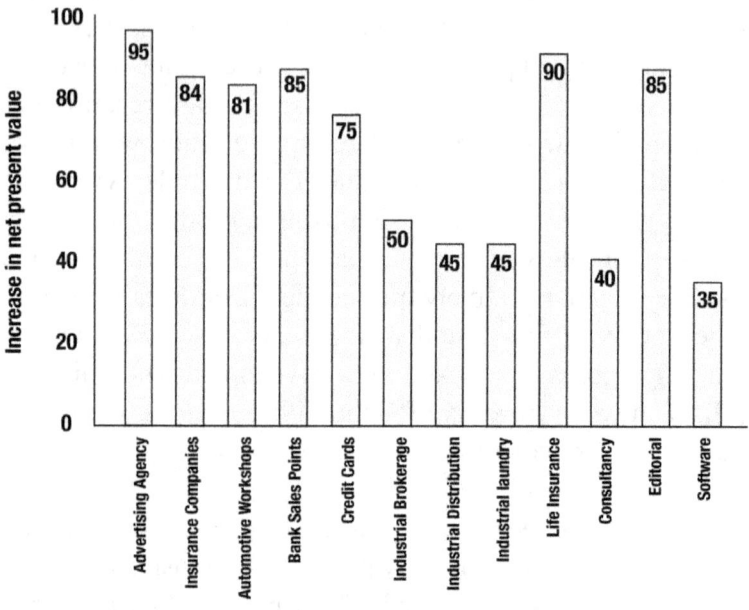

Figure 25: Why loyal customers are more profitable according to data documented by Reichheld (2001).

c. The company's experience curve, learning customer buying processes—intelligence input.

d. The good referrals the client generates, allowing the company to obtain new clients—recommendations.

e. The overprice due to the difficulty of switching and allowing the customer to find an equally reliable supplier—substitution barriers.

5) Brand property assets: refers to the unique elements the company owns that distinguish the brand. They can be tangible (such as patents or registered designs) or intangible (such as reputation and corporate culture).

On the other hand, the brand itself has a financial value that constitutes a crucial asset; it is categorized as an intangible asset, and calculating its monetization requires a complex estimate of future flows based on competitive power.

Three generally accepted methodologies for financially appreciating a brand are Interbrand, BrandZ, and Brand Finance. All of them use multivariable models focused on the net present value of sales projections, considering the brand's impact in the future. To accomplish the latter, they are supported by typically subjective evaluations carried out by experts.

The *Interbrand* model stands out for trying to quantify the influence of the brand on the purchase decision. This is calculated based on the historical roles of other companies in the category that are generally publicly traded. Also, it considers loyalty concerning competitors, measuring it based on the size of the customer base and the desertion rate.

Furthermore, *BrandZ* develops its valuation based on stock futures prices and ongoing quantitative research spanning over 37 million interviews on more than 165,000 brands in more than 50 markets.

Finally, the Brand Finance methodology focuses on what a company would be willing to pay to acquire the commercial rights of a brand. This estimate integrates the relationship with the consumer, market share, and profitability of a real or hypothetical franchise.

As can be seen, the three valuation systems implement 1) qualitative considerations that are quantified with mainly subjective indices and 2) quantitative ones that have to do with future flows. In all three methodologies, it is difficult to determine precisely the relevant qualitative parameters such as emotional connection with customers, the emergence of new brands, the possible decline of products, and strategic updates. To contemplate more accurate valuation scenarios, it is helpful to establish probabilistic models establishing low, medium, and high ranges.

Ultimately, a tangible or intangible value comes from perceptual phenomena that can be identified based on the study and documentation of behavior. Possibly, in the future, the implementation of neurophysiological monitoring instruments can give us significant psychological guidelines regarding the attribution of value.

To complement this exposition, *Figure 26* shows the results of the three methods on the brands they considered to have the highest value in 2022.

	Interbrand	BrandZ	Brand Finance
	Value (*USD Billions)	**Value** (*USD Billions)	**Value** (*USD Billions)
1	Apple $482,215	Apple $947,062	Apple $355,080
2	Microsoft $278,288	Microsoft $819,573	Microsoft $350,273
3	Amazon $274,819	Amazon $705,646	Google $263,425
4	Google $251,751	Microsoft $611,460	Microsoft $184,245
5	Samsung $87,689	Tencent $214,023	Walmart $11,918
6	Toyota $59,757	McDonald's $196,526	Samsung $107,284
7	Coca-Cola $57,535	Visa $191,032	Facebook $101,201
8	Mercedes-Benz $56,103	Facebook $186,421	ICBC $75,119
9	Disney $50,325	Alibaba $169,966	Huawei $71,233
10	Nike $50,289	Louis Vuitton $124,273	Verizon $69,639

Figure 26: The ten most valuable brands in 2022 according to Interbrand, BrandZ, and Brand Finance. [35] [36] [37]

---

35 Interbrand, 2023.
36 Kantar, 2023.
37 Brandirectory, 2023.

In this chapter, we have presented the great relevance of the brand and how it adds value; without a doubt, it is a central and indispensable element for strategic intelligence.

6.5.4.3 Media Plan

The *Media Plan* and creativity are the key pieces for effective value communication. Scope and frequency have already been mentioned as conditions for effectiveness; now, we are going to delve into the choice of media to adequately deliver the messages to the target audience.

The first step is to define "who we are talking to" since, regardless of defining the segment or segments, we must consider the *purchase decision units* and their interrelationship. For example, in acquiring a family car, we could find two purchasing decision units: the person who will use it and the person who pays for it. Therefore, the communication channels and messages must be adapted to the recipients' most significant media and desires. We show a hypothetical case below:

1) PERSON WHO PAYS

Instinctive Desire:
- Control and Organización

Main used media:
- T.V. channels. sports
- National newscasts

2) PERSON WHO USES IT

Instinctive Desire:
- Desire for Protection and Family

Main used media:
- Specialized magazines
- Podcasts on parenting

If we also differentiate media depending on the moment in the purchase path based on the classic communication model known as AIDA[38], a structure like the exercise shown in *Figure 27* results.

AIDA / UDC	PERSON WHO USES IT	PERSON WHO PAYS
Attention	Specialized Magazine	Facebook
Interest	Influencers on Social Networks	Google
Decision	Paid Article	Direct Mail or Email
Action	Test Drive and Dealership	Personal Sales Promotion

Figure 27: Definition of possible means based on the stages of the AIDA model and the means of consumption of the different purchase decision units when acquiring a family car.

As an additional note, spiritual, instinctive, and emotional triggers are especially relevant in the *attention* and *interest* stages, and rational triggers are an important complement to *decision* and *action*.

---

38 Kotler, 2016.

On the other hand, regarding the message to be defined in each media, it is helpful to differentiate based on the following categorization proposal:

Intermission communication: it is one in which companies pay media providers to transmit their messages. The main attraction of the content for the viewer is the transmission that is "interrupted," as it happens with the billions of commercials on television and social networks.

Charm communication: it is about generating interest with the same content as the advertising communication. At times, its commercial nature can be evident, but at other times discreet and aimed at the preconscious. Among several executions of this type are the production of videos (as *BMW Films* did when creating short films), images, books, or articles with engaging and exciting content, or the publication of web pages with rankings of products and services (positioning the brand in first places). Also, it is the case of *product placement* within the plot of television programs, which can have a significant impact on sales, just as *Corona* beer did by placing its logo on the shirts of the fictional team in the popular Mexican production *Club de Cuervos*; or, as brands like *Oreo*, *Nike*, *7UP* and many more did in the world-renowned *Friends* series.

Intermission and charm communication are not mutually exclusive, they can be used in synch, and both rely on creative differentiation and emotional impact to excel and generate results. An advertising guideline will always gain power with an attractive narrative and artistic production with hired repetitions. Nevertheless, it is essential to differentiate the intention since, with the massification of social networks, the role of the *content creator* is often confused with that of the *advertiser*. These are completely different roles: an advertisement depends on the incessant repetition of the same message, while "organic content" depends on its own attractive force. They can even represent very different business models; typically, a content creator monetizes with the payments made by the media and an advertiser with sales of their product or service.

In another sense, the digital era has also offered differentiation between *own* and *paid media*. Currently, a small or large company can easily have communication channels under its control, such as a WEB page or social media accounts.

Now, let's review the grouping of forms of communication by type of media or activity.

The *4 P's of Communication* (not to be confused with the traditional *4 P's of Marketing*) described in *Figure 28* are practical for ordering and defining strategic channels. Let us briefly consider some of its headings below.

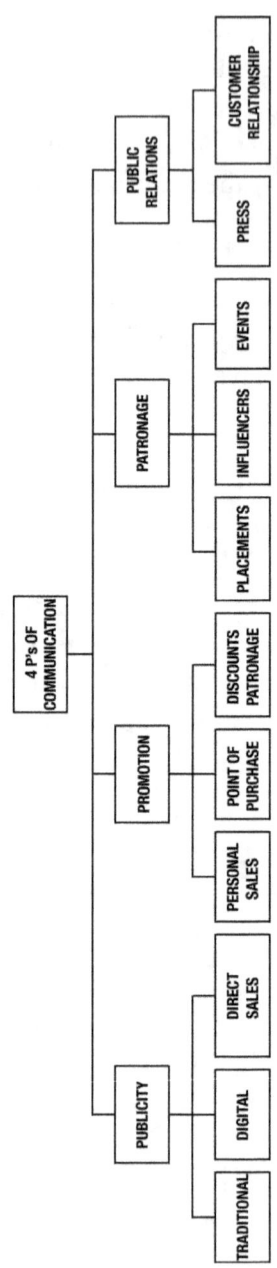

Figure 28: Media by communication activity.

Publicity can be classified as intermission communication, involving the paid placement of non-personalized messages intended to inform and persuade about a product or service. We find advertising in traditional media (open and paid television, radio, newspapers, magazines, etc.) and digital media such as social networks or search engines.

Regarding *personalized direct promotion*, we find traditional postal mail as well as registered and automated emails with the help of a CRM (Customer Relationship Manager). It should be noted that the latter is one of the most effective tools to connect with the target audience more significantly while creating short and long-term relationships.

Personal sales can be very profitable in digital models through e-commerce platforms and traditional models with catalog sales (e.g., Mary Kay). The arrival of big data has favored direct sales since it allows customizing promotions based on individual digital interactions.

The *point of sale* used as a means of communication is enormously influential since it is located at the final moment of the purchase decision. There are several formats for sharing messages on this channel, including signage, banners, displays, vendor activations, and more. In this space, connecting directly with the intuitive impulse and incorporating a rational push through special promotions can be very profitable.

Patronage is relevant in many Marketing tactics, even with a low budget or B2B sales. You can sponsor not only sports teams or special events but also celebrities, universities, social causes, conferences, and much more. A subtle form of sponsorship is *product placement* (placement), which we discussed previously. Yet another is through the so-called *influencers* or *content creators*, which currently represent a medium *per se* with a significant reach; it is an interesting medium if it is validated that its range of impact occurs in our segment and is used as a source of testimonials.

Finally, *public relations* continues to be a recurring medium for all types of companies. The key is disseminating information with news or journalistic value so different media publish it to engage users. For this, press conferences are usually called, or bulletins are sent.

We conclude this section with a list of media to consider when preparing a Media Plan (see Figure 29).

Marketing and Advertising:	Print Media:	Retail Experience:	Public Relations:	Other:	Social Media Platforms:
• Editorial Content • Product Placement • Cinema • Contests • Sponsorships • Digital Promotional Content • Digital Display Advertising • Email • Digital Games • Influencers • Digital Videos • Marketplace Ads • Programmatic Videos • SEM • SEO • Content in Social Networks	• Magazine • Newspaper • Personalized Publication	• Electronic Commerce Platform • Point of Sale	• Press • Events • Opinion Leaders • Sponsorships	• Radio • Direct Mail • Sales Promotion • Coupons • Sampling/Testing • Website • Apps • Street Marketing • Loyalty Programs • Fairs • OOH-Billboards • OOH-Other Outdoor • OOH-Transportation • Packaging and Product Design • Television • Content user generated and reviews	• Blogs • Discord • Facebook • Flickr • Instagram • LinkedIn • Pandora • Pinterest • Reddit • Snapchat • Spotify • TikTok • Twitter • WeChat • WhatsApp • YouTube

Figure 29: List of relevant media to consider.

263

6.5.4.4 Sales

The role of sales in a business model and its contribution to structuring value is decisive. It often marks the central differentiation, especially in the face of competition that relies mainly on pull schemes.

For example, in the cosmetics industry, 32% of sales[39] are made directly through representatives who work on their own, sometimes as part of a pyramid scheme and sometimes individually. In such a competitive and mature category, it is possible to stand out for the advice, relationship, and trust the representatives provide in a context surrounded by participants who invest heavily in branding and communication.

It is typically thought that an efficient sales effort should be fundamentally rational; however, the opposite is true. Like the communication at the point of sale, the intuitive stimulus represents the maximum influence towards the purchase. Let us remember instincts and emotions represent *Plan A* in nature; they are designed to deliberate quickly (consuming little energy) based on information gathered during the evolutionary map. On the other hand, reason is the systematized *Plan B* to operate only in special cases where following the intuitive commands represents an obvious danger. Consequently, to sell, we must speak the intuitive language to engage with ideas and stimuli suggesting the possibility of fulfilled biological desires to finish with logical arguments as a conclusive complement. That is precisely what a good salesperson does whether or not they are aware of it.

The same applies to business-to-business sales; a consultative selling effort charged with realized desires for control and a present feeling of trust is a highly profitable mix. In this

---

39 Euromonitor International, 2022.

industry, the sales process and proper follow-up are crucial to the strategic value proposition. Of course, the rational elements must be part of an impeccable consulting service, but connecting with buyers or decision-makers will be highly difficult without the above.

Selling successfully requires many skills, but the ability to empathize, the way of communicating, and the deep knowledge of the product and market stand out. The representative is a fundamental communication channel in any business model.

In cases of *pull* commercialization tactics where the product use is widely known by the customer and the sale is essentially supported by the brand, logistics, and distribution—as is the case with most consumer products—the role of the seller apparently is not so important; nevertheless, in reality, it also plays a primary role. For example, a *Coca-Cola* vendor seems to only take the order; however, formality, good treatment, and proper conduct in the service are essential to ensure the necessary volume and consistency.

Given the wide variety of tactics between the extremes that *push* and *pull* modes represent, it is advantageous to define the profile and competencies of the sales force. For this, we can consider the following classification (Hunter, 2014):

Hunters: salespeople who take the initiative and actively seek new business opportunities.

Farmers: sellers who develop long-term relationships with existing customers by building solid foundations to ensure a steady income stream.

Both profiles are elemental; the ideal is to find a mixture with an adequate balance of functions between them.

Figure 30 shows a descriptive chart with practical notes on the role of sales depending on each business model's *push* or *pull* trends.

NOTES ON THE ROLE OF SALES REGARDING PUSH OR PULL COMMERCIALIZATION TACTICS	
PULL TACTIC	**PUSH TACTIC**
The sales process is easy to learn and execute.	The sales process is complex to learn and execute.
The sales force is not as relevant to make a sale, which depends mainly on the brand's value, advertising, and contracts in other company areas.	The sales force is of great relevance to making a sale, which depends mainly on the sellers' ability, effort, and motivation.
Farmers: Their activities include services, storage, and maintaining customers.	*Hunter:* His activities include prospecting and developing new clients.
The seller represents some value to the customer.	The seller represents a high value to the customer.
Local vendors or by area.	
Small or straightforward purchases.	Robust and relevant purchases.
Monopolized Selling: it is expensive for the customer to change, or the product is highly differentiated.	*Competitive Selling:* it is not expensive to change, and the product is little differentiated.

Figure 30: Notes on the role of sales concerning push or pull marketing tactics.

6.5.5 Value Maintenance

Maintaining the perceived value is fundamental to generating loyalty, which has a significant financial impact, as we explained in Chapter 6.5.4.2.

The customers' preference over time may vary proportionally to the relationship they have or not with the offer. Understood as a *relationship* to the reiteration of emotional experiences and sublimated meanings occurring in the face of the interaction between customers and the brand, products, or services. Like any relationship, it must be sought and nurtured with frequent contact.

The benefits an active client represents for the company gradually increase over time due to the possibility of cross-selling and the origin of functional and emotional attachments that make it difficult to change towards the competition; it even leads to a consumer willing to pay more. However, retaining clients is a demanding task and requires attentive management that, among other things, ensures the following basic premises:

a. Maintain the quality of the product or service without negative variations over time.

b. Establish permanent communication campaigns aimed at customers.

c. Encourage innovations that constantly captivate interest.

d. Continuously improve the comprehensive experience offered.

Similarly, concerning maintaining value, it must be considered that the context has changed from a seller's market to a buyer's market. That is, in general, the supply is greater than the demand, and therefore, buyers have greater bargaining power. The latter has led to a customer-voter-focused political-economic environment known as *liberal humanism*. As a relevant note, it should be noted that with the emergence of new technologies, such as artificial intelligence, a new major economic paradigm shift is in sight in the near future.

Consequently, it is crucial to take into account external, cultural, and behavioral trends that directly impact customer acquisition and retention; among the most current are:

1. Higher levels of poverty and polarization of wealth.

2. Consumers are better informed and interact mainly through the Internet.

3. Much greater weight of the recommendation and referencing.

4. Search for more intense experiences.

5. Very impatient consumers.

6. The mobile phone has become an extension of the mind.

7. The daily use of artificial intelligence.

8. The client's actions are permanently monitored and recorded.

9. Cultures merge, ratifying the global village, but there is a robust opposite reaction of nationalism and regionalism.

10. Advertising stereotypes have changed, and false perfection is regularly rejected.

11. There is greater awareness of caring for the Planet, animals, and food.

12. Social causes acquire greater relevance.

13. Women have a new leading position in the professional and social strata.

14. Migration is intensifying, impacting security and economic issues.

15. The COVID-19 pandemic marked permanent changes, accelerating the use of technology and working at home.

16. Real income levels have fallen, prompting more caution in spending.

17. Average life expectancy has increased significantly, creating new markets and labor forces.

18. Online education has allowed everyone worldwide access to the best universities, and the virtual classroom has become highly relevant.

19. The metaverse has created an alternate virtual world with new goods, services, and businesses that encourage exchange through cryptocurrencies based on blockchain technology.

20. The possibility of colonizing the Moon and Mars is getting closer.

These 20 phenomena have in common an exponentially accelerated dynamism. 5 years ago, many of them were referred to in a predictive way, but today they are a reality. In addition, we can expect the changes to continue to occur with increasing speed in the coming years. Therefore, to keep customers or generate demand in new markets, we need to consider the transformation of behavior, culture, competition, channels, companies, and much more.

All of the above reinforces a maxim we have stated from the beginning of this book: for a strategy to work, it must be based on constant research and analysis of the biological factors maintained in the face of an increasingly uncertain and unstable environment. The security to ally ourselves with the probabilities in the future is found in the deep natural conditionings of the human being.

6.5.5.1 Demand Generation

Key moments for demand generation

For a customer to remain interested, the company must not only maintain value but increase it through innovation, service, technology, and more. This is a crucial element for financial survival.

However, losing customers for various reasons is natural and must be compensated with a permanent effort to generate demand—the main function of the Marketing area. The growth in the number of people interested in our offer is the most significant indicator of a successful marketing strategy.

Although it is an ongoing task, there are times when stimulating demand becomes critical (see *Figure 31*), the most notorious being when starting a business or introducing a new product or service. *The product life cycle*[40], mentioned in chapter 6.1.3, points us to key moments to strengthen demand generation: at launch, in the maturity stage prior to the decline, and when growth heads to zero.

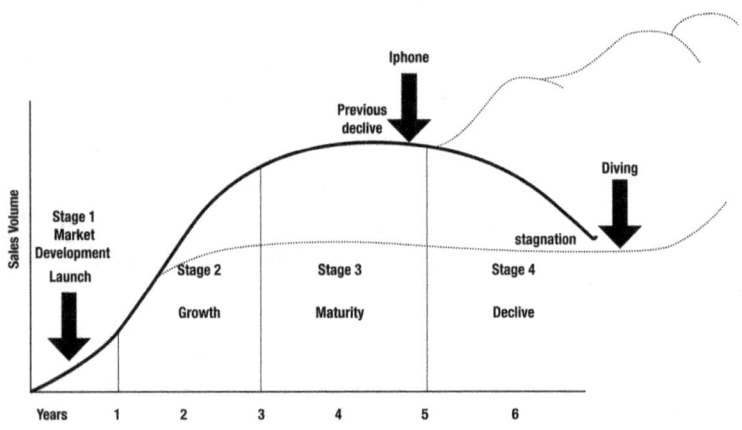

Figure 31: Critical moments for demand generation.[41] (Youngme Moon (2005) adapted by Carlos Chávez (2023).

For example, recreational diving has been parked for over 10 years with 15 million practitioners worldwide. Being an activity that promises freedom, discovery, and pleasure in dreamy places, it would be feasible to significantly increase the size of the category. The barriers to entry, such as some certifications necessary to practice it, are a primary cause of stagnation, which could be reversed with positioning campaigns that appeal to easy accessibility and emotional benefits.

---

40 Vernon, 1966.
41 Moon, 2005.

Another critical moment is before the decline. Innovation is vital to avoid a fall. *Apple* has skilfully achieved this with its *iPhone*: updates are planned well in advance, and its releases allow for constant renewal in the product's life cycle curve. This tactic is known as *planned obsolescence.*

Likewise, a situation requiring consideration and a push in the formation of demand is the generational dynamics. In other words, considering that customers grow old, change their preferences, and even die, conquering new young audiences (even when they are not old enough to decide to buy) is important. An obvious example is sports teams. The *Real Madrid Football School*[42] has nearly 30 academies in 15 cities in Latin America, Europe, Asia, and the Middle East. These centers offer training programs to children between the ages of 3 and 18 of all levels and represent a very effective way of generating future demand. These children are and will surely be *Real Madrid* customers buying shirts, going to the stadiums, and consuming match broadcasts.

Adoption rate when generating demand

In a product launch or effort to generate increased demand, it is practical to consider the *Gaussian Bell*, a symmetric distribution describing the clustering of data around a central value; typically, it coincides with the *rate of adoption of the innovation* and the *life cycle of the product* (See *Figure 32).*

---

42 Real Madrid, 2023.

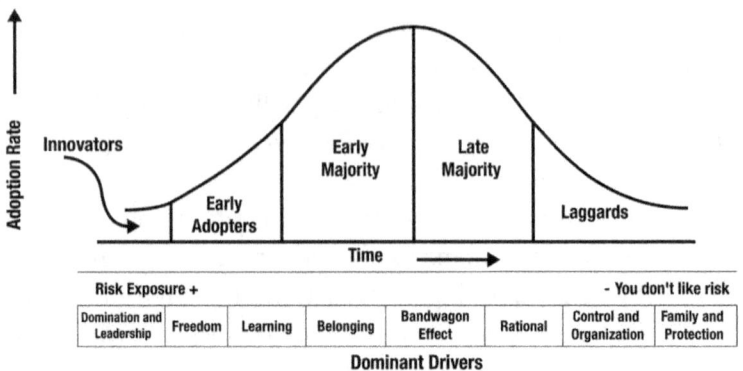

Figure 32: Innovation adoption curve (Rogers, 1995)[43] ccomplemented by instinctive triggers.

This allows us to identify different psychographic groups classified by their inclination to risk (Rogers, 1995) and the primary instinctual triggers at play. The first group, *innovators* (those who buy into a new offering before anyone else), are more likely to take risks to occupy a position of dominance and satisfy their desire for discovery. The following two groups, *early adopters* and *early majority* await the response and learning outcomes of the *innovators*; they are influenced by the desire to belong and the *bandwagon effect*. Finally, the *late majority* and *laggards* prioritize rational analysis (based on the experience of other groups) and risk mitigation, driven by a desire to control. As an additional note, there is typically a direct relationship between the client's age and the proposed categorization: the younger they are, the more they will be inclined to take risks.

What is relevant about the above is that our communication tactics adapt to the motivators of each segment in the different stages to achieve a consistent demand from the launch.

43 Rogers, 1995, p. 262.

Adoption rate when generating demand with technological innovations

Particularly on technological innovations, Geoffrey Moore offers an interesting update on the adoption curve in his book *Crossing the Chasm*. In short, he argues that two *gaps* and a *chasm* between the psychographic segments must be overcome to achieve mass acceptance. (See *Figure 33)*.

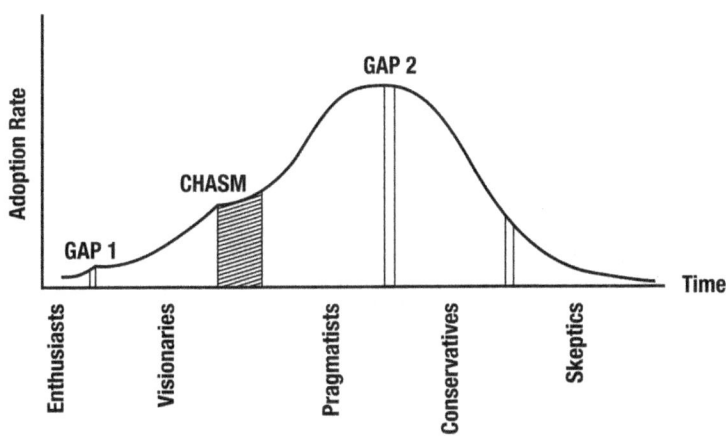

Figure 33: New technology adoption cycle and psychographic groups of adopters.[44]

Moore classifies adopter psychographic groups as:

1. Enthusiasts
- Aggressively pursue new technologies, even before their formal commercial release.
- Technology is a central interest in their life.

---

44 Moore, 1991.

- The pleasure of exploring new options is one of their primary motivators.
- Their approval inspires confidence in other groups.

2. Visionaries
- They acquire new proposals very early, even if they are not technologists.
- It is easy for them to imagine, understand and appreciate the benefits of new technologies.
- They trust their intuition more than references for their purchasing decisions.
- They are a key piece for the acceptance of other groups.

3. Pragmatists
- They show some ability to relate to technology, but practicality is most important to them.
- They know that many innovations are fleeting, so they wait for others to try them before they do.
- They look for well-established references before investing.
- They usually represent almost a third of the market, so doing business with them is important to obtain good business returns.

4. Conservatives
- They are not comfortable with their ability to handle new technologies.
- They wait until something becomes an established standard to adopt it, and even then, they seek a lot of support by buying only from big companies.

5. Skeptics
- They do not want to know or have anything to do with new technologies, which they justify with various reasons— usually reflecting a strong resistance to change.

- They only acquire technological innovations when they are hidden in another product they already use (*e.g.*, automobile accessories).

According to Moore, the *first gap* is between the *enthusiasts* and the *visionaries* since the latter are unwilling to change their usual practices and/or prefer to wait for the technology to improve. This is mainly due to the frequency, complexity, and rapidity of technological changes not allowing for a clear vision. Referrals are essential to cross this threshold.

The *chasm* arises because the product is presented in the same way to the different groups, and their value expectation is very different: the utility of the innovation is not given or clearly communicated. Visionaries are change agents willing to deal with inherent problems. On the other hand, *pragmatists* buy productivity and improvement in their processes; they want evolution, not revolution. For example, cryptocurrencies have been very well accepted by *visionaries* thanks to their innovative ideological and technological framework, but *pragmatists* only acquire them when they see an express economic benefit.

The *second gap* opens when conservatives have difficulty adopting the new technology; ease of use is imperative to mitigate this barrier.

The *OpenAI* development known as *ChatGPT* is a good example of bridging the gaps and chasm to generate demand. *Enthusiasts* see in it a new technology, *visionaries* a tool representing a milestone in humanity, pragmatists an extremely useful ally, conservatives a digital agency they can easily use, and skeptics already use it, without realizing it, in various traditional applications.

In conclusion, to maintain value through demand generation, the strategic development of the offer (brand, product, or service) must consider multi-segment communication, recognizing the different biological desires of each group. The foregoing is required to ally ourselves with the product's life cycles, markets, and in general, face the incessant change.

6.5.5.2 Loyalty

Loyalty is decisive for the maintenance of value and profitability. Revenues increase if customers retain interest due to repurchase, reduced customer acquisition costs, cross-selling, referrals, and willingness to pay a little more for mutual trust.

Reward programs structured with automated information processing and retention systems (CRMs) are traditionally used tools to promote loyalty. However, these instruments do not necessarily generate loyalty by themselves; it is common to find that customers switch brands more frequently than ever.

Therefore, it is convenient to go back to basics and consider the causes of a loyal relationship.

To weave human interaction networks allowing the species to collaborate and gain survival advantages, nature has endowed us with innate behavioral responses such as a *reciprocal conditioning*. In short, we are programmed to give and are motivated to give back. How? Through a compelling sentient reward known as gratitude.

Based on the *Geometry of Feelings* (J.C. Chávez, 2022), *gratitude* is a positive feeling occurring in the face of the well-being of what brings us joys. Therefore, to procure this emotional experience toward us, we must first give.

From biology, the above explains, in part, why it is important to generate value (give) before selling and the relevance of exceeding expectations when buying (give more than expected). Provoking gratitude is a highly profitable tactic because it implies people will be willing to give back: a harmonious win-win.

Consequently, loyalty tactics should focus on fulfilling the customer's desires without demanding something in return and, of course, avoiding the reverse scenario. For example, a bank user who has been paying his credit card on time for more than 10 years will feel especially offended if punished and harassed for a sporadic delay, which will cause the opposite effect of gratitude, and he will probably look for another service provider option.

On the other hand, one way to generate sustained gratitude is to define and foster a shared purpose, something you do not do *for* clients but *with* them. For this, connecting with *spiritual motivators* through a cause bringing a greater good is a forceful exercise. For example, the *Under Armor* sporting goods brand has defined itself as a company that helps athletes achieve their objectives; this customer orientation generates sympathy that ultimately becomes loyalty.

In summary, the strategic tactics established to generate loyalty must transcend the transactional level and connect with the emotional strata. It will help to understand such efforts as gratitude programs (rather than loyalty) to gain clarity on the central objective that will trigger results.

6.5.6 Value Extraction

The role of *pricing* is to harness the value created, generating income primarily to finance current value structuring activities, support research for future value creation, and generate economic benefit for shareholders.

Therefore, we refer to defining the price of a product or service as *value extraction*. For such a task, it is decisive to examine two variables: 1) perceived market value and 2) cost to the organization.

Perceived market value equals the monetized cost of the next best alternative plus (or minus) its differential. Saying it differently, it is the price the customer is willing to pay based on the current price of other options and the comparison of their perceived advantages or disadvantages (channeled fundamentally with the bidder's communication efforts).

As explained in Chapter 3.1.3, it is pertinent to remember monetization attends to quantifying the fulfilled *instinctive desire for power*—the potency to satisfy desires defined with numerical indices. Such quantity is formed in the client's mind according to the accessibility or availability of the product or service in the market and the desires (emotionally manifested) it satisfies.

On the other hand, considering the *cost to the organization* is crucial to establishing adequate profit margins. This factor represents what the company pays to deliver the final product or service. When the price is set below or above cost, there are losses or gains, respectively. It is rarely offered below such limit; however, it occurs with market entry strategies, to harm the competition, or when a product or service is used as a "hook" to promote another. Also, it is possible to aggressively compromise profit margin with promotional tactics designed to increase sales volume, which, taken together, can offset and exceed returns. For example, a 2 X 1 will be convenient if it is possible to sell more than twice the amount derived from it, although care must be taken not to generate a self-destructive dependency with this type of tactics.

Once the above variables have been analyzed, the company can generate a *pricing* solution.

Next, we will examine a method to quantitatively represent the perception of value and identify some variables that influence it.

6.5.6.1 Pricing

Pricing is the last link in the value structure because it closes the purchase cycle.

Traditionally, the price is set considering the product, cost, margin, and competition, as shown in *Figure 34*.

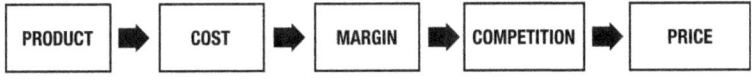

Figure 34: Variables traditionally used to define the price.

As can be seen, the client is not considered at any stage of such process; it follows an in-business approach and is inaccurate. Randomly it can work; however, the chances of success are low because it does not consider the buyer's perceived market value at each stage. In these cases, it is very possible that the development of the product or service has not evaluated the motivators of the user either. It is common to determine cost and margin mainly based on the financial structure of the company and its profitability objectives, but it is usually poorly pragmatic and remains at the level of expectations. Correctly reading the market implies understanding what the client wants, not the company.

On the other hand, cogitating the competition's prices is always necessary, but their cost structures should not be ignored (which generally gives a particular advantage to one of the players in the category). For example, *Jumex*—the Mexican brand that produces juices and nectars—is vertically integrated: it harvests the fruit on its own plantations, while many of its competitors have to acquire the raw material from third parties; this gives them advantages in costs and quality control.

Pondering all of the above, the process we propose—in contrast—to determine prices is focused on customer perception, as shown in *Figure 35*.

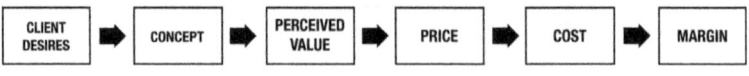

Figure 35: Variables to define price considering the customer's perception of value.

If we start from the *bio-equalization* process and a value proposition has been developed that includes a platform aimed at satisfying what the customer longs for, the recognized value will be competitive. That is, the *perceived market value* by the consumer must be greater than the cost plus the margin to be profitable, and the key is to model the perception through sublimated desires.

The challenge in this process is monetizing the perceived value; for this purpose, we define the method shown in *Figure 36*.

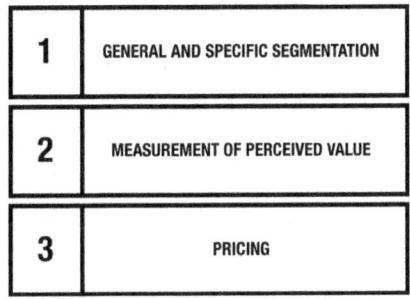

Figure 36: Method to quantify the perceived value.

1. ***General and specific segmentation*** refers to classifying based on sociodemographic and psychographic variables, but also by *consumption occasion* and *purchasing behavior*, as discussed in previous chapters.

2. The ***measurement of perceived value*** can be done through special studies. The simplest is to present the concept or use and ask: how much would you be willing to pay for this product or service? With a sufficiently representative sample of the target audience, an accurate average marks a specific amount. A purchase probability curve can even be illustrated by organizing the responses into blocks from highest to lowest value with their respective percentages, as seen in *Figure 33*, where it is identified that 40% of the market would be willing to pay $7 for the product or service. In this example, if the company wanted to reach 60% of the market, it would have to set its price at $4 and, for 85%, at $3. The drop in the curve from 85% is because there is a price level at which people distrust the quality of the product; in this case, if the price falls below $3, there is a risk of harming the purchase probability. In the sample exercise, it is detected that the profitable scope is between $4 and $7; then, from that range, it can be decided on tactics oriented towards 1) *high margin*, which implies a narrow segmentation with communications connoting quality, or 2) *high volume*, which requires thoughtful care in costs, mass communication, and high-reach channels.

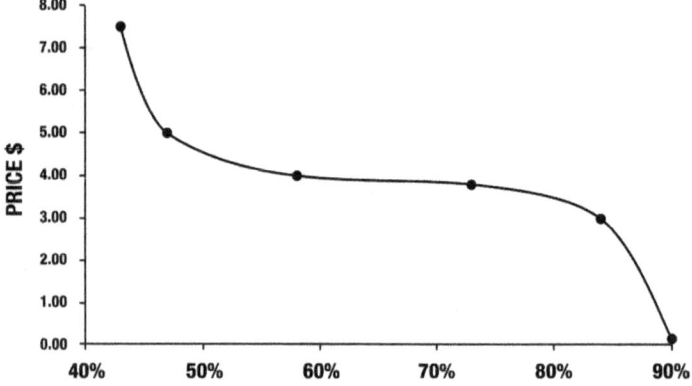

Figure 37: Example of a purchase probability curve.

3. **Pricing** can be assigned by identifying a value coefficient, as shown in *Figure 38*.

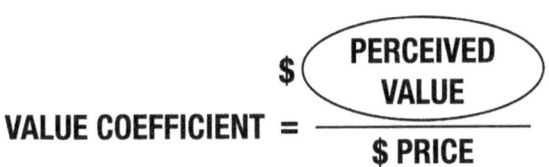

Figure 38: Equation to determine the value coefficient for pricing.

If with the established price, the value coefficient is greater than 1, the customer will be satisfied and will think they have paid less than what the product or service is worth; if it is equal to one, that the price is fair; and less than one, they will not buy or will be dissatisfied.

The suggested courses of action for each scenario, regardless of the possibility of lowering the price, are shown in *Figure 39*.

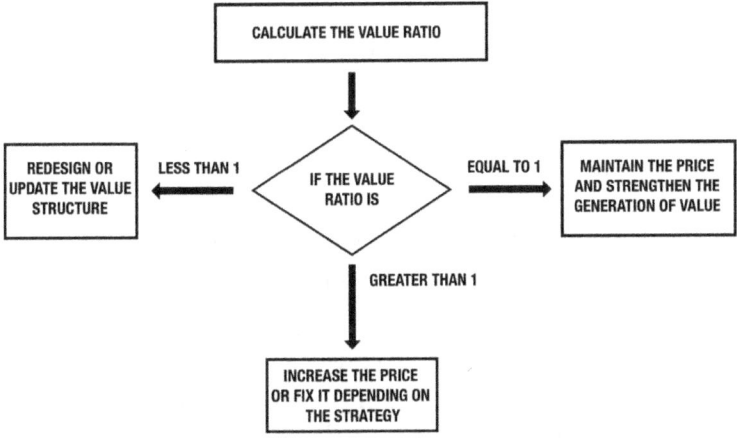

Figure 39: Course of action against different scenarios regarding the coefficient of value.

To conclude this chapter, we list some specifically relevant factors that influence and represent biases in the perceived market value:

a. *Appreciative Reference Bias*

A positive or negative value (expensive or cheap) is always established based on a reference point. In the case of price, a reference related to the direct competition will typically be anchored; however, in the case of new products and services or with weak competitors, it will be compared with indirect elements. For example, juices against soft drinks, or less evident, cinema against amusement parks.

b. *Appreciative Comparison Bias*

When establishing a price comparison is complex, different referents are anchored. For example, for a credit card, the price would be defined by the interest rate, commission payments, annuity, cost for cash withdrawal, reward points, and more; with these characteristics, it will be challenging to establish an abstract value and the decision making will focus on other commercial variables such as communication or ease of acquisition.

c. *Appreciative Cost-of-Change bias*

We consider "our time" very valuable because it is our most important asset as conscious beings; therefore, it influences value quantification. When switching from one brand to another involves a significant investment of time, we will integrate it into the mix resulting in the perception of value. For example, changing from an *Apple* mobile phone to a *Sam-*

sung one (or vice versa) means a new learning curve of use that we will consider to define if the price is appropriate: we will perceive the change option as more "expensive" even if the price is the same. Obviously, the same effect will occur when the changing investment also involves money.

d. *Appreciative Bias in Income Relativity*

The monetary income of each person directly and mathematically influences the perception of value. In other words, spending $120 a month on telephone services could be considered "a lot" for someone who earns $2,000 monthly (representing 6% of their income) and "little" for someone who makes $14,000 (representing less than 1%).

e. *Appreciative Bias of Payment by Third Parties*

Price sensitivity decreases significantly when the user does not pay the bills. For example, this is the case with the so-called *representation expenses* of company executives and employees; indeed, the perception of the grade of the price (expensive or cheap) will be different when traveling paid by others than on your own.

f. *Appreciative Benefit Promise Bias*

When a customer strongly desires something he or she has sublimated into a specific idea and the brand promises to fulfill it, rational price analysis can take a backseat. This is the case when so-called *promise products* offer complex benefits with little effort (like losing weight, making money, and more).

g. *Appreciative Proportion Bias*

In a compound product or service, the price sensitivity of one of its parts will decrease considerably when it represents a small part in relation to the whole. For example, in an industrial assembly, the price of the screws will be less relevant than that of other parts involving a much higher investment.

h. *Appreciative Intuition Bias*

Sometimes intuition can sense a hefty price regardless of rational analysis. For example, the cost of some luxury shoes can be perceived as very high and even absurd for those observers who do not find a desire for domination fulfilled in such an object.

In conclusion, it is crucial to consider the wholly subjective and intersubjective character of the perceived value manifested in price. Ultimately, as we explained before, the price quantifies the opportunity to obtain positive feelings and avoid negative ones derived from biologically conditioned desires. Identifying what originates the perceived value in the psyche of the *Homo sapiens* and knowing how to read the market context with its various actors is essential to establish appropriate strategic pricing tactics.

6.6 Business Plan
Integration, Strategic Axes and Key Resources and Activities

With the pricing and determination of the margin, we have concluded the design of our business model, and we are ready for its execution.

We call *strategic axes* the areas requiring greater attention for implementation, resulting from an analysis of the company's capabilities and limitations. The business model requires skills that are sometimes unavailable or demand greater strength. To go beyond the traditional SWOT model, we propose to analyze blocks, such as those shown in *Figure 40*, which will allow us to qualify the competencies of some relevant company areas for strategic performance.

MARKET SHARE
LOYALTY AND SATISFACTION
COSTS AND MARGINS OPTIMIZATION
OPERATIONS AND MANAGEMENT
DISTRIBUTION
INNOVATION
DIGITAL TRANSFORMATION
ORGANIZATIONAL DEVELOPMENT
PRODUCTS AND SERVICES QUALITY CONTROL
COMMERCIAL INTELLIGENCE
COMMUNICATION AND BRANDING
SALES
RELATION WITH PROVIDERS
DIRECTIVE STRUCTURE
INVESTMENT CAPACITY
DIRECTIVE CONTROL
FINANTIAL STRENGTH

Figure 40: Example blocks for qualifying competencies by area and defining strategic axes.

Qualifying each block quantitatively will require defining punctual objectives or KPIs (Key Performance Indicators), which correspond to a specific execution and monitoring development per project that can be defined at different levels.

We can intuitively rate each block for a brief initial diagnosis based on its strength and alignment with the business model. Thus, the outstanding areas will be identified as requiring improvements or being of remarkable relevance to meet the goals, and they will become *strategic axes*.

For example, if a mobile application is needed in concept development and the company is inefficient in its *digital transformation processes*, the latter will become a *strategic axis* requiring particular monitoring. Or, if the business model considers a robust communication campaign and cannot be carried out with the current operating flow, the *investment capacity* will represent another axis to highlight.

In summary, the *business model* gives us an overview of the attractiveness of the market, and, on the other hand, the conditions of the company's capabilities (identified in this chapter) allow us to define the *strategic axes* to execute it. The latter is based on a structural guide by area, which must be complemented within the particular characteristics of each case.

Integrating the information and decisions generated by the new *business model* and the guide represented by the *strategic axes*, we are in a position to detail, assigning each responsible department the *key resources* and *activities*, which we suggest classifying as material, financial, human, and technological.

With this designation, it will be possible to estimate the necessary costs for the execution and establish the managerial approach of the model in the form of a ***business plan***, ordered thematically and functionally with the fundamental elements we propose below. (See *Figure 41)*

BUSINESS PLAN

1. Analysis of the environment
Economic, social, and political perspectives at the international, national, regional, and local levels.

2. Competitive situation
Positioning map of the players in the industry based on different variables (initially, we suggest using the price comparison and instinctive desires that each player satisfies).

3. Segmentation
Sociodemographic, psychographic, by consumption occasion, and by purchasing behavior characteristics of the group of people most likely to buy (if there is a record, these data are determined by the average of recent clients).

4. Bio-equalization
What does the potential client want, and how can I satisfy it? (Review chapter 2.0)

a. Purpose
What collective good does the project contribute, and how does it protect the vital prevalence?

b. Instinctive Motivators
What innate conditionings can 1 satisfy mainly based on my strengths? (We suggest using the guide to the 12 Instinctive Triggers presented in chapter 2.2)

c. Emotional-Sentient Motivators
What feeling do I seek to anchor each time the potential client interacts with the project's communications, products, and services? (See Chapter 2.3)

d. Rational Motivators
What logical argument is behind my competitive advantage?

---

5. Positioning
Based on the bio-equalization and representing a differentiator, how do I want to be known?

6. Value Structure
(See Chapter 6.5)
- Concept development
(See Chapter 6.5.1)
- Customer relationship
(See Chapter 6.5.2)
- Value Delivery
(See Chapter 6.5.3)
- Value Communication
(See Chapter 6.5.4)
- Maintenance of Value
(See Chapter 6.5.5)
- Extraction of Value
(See Chapter 6.5.6)

7. Functional plans
The specific definition of strategic axes and key resources and activities.
a. Commercial Plan
b. Operations Plan
c. Technology Plan
d. Development and Human Capital
e. Control Board and KPIs
f. Financial Plan
g. Budget and pro forma income statements
h. Determination of profitability

Figure 41: Guide for integrating a Business Plan based on the Strategic Bio-Intelligence model.

6.7 ROI

Profitability and other measures to evaluate the business model.

We are about to conclude a journey that we started from the universe's origins; we contemplated the biological, genetic, neurophysiological, and psychological foundations influencing behavior to apply them in an economic context through the strategy and generation of a business model. Now, let's examine how to evaluate its results.

The most objective financial measure of strategic success is profitability, both on investment and business implementations aimed at satisfying customer desires.

Calculating profitability is a well-known process for those who run businesses, so we will only cite a few ideas to optimize its calculation. This exercise will also help us mitigate future risks from uncertain change manifested in new technologies and variations in human behavior.

We will start with the profitability reflected in the income statement; properly, it is not about the return on investment (ROI) but the profit margin over income, as shown in the following equation:

PROFIT OVER REVENUE *= PROFITS / NET INCOME*

In this case, the profits refer to the last line of the income statement, where taxes, amortization, depreciation, and interest paid to third parties financing the business have already been subtracted. The advantage of calculating it this way is a relevant reserve is contemplated (through amortization and depreciation) for the continuity of the business.

On the other hand, when the profit is calculated before subtracting these last 4 concepts, known as *EBITDA* (earnings before interest, taxes, depreciation, and amortization), we are talking about the ***operating margin***. This measurement shows us how efficient the business operation is and highlights the performance derived from the business model by not considering variables that do not depend on it (such as taxes or interest rates that can present a significant variation depending on the country).

It is indisputable the presentation of the Income Statement and Balance Sheet to the board of directors is crucial; however, based on our approach in this book, indicators are also required to show how the customer evolves and the company's response to such dynamics.

For example, McDonald, Smith and Ward[45] (2013) designed an interesting exercise based on a real company, as shown below. Initially, they present an Income Statement that we can see in *Figure 42*.

Company A Based on sales Income Derived from 5 years						
Returns	Base year	1	2	3	4	5
Income per sale (£ Million)	254	293	318	387	431	454
Cost of sold goods	135	152	167	201	224	236
Gross contribution (£ Million)	119	141	151	186	207	218
General fabrication costs	48	58	63	82	90	95
Sales and marketing	18	23	24	26	27	28
Development and research	22	23	23	25	24	24
Net benefit (£ Million)	16	22	26	37	50	55
Sales returns (%)	6.3	7.5	8.2	9.6	11.6	12.1
Assets (£ Millones)	141	162	167	194	205	206
Assets (% in Sales)	56	55	53	50	48	45
Asset returns	11.3	13.5	15.6	19.1	24.4	26.7

Figure 42: Income Statement of "Company A" in the exercise of McDonald, Smith, and Ward.

45 McDonald et al., 2013.

In the so-called *Company A*, excellent results and good managerial management can be observed.

Subsequently, it is displayed in another table (see *Figure 43*) how Company B satisfies (or not) the wishes of the client and how it adjusts to maintain its value proposition.

Company B Based on 5-year Performance Market						
Performance	Base year	1	2	3	4	5
Base year / market growth (%)	18.3	23.4	17.6	34.4	24	17.9
Company b sales growth (%)	12.8	17.4	11.2	27.1	16.5	10.9
Market share (%)	20.3	19.1	18.4	17.1	16.3	14.9
Customer retention (%)	88.2	87.1	85	82.2	80.9	80
New customers (%)	11.7	12.9	14.9	24.1	22.5	29.2
Dissatisfied customers (%)	13.6	14.3	16.1	17.3	18.9	19.6
Relative product (%)	+10	+8	+5	+3	+1	0
Relative service (%)	+0	+0	-20	-3	-5	-8
Relatively new product (%)	+8	+8	+7	+5	+1	-4

Figure 43: Table with "Company B" indicators in the McDonald, Smith, and Ward exercise.

With this information, it is easy to conclude the performance of *Company A* has been much better than *Company B*, but the authors surprise us by stating it is the same institution. This demonstration concludes that measuring a business model with traditional financial statements is not enough and that it is essential to consider the customer by defining strategic customer satisfaction.

Regarding the ***return on investment*** (ROI), it is a parameter helping us forecast the future of our business model. Its calculation is very accessible as it is a well-established exercise. In simple terms, the formula looks like this:

*ROI = [(Net Investment Benefit - Investment Cost) / Investment Cost] * 100%*

For example, if you invest $1,000 in a business and earn $1,200, then your ROI would be:

*ROI = [($1,200 - $1,000) / $1,000] * 100% = 20%*

The return on investment with consolidated data is a very representative and accurate calculation; however, it is challenging to quantify performance in the coming months or years.

For this, it is convenient to consider the following recommendations derived from our professional experience:

1. The initial investment normally contemplates the purchase of assets and elements such as installation and start-up costs; however, resources for market research and strategic development (the fundamental pieces of any business) must also be integrated. Similarly, technological and human resources must be taken into account to create concepts beyond manufacturing products or implementing services—as we discussed in Chapter 6.5.2.

2. The sales projection for the coming years must estimate the life cycle of the product or service as a tool to know and understand the inflection points, replacing the traditional and misleading linear projection with a sigmoid curve that has proven its relevance in an endless number of analyzed products is a necessary exercise—as we reviewed in Chapter 6.1.3.

3. A curve projected from future flows must calculate probabilities using models of random event generation and derive contingency plans for pessimistic, medium, and optimistic scenarios—as explained in Chapter 6.1.3.

4. Technological innovation as an accelerator of the product or service life cycle has to be incorporated into the financial projection and innovation and development policy—as illustrated in Chapter 6.1.3 (*Kodak* case).

5. It must be taken into account that ROI is not an absolute criterion, especially in innovative projects where profitability could appear years after launch but with extraordinary results; postponing gratification for more significant long-term benefits can be a highly profitable exercise. For example, the latter is the case of several of Elon Musk's companies where, beyond financial analysis, intuition and scientific and human knowledge have proven to be extraordinary allies.

Undoubtedly, financial scrutiny is essential to test the effectiveness of the *business model generator* and provide the long-awaited financial retribution to shareholders, which supports the company's permanence, development, and creativity.

However, we insist on the thesis of this book that exposes the need to see beyond the obvious, in deep biological layers, to achieve both an economic equilibrium and a balanced state of individual and social well-being that protects the prevalence of life: the source of the most sublime gratifications and our central objective as living beings.

POST SCRIPTUM

Thus, we close a collection of systematized ideas with the advances of various disciplinary bases such as Ethology, Biophysics, Genetics, Neurophysiology, Psychology, Economics, Finance, and Marketing.

For what?

In the first instance, to provide the contemporary human being with forceful strategic tools and a privileged vision to ensure the development, permanence, and growth of a business model through profitability.

But, on a more profound and much more significant level, to promote intelligent decisions (away from self-destructive tendencies), critical thinking, vital information flow, creativity, conscious and empathetic leaders and markets, causal understanding of our biological behavioral conditionings and, above all, to defend the prevalence of Life in all its manifestations.

We sincerely hope this book plants a seed in every reading mind that leads to a bright and fertile future; achieving it is in the hands of each of us, from the individual to the collective.

REFERENCES AND BIBLIOGRAPHY

Ariely, D. (2008). *Predictably irrational: The hidden forces that shape our decisions*. HarperCollins.

Bandler, R., & Grinder, J. (2007). *La estructura de la magia, Vol. 1 y 2*. Cuatro Vientos.

Brandirectory. (2023). *Global 500 2023*. Retrieved May 8, 2023, from https://brandirectory.com/rankings/global/

Brynjolfsson, E., Hu, Y. J., & Rahman, M. S. (2013). *Competing in the age of omnichannel retailing*. MIT Sloan Management Review.

Budweiser. (2023). *The Clydesdales brotherhood*. Retrieved from https://www.youtube.com/watch?v=3qMhcpoXxHo

Campbell, J. (2008). *The hero with a thousand faces*. New World Library.

Carroll, S. (2019). *Something deeply hidden*. Penguin Random House.

Carroll, S. (2022). *The biggest ideas in the universe: Space, time, and motion*. Dutton.

Casadesus-Masanell, R. (2019). *Walmart's omnichannel strategy: Revolution or miscalculation?* Harvard Business Publishing.

Catmull, E. (2018). *Creatividad, S.A.* Penguin Random House.

Chávez, C. (2000). *El Palacio de Hierro*. IPADE Business School.

Chávez, C. (2008). *Sport City Fitness Club*. IPADE Business School.

Chávez, C. (2014). *Premios Effie 2013: Buscando competitividad global para el momento México*. IPADE Business School.

Chávez, C. (2017). *Doritos: Ponerle play al target*. IPADE Business School.

Chávez, J. C. (2019). *Creatividad: El arma más poderosa del mundo*. Creativity & Bio-Intelligence Institute.

Chávez, J. C. (2020). *Psyche-Marketing: Inspire and conquer*. Creativity & Bio-Intelligence Institute.

Chávez, J. C. (2021). *Multi-Self: Searching for meaning*. Creativity & Bio-Intelligence Institute.

Chávez, J. C. (2022). *Creative Intelligence Vol. I and II: Geometry of Self Feelings & Freedom*. Creativity & Bio-Intelligence Institute.

Chomsky, N. (2015). *Syntactic structures*. Martino Publishing.

Christen, M. (2001). *Launching New Coke*. INSEAD: The Business School for the World.

Clement, B. R. (2007). *Lifeforce: Superior health and longevity*. The Hippocrates Institute.

Damasio, A. (2016). *En busca de Spinoza*. Ediciones Culturales Paidós.

Damasio, A. (2018). *The strange order of things: Life, feelings, and the making of cultures*. Editorial Planeta.

Damasio, A. (2018). *Y el cerebro creó al hombre*. Ediciones Culturales Paidós.

Damasio, A. (2018). *La sensación de lo que ocurre*. Ediciones Culturales Paidós.

Damasio, A. (2019). *El error de Descartes*. Ediciones Culturales Paidós.

Damasio, A. (2021). *Feeling and knowing*. Pantheon.

Dawkins, R. (2016, 40th anniversary ed.). *The selfish gene*. Oxford Landmark Science.

Deloitte. (2019). *Marketing strategies and tactics at Procter & Gamble*.

Dolan, R. J., & Simon, H. (1996). *Power pricing: How managing price transforms the bottom line*. Free Press.

Eibl-Eibesfeldt, I. (2007). *Human ethology*. Routledge.

Euromonitor International. (2023). *Market trends and insights: Cosmetics industry*. Retrieved from http://www.euromonitor.com/

Foucault, M. (1988). *Technologies of the self*. University of Massachusetts Press.

Freud, S. (2017). *La hipnosis: Textos* (1886-1893). Editorial Ariel.

Gavetti, G., Henderson, R., & Giorgi, S. (2004). *Kodak and the digital revolution (A) case*. Harvard Business School.

Gribbin, J. (1984). In search of Schrödinger's cat: Quantum physics and reality. Bantam Books.

Gupta, S., & Lal, R. (2022). Digital marketing at HBS online. Harvard Business School.

Hassenstein, B. (1973). Verhaltensbiologie des Kindes. Piper.

Hawking, S. W. (2017). Historia del tiempo: Del big bang a los agujeros negros. Alianza Editorial.

Homero. (2013). La Odisea. Penguin Random House.

Homero. (2018). La Ilíada. Wentworth Press.

Holst, E. (1939). Die relative Koordination als Phánomen und als Methode zentralnervöser Funktionsanalyse. Erg. Physiol. 42, 228-306.

Instituto Nacional de Estadística y Geografía. (2016). Encuesta Nacional de Ocupación y Empleo (ENOE).

Israeli, A., & Avery, J. (2017). Predicting consumer tastes with big data at Gap. Harvard Business School.

Interbrand. (2023). Best global brands. Retrieved May 8, 2023, from https://interbrand.com/best-brands/

Iveson, A., Hultman, M., & Davvetas, V. (2022). The product life cycle revisited: An integrative review and research agenda. European Journal of Marketing, 56(2), 467-499. https://doi.org/10.1108/EJM-08-2020-0594

Jung, C. G. (2012). The red book. W.W. Norton & Company.

Kahneman, D. (2013). *Thinking, fast and slow*. Farrar, Strauss & Giroux.

Kantar. (2023). *BrandZ top 100 most valuable global brands 2022*. Retrieved May 8, 2023, from https://www.kantar.com/en-cn/inspiration/brands/2022-kantar-brandz-top-100-most-valuable-global-brands

Keough, D. (1985, April 23). Speech at the Coca-Cola Company gathering at the Vivian Beaumont Theater in New York's Lincoln Center.

Kant, I. (2018). *Crítica del juicio*. Tecnos.

Knutson, B., & Grether, D. M. (1996). Psychological determinants of decision attitude. *Journal of Risk and Uncertainty, 12*(1), 49-68.

Kotler, P., & Keller, K. L. (2016). *Marketing management* (15th ed.). Pearson.

Lacan, J. (2021). *Desire and its interpretation: The seminar of Jacques Lacan, Book VI*. Polity Press.

Lal, R. (2004). *Harrah's Entertainment Inc*. Harvard Business School.

Lassiter III, J. B., Sahlman, W. A., & Misra, S. (2016). *Strava* (9-814-055). Harvard Business School.

Lindley, D. (2008). *Uncertainty: Einstein, Heisenberg, Bohr, and the struggle for the soul of science*. First Anchor Books Edition.

Llano, C. (1998). *La enseñanza de la dirección y el método del caso*. Instituto Panamericano de Alta Dirección de Empresa.

Magnum. (2023). *Discover the pleasure of Magnum*. Retrieved from https://www.youtube.com/watch?v=zeP7yM6nKWg

McDonald, M., Smith, B., & Ward, K. (2013). *Marketing and finance*. Wiley.

Meehl, P. E. (1986). *Causes and effects of my disturbing little book. Journal of Personality Assessment, 50*(3), 370-375. https://doi.org/10.1207/s15327752jpa5003_6

Mi, J. (2017). *A maestro without borders: How André Rieu created the classical music market for the masses* (08/2017-6304). INSEAD Blue Ocean Strategy Institute.

Mitchell, S. A., & Black, M. J. (2016). *Freud and beyond: A history of modern psychoanalytic thought*. Basic Books.

Moon, Y. (2005). *Break free from the product life cycle*. Harvard Business School.

Moore, G. (1991). *Crossing the chasm*. HarperBusiness.

Moss Kanter, R. (2010). *Block by blockbuster innovation case*. Harvard Business School.

Mukherjee, S. (2016). *The gene: An intimate story*. Scribner.

Nike. (2023). *You without limits*. Retrieved from https://www.youtube.com/watch?v=4gncBADVKkw

Noah Harari, Y. (2015). *Sapiens: A brief history of humankind*. Harper.

Noah Harari, Y. (2017). *Homo Deus: A brief history of tomorrow*. Harper.

Noah Harari, Y. (2018). *21 lessons for the 21st century*. Random House.

Osterwalder, A. (2017). *Business model generation: A handbook for visionaries, game changers, and challengers*. Ed Wiley.

Polanyi, K. (2001). *The great transformation: The political and economic origins of our time*. Beacon Press.

Porges, S. *The polyvagal theory: Neurophysiological foundations of emotions, attachment, communication, and self-regulation*. W.W. Norton & Company.

Prager, J. (1998). *Presenting the past: Psychoanalysis and the sociology of misremembering*. Harvard University Press.

Raknes, O. (2004). *Wilhelm Reich and orgonomy: The brilliant psychiatrist and his revolutionary theory of life energy*. American College of Orgonomy Press.

Real Madrid. (2023). Retrieved from https://www.realmadrid.com/football-school.

Rees, R. (1970). *Caso Tlatelolco*. IPADE Business School.

Reich, W. (1946). *Bion experiments*. Farrar, Strauss & Giroux.

Reich, W. (1972). *Ether, God and devil & cosmic superimposition*. Farrar, Strauss & Giroux.

Reich, W. (1980). *Character analysis* (3d ed.). Farrar, Strauss & Giroux.

Reichheld, F. (2001). *The loyalty effect: The hidden force behind growth, profits, and lasting value.* Harvard Business School.

Ridley, M. (2006). *Genome.* Harper Perennial.

Rieu, A. (2023). *Best of Andre Rieu.* Retrieved from https://www.youtube.com/watch?v=fd16sNr9T2Q&list=PLbv4mtcyLmhKdUwHnth1qD2asaJD3rTH

Rogers, E. (1995). *Diffusion of innovations.* Free Press.

Sacks, O. (2009). *Musicofilia.* Anagrama.

Schacter, D. L. (2002). *Seven sins of memory.* Houghton Mifflin.

Schopenhauer, A. (2012). *The world as will and representation.* Dover Publications.

Schrödinger, E. (2019). *What is life?* Cambridge University Press.

Starbucks Corporation. (2023). *Starbucks.* Retrieved from http://www.starbucks.com

Statista. (2021). Number of active Amazon customer accounts worldwide from 1st quarter 2011 to 2nd quarter 2021. Retrieved April 19, 2023, from https://www.statista.com/statistics/948562/amazon-active-customer-accounts-worldwide/

Statista. (2023). *Product life cycle of digital cameras.* Retrieved from https://www.statista.com/

Trout, J., & Ries, A. (2006). *Marketing warfare.* McGraw Hill.

Todorov, A. (2017). *Face value: The irresistible influence of first impressions*. Princeton University Press.

Vernon, R. (1966). *International investment and international trade in the product cycle*. Harvard University Press.

Wedekind, C., & Füri, S. (1997). Body odour preferences in men and women: Do they aim for specific MHC combinations or simply heterozygosity? *Proceedings of the Royal Society of London. Series B: Biological Sciences, 264*(1387), 1471-1479.

Zaltman, G. (2003). *How customers think: Essential insights into the mind of the market*. Harvard University Press.

GLOSSARY

agency: the ability to interrelate and understand thoughts.

artificial intelligence: the faculty to choose appropriately by non-biological entities.

attributes: Ways in which modal systems are represented in consciousness.

Behavioral Biology: the study of the biological phenomenology of behavior.

Being: everything integrating what we know as an "individual living being" (extensive to all species). Including particles, energy fields, or any element we do not know or are not able to identify due to our human cognitive limitations.

Big Bang: the origin of the detectable universe where a big explosion started its expansion and cooling.

Big Data: massive data collection systems.

bioethics: analysis of what is beneficial or adverse concerning the prevalence and resistance of Life in all its manifestations.

Biological Dialectic: vital and existential imperative manifested in a universal pattern of tension-charge-discharge-relaxation.

biological-emotional programming: genetically modeled instructive in synchrony with the Purpose of Life, and that defines the reactive specificity of organisms in front of different stimuli.

biological rhythms: biological conditionings synchronized with universal periods equivalent to planetary movements such as days, months, seasons, and years.

© ***Bioequalization:*** strategic alignment with biological desires.

© ***Business Model Generator:*** strategic map co-created by Carlos Chávez and Juan Carlos Chávez with the fundamental variables in a business model that impact profitability.

© ***Circle of Being:*** a model that illustrates the Four Forces influencing desires and decisions in evolutionary order.

Commercial Strategy: a structured plan to commercialize a product or service.

complementarity or uncertainty principle: the impossibility of specific pairs of observable and complementary physical magnitudes being precisely known at the same time.

conceptual rationale: differentiation and conceptual definition regarding the main elements that generate value in an offer.

conscience: ethical awareness.

conscious: a set of self-perceived mental processes.

consciousness: capacity of the Being to know The Truth and itself; it integrates basic perceptual processes to complex ones such as awareness of awareness.

© ***Creative Dimension of the Being:*** manifestations in the Being of the connection with its ability to create new thoughts from previous thoughts.

creative capacity: the ability to model new thoughts with logical thoughts and previous homeostatic thoughts.

creative desires: the forces motivating the Being to create new thoughts to adapt and become the constant change, thus increasing Life's chances to resist and prevail.

Creative Motivators: biological desires compelled by the psychological ability and behavioral impetus to create thoughts of thoughts impacting inside and outside the mind to transform the future.

creativity: the ability to create thoughts of thoughts that impact inside and outside the mind to shape the future.

CRM: Automated customer-related data management system.

cultural conditionings: behavior patterns derived from shared learning between people and groups.

Cultural Motivators: biological desires compelled by shared learnings between people and groups.

cause-of-causes: those effects whose cause is the effect of another cause, and so on.

Data Intelligence: a strategic deliberation effort based on specialized data collection and processing technologies.

decisions: conscious and voluntary movements (although typically influenced by biological conditioning).

deep structure: complete base (conscious and unconscious) of the mind.

desires: the forces motivating the Being to react in some direction.

desktop research: an exploratory effort to find relevant data through publicly accessible sources.

direct observation: specialized qualitative research without the researcher's intervention in the studied processes.

distortion: considerable differences between the mental representation of an event and what it "really" is.

Economic Ethology: the study of human behavior in an economic context.

elimination: elements excluded during the mental process of representing "reality" and experiences.

emotions: somatic frameworks (bodily states) that correspond to biologically programmed reactions to external and internal stimuli.

emotional desires: the forces motivating the Being to act synchronously with biologically programmed reactions to external and internal stimuli designed to increase the chances of Life to resist and prevail.

© *Emotional Dimension of the Being:* manifestations in the Being of the connection with its reactive biological attributes to external and internal stimuli.

emotionally competent stimuli (EES): any stimulus (outside or inside the mind) relevant enough to elicit an emotion in an organism.

empathy: the ability to perceive the interrelationship of vital phenomenology, including the sentient experiences of other organisms.

entropy: the number of possible microscopic states of a system in thermodynamic equilibrium that tends to increase with time and is reflected in the perpetual expansion and cooling of everything contained in the universe.

experience: internal and external events occurring in relation to a Being.

exteroception: the ability of the mind to perceive and represent stimuli from outside. (images: visuals/sounds/smells/tastes/sensations).

feelings: attributes in the mind when being aware of own emotions.

fixed patterns of action: consistent, species-specific innate motor adaptations.

flux: constant and infinite change.

focus group: specialized qualitative research with groups of around 10 people.

Four Forces: the main forces (or dimensions) of the ©Circle of Being that influence all human decisions: spiritual, instinctive, emotional, and rational.

freedom of conscious decision: the ability of the mind to choose between options.

Freedom of Being: the possibility of fulfilling the objectives of the own biological design.

gene: sequence of letters (nucleotides) that generate a protein or any portion of chromosomal material that can potentially be used as a unit for natural selection.

© *Genetic Drivers:* biological desires compelled by genetically programmed behavioral tendencies defined through natural selection.

generalization: the mental process of representation in which it is assumed that all elements sharing "x" characteristic(s) also share another different characteristic(s). Example: All "x" are "y" (all humans are good).

Germinal-meta-cause: that last cause that has no cause.

hermeneutics: considerations on the interpretation of concepts.

homeostatic thoughts: regulatory and unquantifiable thoughts that reflect the proper functioning of the Being (feelings).

humors: impulses lasting in extended ranges of time.

idea: in the context of the ©Tree of Being model, an idea is a set of thoughts we can share with other minds.

impulses: automatic and unconscious reactions guided by innate conditionings.

individual interview: qualitative research consisting of a free and detailed one-on-one conversation.

innate conditionings: patterns of behavior derived from genetic instructions.

innate releasing mechanisms: consistent behavioral patterns characteristic of each species triggered by specific stimuli.

instinctive acts (or behaviors) (or instincts): behaviors motivated by unconscious innate conditioning, combined with orientation movements and the guidance of individual learning.

instinctive desires: the forces motivating the Being to act in synchrony with its genetic code to protect the survival and reproduction of each gene and thus increase the probabilities.

© *Instinctive Dimension of the Being:* manifestations in the Being of the connection with its genetic programming modeled through natural selection.

intelligence: the faculty to choose adequately.

intelligent information: all those ideas that allow us to get closer to the "truth".

intelligent organisms: beings with the ability to retain and process the information obtained by the representations of their mind to deliberate decisions.

interoception: the ability of the mind to perceive and represent the functioning of its interior. (Feelings).

intersubjectivity: similar perceptions shared between different minds.

intuition: the ability to identify valence through homeostatic thoughts (feelings).

instinctive desires: the forces motivating the Being to act in synchrony with its genetic code to protect the survival and reproduction of each gene and thus increase the probabilities.

joys: feelings that produce a positive sensation in the mind.

judgment: the juxtaposition of quantifiable rational and unquantifiable intuitive thoughts that identify perceived patterns of cause and effect.

kinesic representation: mental representation that is processed in the form of movements.

learning dispositions: phylogenetic conditionings related to learning.

Life: the set of modes composed of genetic material (purines and pyrimidines) capable of auto-replicating.

limbic resonance: bio-emotional influence.

logical thoughts: quantifiable thoughts that seek to detect causes and effects.

Machine Learning: automated learning processes by non-biological entities.

mechanics of affects: a logical model of feelings.

mental representations: neural phenomena that map the experience of a Being deriving in mental images.

meta-cause: the cause of effects that are also causes.

Metamodel: A model proposed by Bandler and Grinder designed to analyze language to identify a person's surface structure and deep structure. It seeks to challenge distortions, specify generalizations, and recover deletions.

Meta-Value: sublimated thoughts representing desires.

mirror neurons: a class of neurons that allow us to simulate states of the body (emotions and feelings, our own and those of other beings).

modeling: in a neural context, planned systematization of mental processes.

© ***Master Campaign:*** communication method that conveys a guiding positioning considering the adequate reach and frequency.

motivation mechanisms: phylogenetic conditionings related to what motivates thoughts and actions.

negative entropy: a term coined by Erwin Schrödinger representing the effort of the subatomic particles of Life to resist and prevail against the constant expansion and cooling of the universe.

neurobiological Motivators: biological desires compelled by the emotional and sentient reactive systematization typical of the species.

nutrition: a set of elements that an organism consumes to obtain resources.

objectivity: utopian antinomy that describes thought outside of subjective mental systems.

organisms with emotions: compound beings created by genes with specific reactive biological attributes to external and internal stimuli.

organisms with mind: beings with the capacity to perceive and represent their exterior (exteroception), the functioning of their interior (interoception), and their own physiological and psychological composition (proprioception).

paradigm: framework on which phenomenology is analyzed.

Path of the Hero: a term coined by Joseph Campbell to define the basic structure of many epic tales worldwide. It represents an initiation journey with marked evolutionary stages reflecting collective unconscious elements.

personalities (or templates): constant behavior patterns over extended time ranges.

© *Psyche-Marketing:* a method designed by the author to identify the main forces that influence decision-making. It considers the behavioral tendencies caused by 1) the integral connection of the Being with the Whole, 2) genes, 3) emotions and feelings, and 4) reason.

psychological conditionings: behavior patterns derived from learnings due to individual experiences.

psychological Motivators: biological desires compelled by the phenomenology of mental processes.

psychological programming: phenomenology of mental patterns of information representation.

preconscious: the set of mental processes not self-perceived but with the possibility of being so.

primary feelings: feelings that precede other feelings and have a specific quality (not a range). For example: 1) feeling of subjectivity, 2) joys, 3) sorrows.

proprioception: the mind's ability to perceive and represent its physiological and psychological composition.

purchase decision process: a conceptual map that marks the customer's steps towards a purchase.

pull (sales): tactics aimed at attracting customers with indirect communications.

push (sales): tactics aimed at closing a sale with direct attention.

qualitative research: a specialized exploratory effort to understand the cognitive phenomenology of small groups and individuals.

quantitative research: a specialized exploratory effort to understand the cognitive phenomenology of large groups of people.

rational desires: the forces motivating the Being to identify causes and effects through their mental representations to complement the behavior process (spiritually, emotionally, and instinctively driven) in the face of context changes as a survival tool for their organism to increase the probabilities of Life to resisting and prevailing.

Rational Dimension of the Being: manifestations in the Being of its ability to identify causes and effects through conscious mental representations.

Rational Motivators: biological desires compelled by the psychological ability and behavioral impetus to identify causes and effects in a logical and quantifiable manner.

reason: the ability to identify causes and effects through quantifiable logical thoughts.

Resilience and Creativity Cycle: diagram showing the apparent chain of command and the evolutionary elements seeking to resist and prevail.

ROI: percentage calculation of the return on investment.

© *Strategic Bio-Intelligence:* an analytical effort to deliberate appropriate decisions based on representative data integrating information on behavioral biology.

segmentation: classification effort based on the characteristics of the persons who make up groups representing the highest purchase probabilities.

self: interpretation of the individuality that differentiates a Being from the outside.

self-control: the ability to control the effects of desires.

semantic memory: memory sector designed for long-term retention of relevant information unrelated to direct experience.

sentient desires: the forces motivating the Being to seek positive feelings and avoid negative feelings to regulate their organism's behavior and thus increase the chances of Life to resist and prevail.

Sentient Dimension of the Being: manifestations in the Being of the connection with its homeostatic thoughts (feelings) representing the consciousness of its reactive somatic frameworks (emotions).

Seven Phenomena of Memory: manifestations that refer to Daniel Schacter's "seven sins of memory".

social feelings: feelings that are defined in conjunction with social interactions and cultural codes.

socialization dispositions: phylogenetic conditioning related to socialization.

somatic balance: ideal chemical and physiological state defined by biological-emotional programming.

sorrows: feelings producing a negative sensation in the mind.

spiritual desires: the forces motivating the Being to act synchronously with Life's Purpose to resist and prevail.

Spiritual Dimension of the Being: manifestations in the Being of its connection with Life at all its levels.

Spiritual Motivators: biological desires compelled by the spatial and temporal relationship with the elements of Life at all levels.

stress: the constant and frequent feeling of fear in the mind.

Strategic Intelligence: the ability of an organization to turn data into solutions.

subatomic particles: any smaller attribute of an atom (including what is understood in the area of physics as particles, waves, or energy).

subjectivity: unique and individual perception of the mind.

sublimation: conceptual and energetic superimposition of different mental constructs.

surface structure: only a part of the deep structure.

sympathy: a set of bodily states (emotions) caused by empathy.

thoughts: conscious neural phenomena in the mind.

The Truth: the knowledge of The Whole.

The Whole: absolutely everything that existence implies.

unconscious: the set of mental processes not self-perceived and with no possibility of being so.

understanding: intuitive, unquantifiable thoughts that identify perceived patterns of cause and effect.

value: quantifiable attribute about what is desired.

value proposition: differentiation and definition regarding the main elements that generate value in an offer.

value structuring: integrating and optimizing different variables that generate value in an offer.

verbal dispositions: phylogenetic conditioning related to verbal communication.

Vision: range of cognitive possibilities.

vital connection: phenomenological pictures on the temporal and spatial interrelationship with Life in all its manifestations.

Will: the set of forces in a Being that obeys the Purpose of a cause.

working memory: memory sector designed for short-term information retention.

© ***Tree of Being:*** a model that complements in more detail © Circle of Being and integrates the elements of mind, consciousness, representations, logical thoughts, homeostatic thoughts, and creative thoughts. It represents an evolutionary map of the creation of the Being and its hierarchies.

© ***Multi-Self Theory:*** a broad and comprehensive vision of the elements and forces that comprise the Being. It identifies that nothing exists by itself and that the Being contains different systems and levels connected to a Whole.

© ***Human Psychological Systematization:*** an abstract model of the psychodynamics of the human mind.

commercial tactics: strategic actions to market a product or service.

counterfactual thinking: mental simulation of alternatives that could have occurred in the past and were not.

creative thoughts: new thoughts modeled with previous logical thoughts and homeostatic thoughts (feelings). They are aware of consciousness.

creative organisms: beings aware of their consciousness and with the ability to create new thoughts from previous logical thoughts and homeostatic thoughts (feelings).

cognitive phenomenology: observable, identifiable, and potentially consensual processes on the mental faculty of understanding.

behavioral phenomenology: observable, identifiable, and potentially consensual processes regarding behavior.

cognitive modes: differentiated categories on the mental patterns of perception, understanding, comprehension, representation, and learning.

episodic memory: a sector of memory designed for the long-term retention of information related to experiential episodes.

motor programs: behavioral movement patterns characteristic of each species.

natural selection: the evolutionary process explaining the phenomenology in which living organisms with new genetically acquired attributes that represent a survival advantage transcend those that do not have them.

positioning map: a comparative strategic graph interrelating two relevant variables.

primary feelings: feelings that precede other feelings and have a specific quality (not a range). For example: 1) feeling of subjectivity, 2) joys, 3) sorrows.

secondary feelings: range of feelings derived from the primary feelings.

causal control: the possibility of consciously intervening on the causes that trigger effects.

alternative possibilities: the existence of alternatives to choose from.

guiding positioning: a forceful phrase that summarizes how we want to be known based on the biological motivators of the client.

auditory representation: mental representation that is processed in the form of sounds.

visual representation: mental representation that is processed in the form of visuals.

resist and prevail: the common effort of all manifestations of Life to maintain order against the constant expansion and cooling of the universe.

phylogenetic adaptations of perception: innate conditioning on perceptions, representations, and understanding of proprioceptive, interoceptive, and exteroceptive information.

CONCEPTUAL CONCENTRATE

BIO-STRATEGIC TOOLS

First Bio-Strategic Tool: understand that the dominant influence on conscious decisions comes from the **preconscious** and **unconscious**, its broader structural basess.

Second Bio-Strategic Tool: understand that **unconscious desires sublimated** in things, persons, or situations, moderate all thoughts, actions, and decisions.

Third Bio-Strategic Tool: understanding that the **meta-value** is a fundamental element that strongly influences decision-making.

Fourth Bio-Strategic Tool: delving into psychological processes, detecting the **multimodal quality of the Being**, and recognizing the dominance of the unconscious, is essential to understand why and how we make decisions.

Fifth Bio-Strategic Tool: Allying with **behavioral biology** to make strategic decisions exponentially increases the probability of completion.

Sixth Bio-Strategic Tool: Understanding that a strong **Purpose** protecting the resistance and prevalence of Life—in all its manifestations—is one of the most potent business tools.

Seventh Bio-Strategic Tool: understanding that **genetic drivers** permanently influences decision-making.

Eighth Bio-Strategic Tool: understanding that **neurobiological conditioning** influences every decision and can be used to trigger emotions in front of the idea of brands, subjects, products, or services to increase the probability of action.

Ninth Bio-Strategic Tool: understanding that **psychodynamic processes** drastically transform the conscious information we use for decision-making.

Tenth Bio-Strategic Tool: understand **reason** is an indispensable ally in decision-making, but it does not represent the most influential behavioral guideline.

Eleventh Bio-Strategic Tool: identify and use codes with **sublimated-collectively-shared values** to connect with distinct cultural groups.

Twelfth Bio-Strategic Tool: understanding that adding **creativity** to anything means adding value exponentially.

BEHAVIORAL CONDITIONING

Axiomatic Conditioning: the map is not the territory; comprehend the axioms that support your conclusions to make better decisions.

Conditioning of subjectivity: All thought is a subjective judgment that integrates individual inclinations; detect and consider them to make intelligent decisions.

Conditioning of valuation: Value (or price) is a mental construct and does not have a direct material root. Human beings value based on biological desires; recognize the own and collective to make better decisions and/or generate demand.

Bio-dialectical conditioning: All physical, biological, and human processes are incessant dialectical cycles; the *Homo sapiens* is designed to seek harmonious resolution in every thought, action, and decision.

Memory fragility conditioning: Memories strongly influence behavior and are formed based on what we frequently experience or generate a high sentient impact. Maxim to permeate long-term memory: repeat and excite.

Generalization conditioning: for psychobiological efficiency and stability reasons, human beings tend to *generalize*. It is essential to detect such biases to not limit understanding, make intelligent decisions, and/or communicate more forcefully.

Distortion conditioning: For psychobiological reasons of efficiency and stability, human beings tend to *distort* the perceived reality. It is essential to detect such biases to not limit understanding, make intelligent decisions, and/or communicate more forcefully.

Conditioning of nominalization: In language, it is widespread to transform improvable dynamic processes into definitive nouns (apparently unimprovable); detecting and reversing this practice gives us new and better possibilities.

Elimination conditioning: Human beings tend to eliminate perceived reality for psychobiological reasons of efficiency and stability. It is essential to detect such biases to not limit understanding, make intelligent decisions, and/or communicate more forcefully.

Instinctive conditioning: Human beings are genetically programmed to behave in specific ways. Identify these conditioning factors to make intelligent decisions and/or motivate actions.

Phylogenetic reaction and perception conditioning: : Humans are preprogrammed to react to stimuli with specific innate releasing mechanisms, motor patterns, and phylogenetic adaptations of perception. Consider these conditions to make intelligent decisions and communicate forcefully.

Conditioning of learning: the tendency to seek learnings that represent sentient gratifications.

Conditionings of socialization:
• *Conditioning of reciprocity*: the tendency to give and receive to create affective bonds.
• *Conditioning of family organization*: the tendency to create mother-father-children ties as the nucleus of society.

• *Conditioning of genetic diversity*: the tendency to seek a partner with a broader genetic correlational difference. For example, aversion toward incest and attraction to certain genetic configurations (C. Wedekind, 1995).

• *Conditioning of dominance*: the tendency to define relational hierarchies.

• *Conditioning of identity*: the tendency to define meeting points to generate a sense of group.

• *Conditioning of territoriality*: the tendency to assume external elements as "own."

Conditionings of communication:

• *Conditioning of concord*: tendency to maintain harmony among members of a group.

• *Conditioning of friendly contact*: the tendency to establish an agreeable initial introduction to other individuals.

• *Conditioning of unity*: the tendency to reinforce social ties through rituals that cultivate shared values and protect against common enemies.

• *Conditioning of imitation*: the tendency to imitate group members to obtain learning.

• *Conditioning of exploration*: the tendency to stretch limits in social norms to restructure them.

• *Conditioning of instruction*: the tendency to teach other members of the group.

• *Conditioning of ranking*: the tendency to place oneself in and protect one's social status.

• *Conditioning of fighting*: the tendency to aggressively defend what is desired.

• *Conditioning of submission*: the tendency to give up in search of reconciliation.

Conditioning of moods: We humans are predisposed to behave in specific ways based on our physiological requirements with different durations and deadlines.

Conditioning of biological rhythms: vital and physiological
requirements are synchronized with universal periods equivalent to planetary movements such as days, months, seasons, and years.

POSITIONING TACTICS:

First positioning tactic: differentiate and add rational and emotional value to the concept of your brand, company, or project using the maximum potential of the **creative** faculty; integrate new thoughts with logical and intuitive thoughts that will forcefully impact inside and outside the mind.

Second positioning tactic: communicate with **clear** concepts including immediate but forceful instinctive significance, connecting in the depth of the unconscious with instinctive, emotional, and sentient values.

Third positioning tactic: repeat, repeat, and repeat.

Fourth positioning tactic: strive to detonate high **emotional intensity** with communications to favor remembrance and impact.

Fifth positioning tactic: Convey that "the majority is in" regarding your goals to add the potent ***bandwagon effect*** to your communication efforts.

Sixth positioning tactic: detect how intuition influences decisions and consider the **sublimated meta-values** of each element used in the communication pieces.

Seventh positioning tactic: Consider whether your perceptions and decisions are biased by available and fleeting data. On the other hand, ensure the constant presence of the positioning you want to establish by turning the availability heuristic and the ***availability cascade*** into strategic allies.

Eighth positioning tactic: Be smartly wary of detecting the unconscious biases that likes and dislikes exert on your beliefs and decisions. On the other hand, align the positioning and value proposition to individual and collective **emotional preferences** to multiply its strength.

Ninth positioning tactic: Detail situations that are easy to imagine vividly to convert the *overestimation* bias into a strategic ally and, on the other hand, privilege statistical data so as not to fall into decision biases.

Tenth positioning tactic: : Carefully configure the context framing the moment of decision aiming for positive emotional reactions and cognitive ease supporting the objective pursued. Likewise, stop to reflect on the momentum and analyze the junctures with a broad vision to avoid the biases of the *framing* effect.

Eleventh positioning tactic: Generate a sense of belonging concerning your offer to create human ties well protected by *loss aversion* (*e.g.*, loyalty programs). Also, consider the long term so as not to fall into biases derived from fear of immediate loss.

Twelfth positioning tactic: We humans tend to commit to what we have invested effort into. Strive for involvement and time invested from other minds in your positioning to encourage affiliation and demand. Also, be aware of the bad decisions that *escalation of commitment* and *sunk cost fallacy* can cause.

Thirteenth Positioning Tactic: Determine the starting mental reference points in advance to limit the range of behavioral responses you seek. Consider if there is a preset value

for the *anchoring effect* dissembling your decisions unconsciously.

Fourteenth positioning tactic: Intelligently use codes with
controlled sublimated values to generate a first impression
leading to the response you are looking for. Consider the
symbolic elements that unconsciously influence your decisions due to the *priming* effect.

Fifteenth positioning tactic: Team up with the *halo effect*
by detonating and maintaining a positive perception of what
you represent. Regarding individual decisions, identify those cumulative biases present in the foundations of your judgments, beliefs, opinions, and decisions..

Sixteenth positioning tactic: Pay close attention to the causal constructs you form and validate them with critical thinking to prevent *judgment heuristics* from adversely biasing.
In communication, understand the phenomenology of such
heuristics to guide perceptions and decisions.

Seventeenth positioning tactic: model intersubjective thoughts with the help of current belief systems to facilitate their
impact. On a personal level, reflect on whether you really
knew what you think you knew to avoid the adverse effects
of *hindsight bias*.

Eighteenth Positioning tactic: Before assuming something
is true, question it rationally to avoid negative effects due to
confirmation bias. In communication, always consider the
immense power of the first intuitive impression; the mind
tends to believe anything; use that pattern responsibly.

Spiritual heuristics: we human beings, due to our germinal and biophysical interconnection with Life as a whole, tend to protect it in all its manifestations. When choosing between options—especially when they are very similar—we are conditioned to prefer those defending vital prevalence and resistance. For example, a product that takes care of the Planet will be more attractive to us than one that does not.

Instinctive Heuristics: *Homo sapiens* follow genetically defined innate behavioral tendencies that have represented a survival advantage on the evolutionary map. When we decide, we will be inclined to opt for what satisfies our instinctive—egotistical—desires. For example, a luxurious watch that provokes admiration will be attractive due to our innate predisposition for domination and territoriality. As a side note, we might as well propose a specific heuristic for each identifiable instinctual conduct tendency..

Emotional heuristics: emotions are automated physiological reactions aiming to regulate their organisms' optimal functioning and behavior. When looking for answers, we are prone to privilege those eliciting body frames interpreted as positive mental states. For example, a food that, due to its ingredients, causes the release of dopamine—such as chocolate—will be more appetizing. The same happens with concepts loaded with sublimated meanings; likewise, they increase—on a greater or lesser scale—the levels of specific biomolecules that trigger emotions.

Sentient heuristics: the mind translates emotions into feelings. Human judgments and decisions are heavily charged with limbic resonance; that is, they tend to be defined based on what produces positive sentient experiences. For example, we will prefer the drink that, due to its brand architecture, connotes a longed-for feeling over another that simply highlights its formula.

Rational heuristics: reason is the biological collaborator in charge of determining the convenience of innate conditionings based on a present context. In other words, it has the primary function of temporarily mitigating behavioral tendencies driven by instincts and emotions when they become out of context and self-destructive. For this, its main tactic is the identification of congruent causes and effects. The human being tends to prefer what logically supports his or her convenience. For example, we will be more willing to buy a real estate asset—which we already instinctively desire—if we are told of its particular financial benefits.

CONCEPTUAL MAPS

STRATEGIC BUSINESS MODEL GENERATOR 5.0

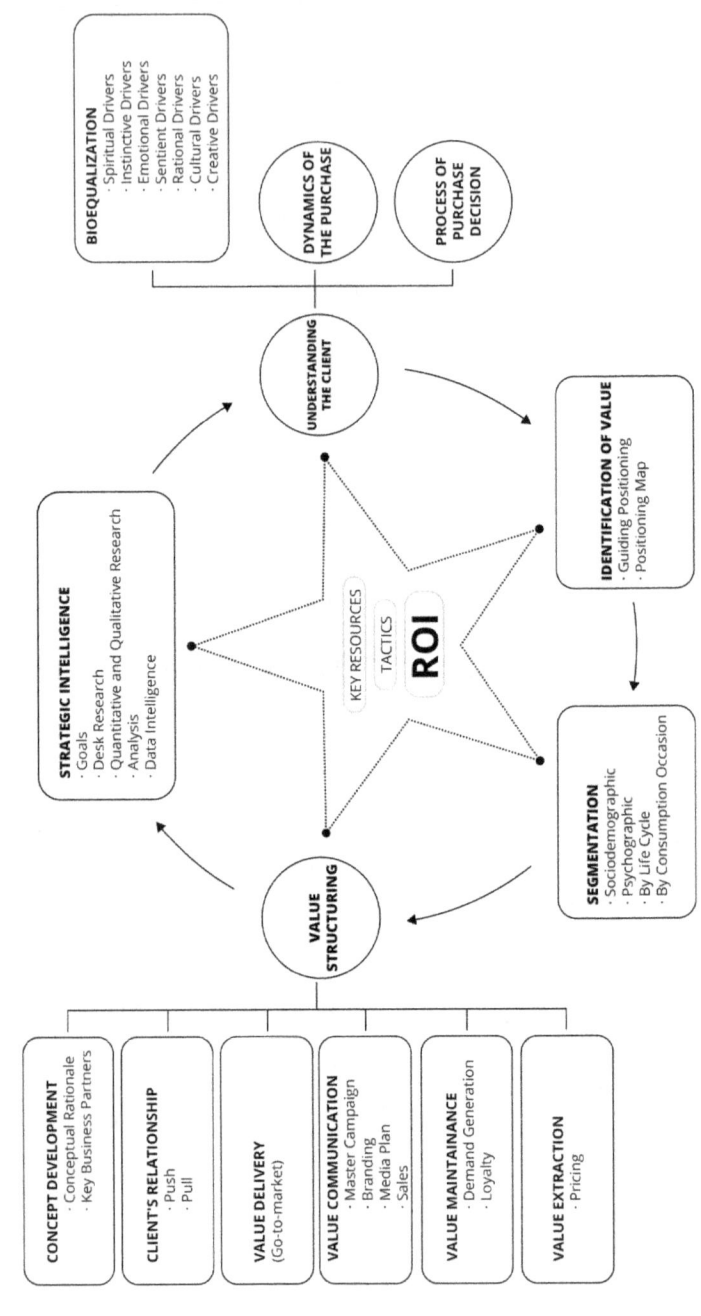